Praise for Mariano Rivera's

The Closer

"An engaging memoir.... His tale transcends team loyalties. It even transcends baseball. It is the story of a humble man of deep faith doing great things under enormous pressure. 'I am an imperfect man on an imperfect journey,' he writes. And what a journey it's been."
—Steven V. Roberts, *Washington Post*

"Rivera was known as perhaps baseball's classiest act. He keeps up that reputation here.... Rivera emerges on these pages as a wordsmith.... It's the kind of baseball odyssey that leaves readers with a sense of the Homerian that later extends to the stuff of clutch strikeouts, 'Casey at the Bat'–style grandeur, and fallen records."
—Colin Fleming, *Los Angeles Times*

"A warmhearted, charmingly frank baseball memoir.... *The Closer* describes such a devout, decent, and admirable guy.... It's as inspiring as it is exciting."   —Janet Maslin, *New York Times*

"A deeply personal tale about hard work, perseverance, and an unbridled passion for baseball.... For baseball fans, and casual observers, Mr. Rivera's nineteen-year career is a marvel to behold. Every page of *The Closer* reveals another layer of this surprisingly humble man with an incredible talent he only discovered in adulthood. Yankees fans like me are eternally glad that he did, and thank him for all the wonderful memories he gave us."
—Michael Taube, *Washington Times*

"Rivera recounts his journey with humor and humility."

— Ben Teitelbaum, *Daily Beast*

"Classy, earnest, and spiritual."

— *Sports Illustrated*

"In *The Closer*, Rivera comes across as a fellow who's made the transition from poverty in Panama to spectacular wealth and success in New York without abandoning the humility that has apparently characterized him almost since childhood."

— Bill Littlefield, *Boston Globe*

"Intensely competitive and a gifted athlete, Rivera will delight baseball fans....In an age of bravado and bluster in professional sports, he is one of the few athletes who has earned a right to brag. Yet Rivera's elegance and class manage to somehow outshine his accomplishments."

— *Publishers Weekly*

"*The Closer* is a reflection of Rivera—calm, focused, and workmanlike."

— Bob D'Angelo, *Tampa Tribune*

"Even if you're not a Yankees fan (or you're even a Yankees hater), you can't deny that Mariano Rivera is one of the nicest guys in the game and easily the greatest closer of all time....*The Closer* is the story fans have been wanting to read for a long time and one Dad will definitely dig."

— Scott Neumyer, *Parade*

"*The Closer* is quick, simple, to the point. Just like the way he pitched."

— *Yankees Magazine*

The Closer

MARIANO RIVERA

with Wayne Coffey

BACK BAY BOOKS
LITTLE, BROWN AND COMPANY
New York Boston London

Back Bay Books / Little, Brown and Company
Hachette Book Group
1290 Avenue of the Americas, New York, NY 10104
littlebrown.com

Originally published in hardcover by Little, Brown and Company, May 2014
First Back Bay paperback edition, May 2015

Back Bay Books is an imprint of Little, Brown and Company. The Back Bay Books name and logo are trademarks of Hachette Book Group, Inc.

The publisher is not responsible for websites (or their content) that are not owned by the publisher.

The Hachette Speakers Bureau provides a wide range of authors for speaking events. To find out more, go to hachettespeakersbureau.com or call (866) 376-6591.

Unless otherwise noted, all photographs are courtesy of the Rivera family.

ISBN 978-0-316-40073-2 (hc) / 978-0-316-40460-0 (large print) /
978-0-316-27761-7 (Spanish edition) / 978-0-316-40074-9 (pb)
Library of Congress Control Number 2014934754

10 9 8 7 6 5 4 3 2

LSC-C

Printed in the United States of America

To my Lord and Savior, Jesus Christ,
and the family He has blessed me with:
My beautiful wife, Clara, and our
three wonderful boys, Mariano Jr., Jafet, and Jaziel

Contents

The Closer

Prologue

You don't mess around with machetes. I learn that as a little kid—decades before I'd ever heard of a cut fastball, much less thrown one. I learn that you don't just pick up one of the things and start swinging it as if it were a bat or a broomstick. You have to know how to use it, know the right technique, so you can be efficient and keep it simple, which, if you ask me, is always the best way to go, in all aspects of life.

Keep it simple.

My grandfather Manuel Giron teaches me everything I know about using a machete. We would head out into the sugarcane fields and he'd show me how to grip it—how to bend my knees and bring the blade around so it is level with the surface you want to cut, not a random whack but something much more precise. Once I get the hang of it, I cut our whole lawn with a machete. The lawn isn't big—much closer to the size of a pitcher's mound than an outfield—but I still cut every square inch of it with that handheld blade. It takes an hour, maybe two. I don't rush. I never rush. It feels good when I am done.

I do not have my machete with me on the late March morning in 1990 when I walk out into the rising sun and get the day's first whiff of fish. I don't think I will be needing it. I am twenty years old and I have just signed a professional baseball contract with the New York Yankees. I have no idea what this means.

None.

A few weeks earlier, a Yankee scout named Herb Raybourn sits in the kitchen of our two-room cement home. The house has a tin roof and a couple of chickens out back and sits on a hill in Puerto Caimito, the poor little Panamanian fishing village where I've lived my whole life. My parents sleep in one room, and the kids, all four of us, sleep in the other.

Before Herb arrives, I have a quick talk with my father.

A gringo wants to talk to you about me playing pro baseball, I say. I don't know much more than that.

Let's listen to what he has to say, my father says.

Herb is actually Panamanian and speaks Spanish, even though he looks white. He puts some papers on the table. He looks at me, then my father.

The New York Yankees would like to sign you to a contract and can offer you $2,000, Herb says. We think you are a young man with talent and a bright future.

Herb adds that the Yankees will include a glove and baseball cleats in the deal. I am making $50 a week working on my father's commercial fishing boat. This is not a negotiation. It is what the New York Yankees are offering, the only number that would be mentioned.

Because you are twenty, we're not going to send you to the Dominican Republic, the way we do with teenagers, Herb says. We're going to send you right to Tampa for spring training.

I believe I am supposed to take this as good news, but Herb has no clue how clueless his new signee is. I have never heard of Tampa. I know almost nothing about the Dominican Republic. My world isn't just small. It is the size of a marble. The biggest trip of my life to that point is a six-hour car ride to the border of Costa Rica.

Honest to goodness, I think that when the Yankees sign me I will continue to play my baseball in Panama. I figure that maybe I'll move to Panama City, get a little upgrade in uniform, along with a legit glove and a pair of shoes that don't have a hole in the big toe—like the ones I'd had my Yankee tryout in. I'll get to play ball and make a little money for a while, and then go off to mechanic's school. That is my plan.

I am pretty good at fixing things. I like fixing things. I am going to be a mechanic.

The extent of my knowledge of the big leagues—*las Grandes Ligas*—is close to nothing. I know it is where Rod Carew, Panama's greatest ballplayer, once played. I know there are two leagues, American and National, and that there is a World Series at the end of the season. I do not know much more than that. I am already in the major leagues when I overhear somebody talking about Hank Aaron.

Who's Hank Aaron? I ask.

You're not serious, the guy says.

Yes, I am. Who is Hank Aaron?

He's baseball's all-time home run leader, the guy who hit 755 homers to beat Babe Ruth's record.

Who's Babe Ruth? I ask.

The guy mutters something and turns away, knowing better than to try Honus Wagner on me.

So Herb has to spell everything out for me, a kid as skinny as a Q-tip, and utterly naive: No, you won't be staying in Panama. When you sign with a big league organization, the deal is that you move to the United States. You go buy some shirts and underwear and a cheap suitcase. You get a work visa and try to act as if you know what you are doing when you are filling out the paperwork. You will be scared and nervous and sad and have no idea how you are going to manage in a foreign country when all you know how to say is, "I no speak English."

It isn't just daunting. It's terrifying. I try not to let on. I have always been good at hiding my feelings.

Weeks pass. The plane ticket to Tampa arrives. Now it is getting real.

Now it is time.

Let's go, Pili, my mother says. Pili is the name my sister, Delia, gave me when I was a baby. Nobody knows why. It's what my family has called me my whole life. My father starts up his white Nissan pickup truck. Turbo is our name for it. It's ten years old, rusty and battered and not anybody's idea of a race car, but we still call it Turbo. Clara Diaz Chacón, my longtime girlfriend, is sitting between my father, Mariano Sr., and my mother, also named Delia. I throw my new suitcase in the flatbed and then climb in myself, along with my cousin Alberto. My father puts Turbo in reverse and we pull out of the driveway, onto Via Puerto Caimito, the one road in and out of our village, the only road that is paved. All the rest are dirt, most of them looking more like paths than anything you would drive on. We proceed through Chorrera, a much bigger town five miles away, and then make our way on a twisty, rutted road, past goats and plantain trees and swatches of rain forest, Alberto and I bouncing around in the back as if we were coconuts, anchored by nothing, only a skimpy railing stopping us from tumbling out.

I know where *we* are going—Tocumen International Airport in Panama City—but I am much less certain about where *I* am going.

I am a high-school dropout. I don't even make it out of ninth grade in Pedro Pablo Sanchez High School, a U-shaped building in the heart of Chorrera with three floors and a courtyard in the middle, and dogs sleeping wherever they can find shade. It is a terrible decision to leave school, but I get fed up one day and just bail on it, walking right out past the dogs in my pressed blue trousers and crisp white shirt. (I iron the uniform myself; I like things to be neat.) I am not thinking through any of the consequences of walking out of school, and I am not getting much direction from my parents, working-class people who are smart but not very familiar with formal education.

My last school lesson—and the last straw—comes in Mrs. Tejada's math class. At least I think that's her name, but honestly I am a bit fuzzy about that, just because I try not to think about her very much. She isn't my biggest fan, and she doesn't try to hide it, glaring at me as if I were the bane of her teaching life. I hang around with kids who aren't full-fledged troublemakers but are definitely into mischief. It is guilt by association, I guess. One day a few of us are fooling around in the back of the classroom, paying little attention to the Pythagorean theorem and a lot of attention to a kid we are giving the business to. One of my friends crumples up a piece of paper and tosses it at the kid, hitting him in the head.

Hey, cut it out, the kid says.

I do no throwing, but I do do some laughing.

Mrs. Tejada notices.

Rivera! She always calls me by my last name.

Why did you throw that?

I didn't throw anything, I reply.

Don't tell me you didn't throw it. Now come up here.

I didn't do anything wrong. I am not going anywhere.

Rivera, come up here! she repeats.

Again, I do not obey her command, and now she is really ticked off. I am no longer a mere paper-thrower. I am an all-out insubordinate. She walks to my desk and stands over me.

You are to leave this classroom right now, she says, then escorts me out into the hallway, where I spend the rest of math class, definitely doing no math.

After I walk out that day, I wind up being suspended for three days, and I never return to Pedro Pablo Sanchez High School. I never see Mrs. Tejada again, either, until I run into her in a market after I'd been in pro ball for several years.

Hi, Mariano, she says. Congratulations on your baseball career. I've followed how well you are doing.

There is no glare. No scolding voice. She greets me with a warmth I've never seen from her before.

Is this really Mrs. Tejada, or just a Mrs. Tejada look-alike with a much better disposition? I think.

I smile weakly. It is the best I can do. I've never liked it when people treat you according to how successful or prominent you are. The whole time I was in her class, she regarded me as a borderline juvenile delinquent. Maybe I wasn't going to make anybody forget Albert Einstein, but I was nowhere near the kid she had typecast me as.

Please don't act like you care about me and like me now when you didn't care about me or like me when I was a student, I think.

Thanks, I say, heading right past her to the fruit aisle, hoping she gets the message.

But Mrs. Tejada isn't really the main reason I dropped out. The bigger problem is the fights, which are a regular occurrence. I enjoy learning and do pretty well in school, but the fights just get to be too much. In the hallways, in the schoolyard, on the way back home — they break out everywhere, almost always for the same reason, kids teasing me that I smell like fish:

There he goes, the fishy boy.

Hold your nose, the fish are getting closer.

I thought we were in school, not on the fishing boat.

My tormentors are right. I do smell like fish. Plenty of Puerto Caimito kids do. We live by the water, not far from a processing plant that makes fish meal out of sardines — or *harina de pescado,* as we call it. My father is a captain on a commercial fishing boat, his twelve-plus-hour workdays spent throwing his nets and hauling in all the sardines and anchovies he can. The smell of fish overpowers everything in Puerto Caimito. You could shower for an hour and plunge yourself in cologne, and if a droplet or two of water from the fish plant touches your clothes, you are going to stink all night. Fish keep the local economy from drowning. Fish are what supply jobs for many of the parents of the kids who are taunting me. I could've, should've, ignored them. I do not.

They bait me, and then they reel me in. I'm not proud of this. It's really dumb on my part. My grandmother had just died and I am a little adrift, and get overcome by a self-destructive impulse. I should've finished out the school year, should've turned the other cheek, as the Bible teaches. I do not know much about the Bible at this point. I do not know the Lord at all. I am young and headstrong, intent on doing things my own way. His way? The power of Scripture?

I am not there yet.

We continue the drive to the airport. On the autopista, I feel the warm air rushing into my face in the back of the pickup. I am getting sadder. We drive past groves of cassava and pineapple trees, and the occasional cow, and it's almost as if my boyhood is passing by, too. I think about playing ball on the beach with a glove made from a milk carton, a bat made from a stick, and a ball made from tightly wound fishing nets. I wonder if I've played my last game on El Tamarindo, another dirt patch of a ball field where I played, a field named for the tamarind tree by home plate. I think about what would've happened if I'd kept playing soccer, my first sporting love, trying to beat defenders with a ball attached to my foot (with or without shoes), imagining myself the Panamanian Pelé, a dream that lasted until I got smacked in the eye with the ball during a game and temporarily lost vision. I kept playing and, twenty minutes later, went up for a header, collided with a guy, and wound up in the emergency room, where the doctor closed the cut and told me the eye looked very bad and needed to be seen by a specialist.

My soccer career didn't go for very much longer.

We are just a half hour away now. I look into Turbo's cab, at Clara sitting between my parents. Clara is always close by, steadfast and strong. You know how it is with some people, that you can just feel their strength, their goodness? That is how I feel about Clara. We grow up just a few houses apart in Puerto Caimito; I've known her since kindergarten. Friendship turns to romance on the dance floor of a club one night. Clara had not spoken a word to me since I'd dropped out of school. She would even move in the other direction if she saw me coming. I think—no, I know—she is disappointed that I'd just quit like that. I think she expects more from me. The deep freeze lasts until a bunch of us guys and girls are together in the club, and Clara and I wind up dancing. The lights are low. The beat pulses hard. As the dance is ending, I am about to head off the floor when our eyes lock. She reaches out for my wrist. I can't really describe what happens in that moment. We don't dance the rest of the night together. I don't walk her home and we don't have our first kiss beneath swaying palm trees, or in the midnight quiet of El Tamarindo.

But something happens. Something powerful. It is the Lord who brings us together, I am as sure of that as I am sure that my name is Mariano Rivera. It was, and is, the will of the Lord that Clara and I are together. Why else would she have started speaking to me again? Why else would she have even been at the club that night? She hardly ever went to clubs, didn't like the club scene much at all. But there we were, dancing, a connection being forged even though neither of us knew it at the time. You can call it a coincidence if you like, a random spin of the universe's roulette wheel, but I believe the Lord has a plan for us, and this is the start of it.

After I drop out of school I hang around the clubs in Chorrera a lot—when I am not out to sea on my father's boat. I drink a little and dance a lot. I love to dance, Merengue Mariano, out there on the floor, not closing games, just clubs. As with most places where liquor and testosterone are flowing, fights are commonplace. The cops are regular visitors. Guys pack ice picks. They pack knives. One night I am there with a big group, fifteen kids, maybe more. One of the guys in my group gets into an argument with a kid who is with a big group of his own. I don't know how it starts, probably a look or a comment about somebody's girl, the usual stuff. It's getting heated. They are about to go at it, and I step in to calm things down.

Guys, let's just have a good time. We're here to have fun and dance, not fight. Let's not get anybody hurt or do anything foolish.

They posture and act tough and curse at each other, before things seem to settle down briefly. Then someone in the other group pushes his way to the front. He is carrying a machete. The look on his face suggests he wants to use it, and not on a patch of grass. Apparently he wants the fight to go on and is not pleased with me.

Where's that skinny kid, the peacemaker? he yells, brandishing the machete.

I am back in the crowd by now, but I see him and I hear him. I have no weapon, but I do have good sense, and a lot of speed. I take off running. The guy chases after me. I leave him in the dust, and duck into a nearby house for refuge. The guy with the machete never finds me.

This incident is not atypical. I am not a bad kid. I never get hauled off to jail, but could that have happened?

Sure it could have happened. Some of the kids I hang around with wind up spending far more than a few hours or a night in jail. Getting chased by the kid with the machete is another wake-up call. Clara and I start seeing each other more and more, and everything changes. We go out for quiet dinners, lie in the hammock (it's made out of fishnet) beside my parents' house. We talk all the time, and I marvel at how easy it is, talking to this girl. I begin to cherish those times, and a realization isn't long in coming:

Nothing good is going to happen if I keep dancing the night away in the clubs.

I truly believe if it weren't for Clara, I would never have become a New York Yankee.

My father wheels Turbo into the airport and parks. Alberto and

I clamber out of the back. We all walk toward the terminal. What's about to happen is all starting to hit me for real.

I am leaving home. Leaving Panama.

Leaving Clara.

I am a professional baseball player from this moment on, all six feet and one hundred fifty pounds of me. I don't know how long it will last. There is no concealing anything now; I am scared. I know I love to play ball, but have no idea how I will measure compared to the other players I am going to go up against. I am not a worrier by nature, but I am a realist. Who else has made this transition, from a Panamanian fishing boat to the New York Yankees?

I came to Puerto Caimito to be a fisherman, my father tells me. I started at the bottom, cleaning up boats, sweeping up garbage, getting paid pennies, but I worked and worked, and I advanced and finally became a captain. You will do the same thing, Pili. It won't be easy, but you are going to work your way to the top.

I hug my mother goodbye and shake my father's hand.

I am not going to see Clara for five months. It feels as if it will be five years.

I tell Clara how much I love her and how much I will miss her.

I will write and I will be back soon, I say, and then I wrap her in my arms and kiss her goodbye and try not to cry, but I do anyway.

She is crying, too.

I love you, Pili. I will be here, waiting for your safe return, she says.

I make my way through the ticket counter and security and go up an escalator.

There goes our boy. I wonder where this is going to take him? It's the voice of my mother, though it's hard to make out her words.

I see them move upstairs toward a viewing deck to watch the plane take off. I turn and walk down an alien passageway, into the plane. Soon I am airborne, the first flight of my life. My tears are almost dry. I do not look back.

1

Fish and Consequences

My country is a curvy strip of earth at the southern tip of Central America that doesn't look much wider than a shoelace when you see it on a map. It has 3.6 million people and one famous canal that meanders for forty-eight miles and connects the Atlantic and Pacific Oceans, a shortcut that saves the world's ships about eight thousand miles of sea travel. Costa Rica is the neighbor to the north, and Colombia to the south. Panama isn't just a place where two oceans meet; it's a place where two continents, North and South America, meet. For a nation that is a little smaller than South Carolina, it has a lot going on.

Puerto Caimito is about twenty-five miles from the canal, on the Pacific side of Panama, and about fifty miles from a volcano called El Valle. It is a village put on the map by fish. If you aren't an actual fisherman in Puerto Caimito, then you probably work at the ship repair shop or the fish processing plant, or take the fish to market. Just about everybody is connected to fish, and everybody eats it.

I ate fish every day, and that's what made me strong, my father says. His father lived to be ninety-six, and my father says he is going to go longer than that, and I wouldn't bet against him.

My father comes from tough farmer stock. One of fifteen children, he was born and raised in the province of Darién, near the Colombian border, and after he left school following sixth grade, he spent eleven hours a day, six days a week, working on the small family farm. They grew rice and corn and plantains, and an assortment of vegetables, and did all of it without a tractor or any other sort of power equipment. Shovels, hoes, rakes—that was the high-end gear, tools for the well-to-do farmers. My father and his family used a machete to cut the brush and the weeds, and sharp sticks to till the soil. Each week they would take their goods to the market, an all-day trip in a boat powered by a pole in the water, gondola-style.

It was a hard, even brutal, life, and by the time my father was a teenager, several of his brothers had already moved to Puerto Caimito, because fishing was considered a more prosperous line of work. At age seventeen, my father joined them. He started out by getting whatever fishing odd job he could, and he was still trying to get to know his way around when he went for a walk one day and came upon a girl who was washing dishes and singing in front of her home. The girl, one of eight children herself, was fifteen years old, and my father will tell you that he fell in love with her in that instant. Her name was Delia Giron, and two years after she stole my father's heart with her singing, she gave birth to a baby girl.

Two years after that, she gave birth to me.

My own life in Puerto Caimito is simple, and smelly. For my first seventeen years we live on the shore of the Gulf of Panama, in a dingy cement home on a dirt road, two rooms with a beat-up tin roof, just a long throw from the fish-meal plant. There's a whole lineup of such homes in the village, most of them occupied by my aunts and uncles and cousins. When my parents move in, the home has no electricity or running water; there is an outhouse in the back and a well for water a short walk away. Light comes from a kerosene lamp. By the time I come along in 1969, we have electricity and water, but the outhouse is still the only bathroom option. Steps away is a big gritty beach strewn with broken shells, pieces of old boats, and fragments of discarded net. It is not a beach you see in a Corona commercial or a tourist book—no turquoise water or tropical trees or sand as soft as talcum powder. It's a working place, a storm-battered boat here, half a dead fish there, the humble soul of a village where people are trying to eke out a living from the sea.

This shore is where I become an athlete. At low tide it is the best playing field in Puerto Caimito, flat and big, a place where you could run forever on the mudflats. I play soccer here. I play baseball here. I play all kinds of games, really, and my favorite is the one where we get a piece of cardboard and cut three holes in it, and string it up between two sticks in the sand. Then we stand back about twenty or thirty feet and fire rocks and see who can get the most rocks through the holes.

My aim is good.

We learn to be creative on the shore, too. We have no bat, so we find an old piece of wood or saw off a branch of a tree. We have no ball, so we wrap up a rock with fishnet and tape. We have no baseball gloves, but it's amazing what kind of pocket you can make out of a cardboard box or a six-pack carton, if you know how to fold it.

This is how I play ball for almost all of my childhood; I don't put a real glove on my hand until I am sixteen years old. My father buys it for me, secondhand, right before we move away from the shore, up the hill about a third of a mile, to another cement block home but in a quieter location, without so much drinking or as many men hanging around the shore all hours of the night.

Neither of our homes has a telephone (I don't have a phone until I move to the States), or a single amenity to speak of. There is a plantain tree hanging over the roof. I don't have my own tricycle or bicycle or any kind of cycle, and really, I have only one toy for most of my early childhood. It's called Mr. Big Mouth. You touch his belly and his big mouth opens and you put a little chip in it. I love touching Mr. Big Mouth's belly. I don't feel deprived, because I am not deprived. It's just the way life is.

I have everything I need.

My favorite time of year is Christmas. As the oldest boy in the family, my job is to get our Christmas tree. I do it every year, and know just where to go. Behind our house is a *manglar*—a swamp—that has a lot of little trees growing in the muck. You aren't going to find a Fraser fir in the swamp, of course, so the next best thing is to scope around for a decent three- or four-foot tree, yank it out, and bring it home. After it dries out, we wrap the branches in cloth so it looks festive, not like some sad little swamp bush. Santa Claus doesn't make it to our part of Panama—maybe because there are so few chimneys—but Christmas Eve is still magical, with lights twinkling and Christmas songs playing and all the anticipation of the big day. For years I get the same present—a new cap gun. I am happy to get it. I like the pop-pop-pop sound it makes. I like firing it when I am watching my favorite television show, *The Lone Ranger,* about a do-gooder in a black mask, though the truth is that I like his companion, Tonto, even better. Tonto is smart and loyal and so humble that he doesn't care about getting credit. You can't find a more trustworthy person in the whole Wild West than Tonto. I think that is pretty cool.

I discover early on that I love to run, and I love to be in motion. If I am not playing soccer or baseball, I am playing basketball. When the tide is in and the beach shrinks, we switch to El Tamarindo, just far enough off the shore to let us play without being ankle-deep in mud. Whatever I play, I want to win badly. When a baseball victory is about to turn into a defeat, I throw the ball into the Gulf of Panama and declare the game a tie. It doesn't win me any sportsmanship awards, but it does prevent an outright loss.

If the tide is in, I do the next best thing to sports and hunt iguanas. They are everywhere in Panama, green and spiky and leathery, six-foot lizards that lounge on branches and hide in the vegetation. I know exactly where to find them, and how to hunt them. All I need is a rock and my right arm. Iguanas are very fast when they get going, and they are amazingly resilient; they can fall forty or fifty feet out of a tree and run away as if all they've fallen off is a park bench. Mostly, though, iguanas stay stationary on the upper branches of trees, and that makes them an easy target. Most times I'd have a direct hit on the first try, then pick it up and sling it over my shoulder to bring home for dinner. Iguana—chicken of the trees, they call it—isn't as much of a staple as coconut rice or tamales, and you aren't going to find fast-food restaurants selling iguana nuggets, but it's one of my favorite dishes.

I never stop and figure out how many relatives I have in Puerto Caimito, but all I can tell you is that my cousins might outnumber the iguanas. It makes for an instant stash of playmates when you want to start up a game, and a total small-town feel, where, if everybody doesn't know your name and what you are up to, they at least know somebody who does. It's a great comfort to grow up this way, surrounded by friendly faces and people who are looking out for you, the only trouble being that it is almost impossible to do anything without three-quarters of the town knowing about it.

This is not always a good thing when you have a father like my father.

My father has taught me so much in my life. He's not big on speeches and parental declarations, but his actions have imparted many lessons that have shaped who I am. A strong sense of discipline, doing things the right way, sticking with a task no matter how difficult it is—he models all of these things for me. He is a great provider, getting up at 5:00 a.m. on Monday and staying out on his fishing boat all week, not coming home until Saturday, spending twelve- or fourteen-hour days (or longer) hauling and dragging the nets, a man of the sea right to the core. I'm sure there were times he didn't feel like going out, but I don't remember him ever taking time off.

Vacation? Weekend getaways? Sick days?

No such thing. He is a fisherman. Fishermen fish. He takes care of business, day after day after day.

You don't appreciate all these things so much when you are a child, though. You are too busy kicking soccer balls or feeding Mr. Big Mouth, or trying to pry the family bicycle away from your sister. As a kid, mostly what I associate with my father is fear. He is a big, strong man. I am a small, skinny kid. He has a barrel chest. I am all rib cage. He walks in the house on Saturday, and the stench of fish is with him, and I immediately look at his hands.

They are thick, powerful, workingman's hands.

They are hands that petrify me.

They are hands that hit me. Hands that have me walking on seashells, because you never know when they are going to strike. As the oldest boy, I am his favorite target. Sometimes I feel as if I am my father's personal piñata. I don't keep track, but I get the beatings often. Before leaving for the boat, my father gives me a list of things to do around the house and yard. They don't always get done. And when they don't, it is not pretty.

Pili, why did you not do what I asked? my father demands.

I did most of it, I say.

You did not do everything I asked you to do.

I'm sorry, Papa. I will do everything next time, I promise.

But there is no slack with my father.

Bend over, he says.

They are the words I dread more than any others. A close second is when my mother says: Wait until your father gets home.

When he does get home and gets a less than favorable report, there is rarely a delay. My father's thick hands go to his waist and unfix his belt. And then it begins, three or four hard lashes to my backside, sometimes more. I try not to cry, but sometimes I do.

I get the belt for a variety of offenses. Break something playing ball? Misbehave in school? Get into some mischief with my sister and brothers? It doesn't take much. One time I pass a friend of my father's in town. I don't really know him, but he looks a little familiar. Or maybe my mind is somewhere else, I don't know. Anyway, I don't wave or say hello to this man. He mentions it to my father the next time he sees him.

My father comes and finds me.

Pili, why did you disrespect my friend? He said he saw you and you said nothing. You didn't even wave hello.

I wasn't sure who it was, I say.

That doesn't cut it. The belt comes off. It is the last time I do not say hello to one of my father's friends. Now I wave to everybody. I also develop a key pain-prevention technique. When I know I've messed up and that the belt is coming, I put on two pairs of pants.

Sometimes I put on three pairs of pants. You need all the cushioning you can get against the belt.

The worst beating I get comes late one February, during Panama's Carnival celebration. There is a big dance in town to commemorate the occasion. I am fourteen years old. My parents have opened a small bodega out of our house to make a little extra money selling fruit and groceries and sundries. They head to Carnival and leave my sister, Delia, and me to mind the store. We stay open for a while, but business is slow, with everybody at the celebration. It doesn't make any sense to stay open when there are no customers.

It makes even less sense knowing there is all this fun and dancing going on and I am not part of it.

Let's close up and go to the dance, I say to my sister.

We can't do that. Do you know how much trouble we'll get in? she says.

I know, but it's Carnival. It's the biggest party of the year. And you might as well come with me, because even if you stay behind you're going to get in trouble for letting me leave.

My sister isn't so sure of my reasoning, but we change our clothes and go to the dance. The merengue music is blasting. The spirit is festive, the dance floor packed. It is all I had imagined it would be. I am out there in the middle of it before you can bang a conga drum, feet flying to the beat, having the best time.

And then I feel a hand on the back of my neck.

A big, strong hand. A hand that feels like a clamp.

If I'd seen it coming, I would've run, but I had no chance. I do not even turn around. There is no need. Only one person in the world grabs me this way. My father is right in my ear, hollering over the music.

What are you doing here? Weren't you told to work in the store?

I do not talk about the slow traffic in the store. I don't offer any defense whatsoever, because there is none. I have disobeyed him. I figured this moment would be coming. I'd just hoped to get a little more dancing in before it did. My father has been drinking, and that makes me even more apprehensive. He is always rougher after he's had something to drink.

He clamps down on my neck ever harder, pushes me forward. He rams my head into a pillar, a direct hit. A big bump pops up on my forehead. A surge of anger courses through me. Part of me wants to lash out at him, punch him, but I know better than to do anything or say anything. It would only make things worse. Much worse. I do not go back on the dance floor. I know the belt will be coming later, when my father returns from the party.

Our house is just five hundred yards away. I walk home through the tropical darkness, sad and hurt.

I think, *Why does my father have to be so harsh? Why can't he understand what it's like to be a kid and how much it meant to me to be at Carnival? Why does he want to hurt me all the time?*

I know it's a parent's job to instill discipline and teach kids right from wrong. But is this how it has to be done? I don't know. I am confused. Maybe it's in the genes. My father's brother—my uncle Miguel—lives next door to us. He is very tough on his kids, too. He works on the boat with my father. I am very close to him and his family, and one time I decide to ask my uncle straight-out.

No way would I ever think to ask my father.

Why are you and my father so rough on your children? Do you want us to live in fear of you?

My uncle thinks about it for a few moments. I can tell he wants to answer the question the right way. He seems more reachable to me than my father.

I know that we are tough guys, your father and I. But if you think we are tough, you should've seen how our father was with us, he says. This is not an excuse, but this is all we know, because it is how we were raised. We left home as soon as we could—to get away from it. He doesn't give me many details, but I know they lived inland, in a farming area, and they practically had to flee, things were so bad.

I think about my father as a kid, being afraid of his own father, going out on his own when he wasn't much more than a boy. It is hard to imagine him as small and vulnerable, but listening to my uncle helps. I never doubt that my father is trying to help me find my way in life by hitting me. I don't doubt that he loves me, even though those are not words that he says when I am a child. It's just so...so...hard all the time. I walk away from my uncle Miguel feeling compassion for my father, feeling love for my father. I know how much he cares, how much he is trying to teach us what we need to be a success in life. Even so, I know one thing.

When I have children, I will discipline them and I will teach them, but if I do nothing else, I am going to do it in every other way than through outright fear. And I will pray that, with their own children, they are even better parents than me.

2

Water Torture

You are not supposed to fish near the Panama Canal. There is way too much traffic on the seas there, and the other boats don't slow down. When your boat is the size of my father's—90 feet in length and 120 tons in weight, with nets that stretch out a thousand feet—it's not easy to get it out of the way if you have to.

But the way my father looks at it, you do what you have to do. As a fishing boat captain, he has a mantra I've been hearing my whole life:

The nets don't make money on the boat. They only make money in the water.

I am eighteen years old, the youngest of the nine crew members, working on my father's boat full-time. It's a hulking steel vessel named *Lisa,* with a banged-up hull and a rusty patchwork of dents and dark paint. It has seen better days, lots of them. I am not on board because I want to be. I am on board to make my fifty dollars a week so I can go to mechanic's school. I have already decided that the fisherman's life is not for me. I don't like being out at sea all week, or the monstrous hours or monotony, and that's not even getting into the risks involved.

Did you know that fishing is the second most dangerous occupation out there, behind logging? a friend tells me. *That it's thirty-six times more dangerous than the average job?*

I did not know that, I reply. But I am not surprised. Then I tell

him about the family friend who had his arm ripped right off his
body when it got caught between two boats.

There is another reason I am not keen on being a fisherman. I
hate being away from Clara. Six days a week out at sea, and one
day a week with Clara? Can we reverse the ratio?

Right now I don't have a choice, though. I need money and this
is how I can earn it. Our nets are in the water, in the Gulf of Panama, and we are not having a good day of it. For hours we've been
in one of our regular sardine hot spots, called La Maestra, but we
haven't caught anything and are heading back to our base island.
We are about twenty minutes away, not far from the Canal, when
the fish-finding sonar lights up.

If the sonar is orange, it means you've come across a lot of fish.
If the sonar is red, it means you have hit the fish lottery. The sonar
is red. They are everywhere. We go all day with no action, and suddenly we're right on top of the mother of all sardine schools. Even
though we're near the Canal, my father figures that at this hour—
it's after 11:00 p.m.—the boat traffic won't be a problem. You only
make thirty-five dollars for every one hundred tons of fish, so you
don't want any swimming away.

Drop the net. Let's go. The fish are waiting, my father hollers.

We cast the net out in a huge circle, the idea being to surround
the fish with it, and then quickly close it up with two massive ropes
that get pulled in by hydraulic winches on either side.

It takes a bit of time, but we have a huge haul, maybe eighty or
ninety tons of sardines, the net just about bursting, our boat sitting
so low it's practically submerged in the water. We have so many
fish, in fact, that my father radios for another couple of boats to
come so we can transfer our haul to them and go back out and
catch more. The other boats show up, and we unload the sardines
and go back to the hot spot. It is now close to 4:00 a.m. It's not normal to fish at such an hour, but we are not stopping now.

Not when the sonar is flaming red.

My father circles the spot again and we drop the net. He has a hard time maneuvering the boat in the strong current, but we get where we need to be. There is one guy in the back and one in the front working the ropes—huge hunks of interwoven line that do the heavy lifting, bringing the bounty up to the boat. The ropes are guided by a pulley system, and at the top of the pulleys there are flaps that lock into place so the ropes won't fly out of control once the winch starts reeling them in. When the ropes start coming, they move at a blinding clip, like cars on the Daytona straightaway.

We are working in complete darkness, the sun still two hours from coming up. Our deck lights are not on because lights would alert the fish to our presence and then they would swim away. We are about to close the net and fire up the hydraulic winches and bring the fish up. I am near the middle of the boat, about six feet from my uncle Miguel. It's a bit tricky working in the dark, but we're all so familiar with what needs to be done that it isn't usually a problem.

Except that one of the pulley flaps is not secure. In the daytime somebody definitely would've noticed. In the darkness nobody does.

The ropes have to close the net in tandem, one after another, and when I notice that one rope is too far ahead, I tell the crew member on the second rope to let go of his rope. He lets go, but because the flap is not secure, when the winch starts reeling it in, the rope takes off, coming at us like a braided bazooka, ripping out of the water and onto the deck. It happens in an instant. There is no time to get out of the way. The rope blasts into my uncle at chest level, knocking a 240-pound man across the ship as if he were a palm frond. My uncle crashes face-first into the metal edge dividing a large salt-water-filled bin in the middle of the boat. The rope lashes into me a microsecond later, also hitting me in the chest, and I go flying even farther, but I don't hit the metal edge, just the divider itself.

I get a tooth knocked out and get scraped and bruised but otherwise come out unscathed. It has nothing to do with athletic ability or anything I do to minimize the damage; by the grace of God, I simply land in a relatively safe place.

My uncle is not so fortunate. His face is split open, blood gushing everywhere. He is badly hurt. He is screaming in pain. It is the most horrific thing I've ever seen.

Stop! Help! Miguel is hurt! somebody yells.

Call for help! Quick! He's hurt bad!

Everybody on board is screaming. My father, who is at the helm in the cabin upstairs, races down to find his brother looking as if he'd taken a machete to the face. I keep replaying the nightmarish sequence of events. An unfastened flap, an out-of-control rope, and seconds later, an uncle I love—the man who gently explained to me why my father is so strict and quick with the belt—seems about to die before my eyes. I wish I could do something. I wish I could do anything. My father radios the Coast Guard, our first responders, and they arrive within minutes and take my uncle to the nearest hospital. The sun is coming up now. I can't get the brutal images out of my head.

My uncle is a diabetic, and that massively complicates his recovery. He seems better on some days, and on others slips back again. He fights for his life for a month. He does not win that fight. The funeral and burial are held right in Puerto Caimito. People show up by the hundreds.

Miguel has gone home to be with the Lord, the priest says. We grieve for this loss, but we have to remember that the Lord has prepared a room for him and he has gone to a better place. There are nine prayerful days of mourning. It is the first time I remember seeing my father cry.

We are back out on the boat a few days later, because the nets only make money in the water. We return for the final day of mourning. The perils of the job are nothing we can change. This is just what we do, day after day, week after week.

Close to a year after my uncle died, we are supposed to be off on a Friday, only my father doesn't know it because he never gets the message from the company that owns the boat. We spend the first part of the day repairing the nets and then set out in the direction of Contadora Island, in the Pacific Ocean, heading toward Colombia. The nets fill quickly and we start back toward our base island to unload our haul. We have not gotten far when the belt on our water pump stops working. We try a backup belt that we have, but it doesn't fit properly. The pump is still not working.

This is not good.

The pump is what gets the water out of the boat. You do not stay afloat for long if your pump is not functioning.

We're carrying about a hundred tons of sardines and we're sitting low and taking on water. Without the pump, we immediately begin taking on a lot more water. We are about two thousand feet off an island called Pacheca, which is next to Contadora. We are starting to sink.

There is no time to deliberate. My father has an immediate decision to make—a decision no captain ever wants to make.

We're going to bring the boat into Pacheca, right onto the sand, my father says. There isn't time to do anything else.

He heads directly for the island and we are about halfway there, maybe a thousand feet away, when the belt mysteriously starts working again. Nobody knows why, and nobody is launching an investigation. Water begins to get pumped out and the boat rises in the water. My father is relieved, and you can see it on his face; he knows all about the risks involved with trying to pilot such a big boat onto shore. We could hit a rock or a coral reef, and the hull would get shredded like cheese in a grater. We'd take on too much sandy water, and the engine would be gummed up for the rest of time.

We are two hours from our base island of Taboguilla, and with the pump back in commission, my father says we're going back to Contadora. The wind is picking up and the swells in the ocean are getting bigger, but he is confident it will be no problem.

We need to get back and unload the fish, he says. As long as the belt is good and the pump is good, it will be fine.

My father has been fishing these waters for years, and has keen instincts about what's safe and what isn't. Those instincts have served him well, but that doesn't mean they are always right. He reverses field and pulls away from Pacheca. We don't get more than fifteen hundred feet before the pump stops again.

It is almost 9:00 p.m. now. The water in the boat starts rising, of course. The wind keeps getting stronger, and soon the swells are eight or ten feet, crashing over the sides of the boat. The conditions are worsening by the second. The boat is taking on water at a terrifying rate.

Now there is no decision to make, because there is only one alternative.

We're heading back to Pacheca, my father shouts. He turns the boat around. The shoreline has literally become our only port in the storm.

It is not going to be an easy or fast trip, not with the water on board and the seas so heavy.

Let's just get to safety, get to shore, no matter how slow going it is. I know this is what my father must be thinking.

And then the engine knocks off.

It doesn't sputter or wheeze. It just dies. The engine is in the front of the boat and probably just got drowned by all the water.

Now what do we do? I ask my father.

We get down there and try to crank-start it, he says. He seems remarkably poised, given the circumstances.

We clamber down the metal steps into the hull, through the wet and darkness, and I grip a thick metal handle and start cranking and cranking on a device that pumps air to generate power to jump-start the engine.

Nothing.

I crank some more. The engine is still not responding.

Our ninety-foot boat is bobbing in the water like a cork now. It is sinking fast. There is no more time for cranking. We scramble up and out to the main deck, almost waist-high in water.

Everybody onto the lifeboat, my father hollers.

The lifeboat is made of iron, deep-hulled and fifteen feet long. We fight the wind and walls of water and finally wrestle the lifeboat into the sea, and all nine of us get in. It is supposed to be equipped with life jackets, but it isn't. My father starts the engine and steers us slowly away from *Lisa*, waves crashing and cresting, tossing the lifeboat as if it were a bathtub toy.

Behind us, I see my father's boat—and our family's livelihood—keel over on its side and then turn upside down. In minutes it disappears completely.

Pacheca is off in the distance, maybe eight hundred feet away. It might as well be on the other side of the earth. I am on the right side of the lifeboat. It is sitting so low with all of us in it that now it starts to take on water, too.

I look out toward the lights of Pacheca. I wonder if I am going to have to swim for my life. I wonder how many of us—or if any of us—will make it. The swells are one thing. The sharks are another. We have fished these waters many times. Hammerheads, reef sharks, tiger sharks: We have seen all kinds.

There are sharks everywhere.

The best hope for us is to get to shore via the back side of the island, where there is some protection from the wind and the seas figure to be much less rough. That is exactly where my father tries to take us. It is slow going. Up and down the swells we go. The big boat is already gone. Is this one going down, too?

I can't stop staring at the churning sea. It looks so angry. I don't scare easily on the water, but I am scared. We are getting a little closer to the back of the island, but it still seems hopelessly far away. The wind and water continue to pound us. Nobody on the boat is saying a word. I am so racked with fear I can barely breathe.

I can't believe I might die because of a faulty water pump.

I knew I wanted no part of being a fisherman, and this is exactly why. I think about my uncle, and what the fishing life has cost our family. I think about my mother and brothers and sister. Most of all, I think about Clara. She is my best friend, the person I want to spend my life with, even though I've never told her that. The thought that I might never see her again is almost too much to bear.

A wave of water soaks me as I hang on to the side of the boat. Do I want to drown to death, or get eaten by a shark? Nineteen years of age, and these are my options.

Somehow my father keeps the lifeboat creeping forward, plowing and dipping through the waves. I try to steer my mind away from the options. He is actually making progress somehow, even in a glorified dinghy that is far from the ideal vessel in such harsh elements. Maybe he will get us to the calmer water, after all. Maybe we aren't going down.

Is it five minutes later? Ten minutes? I don't know. I just know we are much closer now, probably three hundred feet from land. The wind is subsiding and the surf seems to be in retreat. We pick up a little more speed. We are heading toward a sandy beach.

We are going to make it to Pacheca.

My father lifts up the motor and guides the lifeboat onto the beach. I jump out and shout with joy.

Land! We're on land. Land has never felt so good!

We begin hugging each other. I even hug my father—that's a first, as far as I can remember—and thank him for doing such a masterful job navigating us through. My father had radioed ahead, so the police and Coast Guard are waiting for us and check to make sure we are okay. They take us to a hotel—Pacheca is a tourist island, so it has plenty of nice places to stay—where they let our whole shivering and grateful group get a hot shower and dry clothes. It's sad about the boat sinking, but this ending beats any scenario I could've imagined even a few minutes earlier.

Eventually my father gets a new boat from the company he captains for, but for the time being, our fishing season is over. We spend our time repairing the net. It's tedious and time-consuming, but I am in no rush to get back out on the water. And I am happy to be doing anything, alive.

The near-calamity brings one other positive result: Without our six-day excursions on the boat, I get to play more ball with my team, Panama Oeste. I play ball all the time as a kid, but in a place as poor and remote as Puerto Caimito, it's much more likely to be a pickup game on the shore than anything remotely organized. I am one of the stronger players from our village, and at thirteen I begin to travel around Panama as a member of our provincial team, playing teams from other provinces. I am a good local player, but it's not as if people are touting me as the next Rod Carew or Rennie Stennett. When I reach eighteen, I am invited to play with the

Panama Oeste Vaqueros (Cowboys) in Panama's top adult league. I play whatever position the Cowboys want me to play. One game I am in right field, the next game at shortstop, and the next one after that I am behind the plate. I usually bat leadoff or No. 2. I can run and hit the ball in the gaps.

My favorite position, though, is the outfield, because there's nothing better in baseball than running down a fly ball. I am stationed in right field for an important game in the league playoffs. We have our best starter on the mound. We are sure he's going to be dominant, but today they are all over him, smacking hits from here to the Canal, and we are getting into a big hole. The manager comes out to the mound, looks around for a moment, and then motions to me in right field.

Why is he looking at me? I think. *He can't mean me. I am not even a pitcher.*

He points at me again. He waves for me to come in. He does mean me. I have no clue what is going on, but I trot in.

I know you aren't a pitcher, the manager says, but we're in a bind, and all we're looking for is for you to throw strikes. Don't worry about anything else. You throw the ball over the plate and you'll be fine.

Well, I'll try, but I really don't know what I'm doing, I say.

Throw strikes and you'll be fine, he says again.

Okay, I'll do my best, I say.

I've always had a good arm, a loose arm, and I can pretty much put the ball where I want. But I am far from the hardest thrower around, and I haven't pitched since I threw a few innings for the provincial team when I was fourteen. It feels totally bizarre to have my foot on the rubber, to try to come up with some motion on the spot.

I come on in the second inning and go the rest of the way. I do not allow a run. I am doing nothing cute. I have no curveball and sure don't have any dipsy-do windup. I get the ball and throw it, probably no more than eighty-five miles per hour, but I am getting ahead of everybody, hitting corners, pitching quickly.

We wind up winning the game.

Great job, the manager says. You kept us in it and gave us time to come back. You saved the game for us.

I do not think any more about it. As far as I'm concerned this is a one-day fling. Next time out, I will be back at short or left or wherever.

I go back to fixing the nets and playing as much ball with Oeste as I can, vaguely figuring out a timeline for when I am going to enroll in mechanic's school. About two weeks later, I spend a quiet Sunday afternoon at the beach with Clara and my family. At the end of the day we walk back up the hill to the house, and when we arrive, Emilio Gaes and Claudino Hernandez, the center fielder and catcher from Panama Oeste, are waiting for me. They want to speak to me, and, since we have no phone, showing up is the only way that will happen.

What are you guys doing here? I say.

We've arranged a tryout for you, Claudino says.

A tryout? What are you talking about? With who?

With the New York Yankees.

The New York Yankees?

Do you really expect me to believe this? I think.

Yes, they want to see you pitch, Claudino says.

We told them how good you looked the other day and they think you are worth checking out, Emilio says.

This is getting more absurd by the second.

See me pitch? But I am not a pitcher, I say. If you guys are joking, please stop it.

We are not joking. We're serious, Mariano. They want to see you pitch and the tryout is tomorrow, Claudino says.

I look at my teammates in complete disbelief. I couldn't be

more shocked if Clayton Moore and Jay Silverheels rode into Puerto Caimito and said I was going to get a chance to be on *The Lone Ranger*.

When I press for more details, Claudino tells me he was so impressed with what he saw from me in that game that he and Emilio got the idea to call up Chico Heron and tell him about me. Chico is a local coach and part-time scout for the Yankees, one of those baseball lifers who are always at one field or another. Emilio and Claudino are really good guys, but they also are looking to get a little piece of the action, if there is any. Turns out, if you refer a player to the Yankees who winds up signing, you get a finder's fee of two hundred dollars.

So what do you think? Claudino asks.

What I think is that it's one of the craziest things I've ever heard. But nets don't make any money when they are on the boat. And I love playing ball.

I'll see you tomorrow, I say.

3

Two Buses, Nine Pitches

THE YANKEES TRYOUT IS held in Estadio Juan Demóstenes Arosemena, a fabled old park with ornate turns of stone in its stucco façade. It dates to 1938 and is named for the Panamanian president who built it. The Latin words *Citius, Altius, Fortius* (Faster, Higher, Stronger) are etched into the stone by the main entrance. I'm not convinced I am going to be any of the three, but I am here to give it a shot. Many of the top Central American and Pan American championship tournaments are held in Juan Demóstenes Arosemena. I spend the first half of the day repairing nets with my father, who isn't thrilled that I am leaving but grudgingly gives me permission.

Get as much done as you can before you go, he says.

I set out for Panama City at 1:00 p.m. I take a bus from Puerto Caimito to Chorrera for 45 cents. Then I switch and get on another bus that takes me to Panama City, for 65 cents. The trip takes an hour and a half, and by then I am hungry, so I stop at a bodega and get six little rolls—*pan de huevo,* we call them—for a nickel apiece, and a 25-cent container of milk. It means I won't have the full $1.10 I need for the bus trip home, but the drivers are usually good about letting you slide until the next time.

It's a twenty-minute walk from the bus stop to the stadium. Much of it is in a barrio called Curundú, a ragged section of the city with run-down houses, vacant lots, and starving stray dogs almost everywhere you look. Garbage is scattered all over the place. You see drunks, homeless people, and street hustlers. Crime is widespread. It's not a neighborhood you want to linger in, but people tell me that nobody messes with ballplayers. I walk fast and don't stop. I get through the barrio with no problem.

It's a good thing the Yankees don't have a dress code for tryouts. If they did, I would've been sent right back to Puerto Caimito. I show up in old green pants, a frayed shirt, the shoe with the hole... and no glove. There are about twenty other prospects there, and when I arrive in my ragamuffin outfit, I see them pointing and laughing at me.

Hey, look, they're giving a tryout to a hobo, I imagine them saying.

I've played games in the park before. I know the layout and the size — it seats twenty-five thousand people — so the surroundings are familiar enough. The first thing I do is look up Chico Heron, the Yankee scout who has organized the tryout. Chico is a small, round man who always has a Yankee hat on his curly mop of hair. I've known him for years; you can't be a ballplayer around Chorrera or Puerto Caimito or any of the surrounding towns and not know him. I shake hands and say hello.

I am glad you're here, Mariano. We're taking a look at some players and I'd like to have you throw to me. I hear you looked good in relief the other day. So you are doing some pitching now?

Well, a little bit. It's not like I pitch every day or anything. Really, I just pitched that one time, because the team needed me.

Okay, fine. Get out there and warm up and we'll get started.

Chico had scouted me once before, about a year earlier. He was looking at me as a shortstop when I played some games there for Oeste. I made most of the plays, and had a couple of hits, but Chico didn't see enough to recommend me as a prospect. He was concerned that I wouldn't be enough of a hitter to be a pro prospect, and because he'd scouted me previously, he wasn't all that fired up when he got the call from Claudino and Emilio.

I've already seen Mariano Rivera as a shortstop, Chico told them.

You haven't seen him as a pitcher, Emilio said. You need to take a look.

Trust me. I caught him, Claudino said. This is a kid who can put the ball wherever he wants.

I recognize quite a few of the guys at the tryout from playing against them. At twenty years old, I am one of the oldest players there. The guy they really want to look at is a big kid pitcher named Luis Parra, a really hard thrower. There's another pitcher they like a lot, but I don't even know his name. I ask one of the guys if I can borrow a glove and start to warm up. I am not worried about Luis Parra or anybody else. It is not even in my mind to make an impression, or do anything but play ball. Performance anxiety is not in my makeup. What is the worst thing they can do if they don't like me—send me home? I am not thinking that this is my big chance to escape Puerto Caimito and change the course of my family's life forever.

All I am thinking is: *Let's play ball, and then I'll get on the buses and go home.*

After a few minutes, Chico calls me over.

Why don't you get on the mound and throw some pitches?

Okay, sure.

I head out to the mound and dig in front of the rubber a little. When I look down I see my big toe poking out of my right shoe, but I pay no mind. I face the plate, pitch from the traditional windup position. I rock back with my left leg, raise my hands up slightly, then bring my left leg forward and push off with my right. I wind and deliver—a fastball on the corner. I get the ball back from the catcher and throw again, another strike on the black that pops into the catcher's glove. I am throwing easily, fluidly, with no grunting or flailing limbs, and seemingly little effort. I may be built like a pipe cleaner, but the ball seems to know where it needs to go.

I throw a total of nine pitches. They are all fastballs, because that is the only pitch I have.

That's good, Mariano. That's all I need, Chico says.

I am not sure what he means. Nine pitches? That's it? Is it time for me to get back to the fishnets now?

A few minutes later Chico pulls me aside.

I like what I saw from you today. I would like you to keep coming back for the rest of the week, and then have Herb Raybourn, director of Latin American scouting for the Yankees, take a look at you. Herb is the one who has to make the final call. What do you think about that?

That's fine, Chico, I say. As long as I can get off of work, I'll come back. Thank you for having me in today.

I hope I see you tomorrow, Chico says.

I walk back through the barrio, dodge a few panhandlers, and get on one bus and then another (and talk the driver into accepting a reduced fare of twenty-five cents for today). My father signs off on the additional tryout sessions. The rest of my week follows the same schedule. I repair fishing nets in the morning, then take two buses and walk through Curundú to get to Estadio Juan Demóstenes Arosemena in the afternoon. I work out for Chico all week, and it's all good. I get to play ball every day, and get time off from the nets—always a welcome thing. Herb Raybourn shows up at the end of the week. I find out I will be pitching against the Panamanian National Team. I don't know much more, except that I am sure I will be pitching last. Parra is obviously the pitcher they are most interested in, and there are other guys whom they've been looking at a lot more closely during the week, guys who are throwing more and getting much more feedback.

I am a bottom-of-the-barrel guy. That much is very clear to me.

And that's fine. I don't burn to teach them a lesson for underestimating me. I don't fill up with private fury at the sight of Luis Parra or the other guys. Nothing is really registering with me about what doing well here could mean. It's as if they are talking in a foreign language, like English, whenever they speak to me. I am just doing what they ask. They tell me to go here, and I go here. They tell me to go there, I go there, and when they tell me to pitch, I pitch. I don't see the future. I can't even imagine it.

Why aren't the possibilities on my radar?

What's radar?

On the final day, I ride the same two buses, and stop for the same *pan de huevo* and milk. When I get to the stadium, I see Herb talking to Chico. Herb has white hair and a medium build, and his radar gun is ready to go. Like Chico, he is surprised to see me as a pitcher, because he had looked at me as a shortstop, too. I know Herb a little bit. He used to work for the Pittsburgh Pirates and signed several Panamanian big leaguers, including Omar Moreno, Rennie Stennett, and Manny Sanguillen. But mostly I know him because he once signed my cousin Manuel Giron, my mother's nephew. Manuel was also a pitcher, and a lot of people thought he'd be the first player from Puerto Caimito to make the majors. He played three years in the Pirates' system and then got released. He came back to Puerto Caimito and went to work— where else?—in the fishing business. My cousin never talked much about his baseball career, and I didn't ask him. He was back home, which happened to almost everybody, and that was that.

About a half hour before the game is going to start, Herb finds me in the dugout.

You're going to pitch first, so you should warm up soon, he says.

I am shocked.

I am starting?

Yes. I want to put you right out there and show these guys some pitching, Herb says, smiling.

He's got to be kidding, I think.

I get my arm loose and I feel good as I walk out to the mound. Herb settles in behind home plate with his gun. I don't know what he's expecting, or what numbers the gun will spit out. I'm not worried about it, either. As inexperienced as I am, I understand pitching enough to know that it involves much more than what digits you put up on a gun.

The leadoff hitter steps in and I get ahead right away. I settle into a groove quickly, throwing strike after strike, hitter after hitter. There is no deception to anything I am doing. The ball is going exactly where I want it to, on almost every pitch. The strike zone looks as big as the side of a house. My approach, even then, is to keep it simple, and get out of there quickly.

I go three innings and strike out five and give up one hit. I'm not counting, but I probably don't throw more than thirty or thirty-five pitches, almost all fastballs with one or two very primitive change-ups mixed in. When I walk off, Chico shakes my hand.

Good job, Mariano. You're done for the day. We're going to look at some of the other guys now.

I thank him and sit in the dugout and watch Parra and the others, wishing I could get out there and play some more, maybe run around the outfield. Not to make an impression. Just to play. I'd always rather play than watch. After the game, Herb asks me if we can talk for a few minutes.

Sure, of course, I say.

You looked very good out there today, he says.

Thank you.

You made some good hitters look pretty ordinary.

Thank you.

I think you have a future as a pitcher. I'd like to talk to you and your parents about you signing a contract with the New York Yankees. Can you come here tomorrow and meet me, and then we will go to your house so we can all meet and discuss this?

Yes, sure. That would be okay with me, I say.

I am not sure why Herb wants me to meet him, instead of just driving to Puerto Caimito himself, but I do as he asks. After I get to the stadium, we ride together through the hills and the sliver of rain forest, through Chorrera and finally back into my village. My father is down at the boat when we arrive, so I have to go get him. Herb has a small briefcase with him. I wonder what is in it, and wonder what this all means, because it is still not at all clear to me.

When we all get to our little block house, Clara is there, too, and that's a big comfort. If something important is happening to me, I want her there. Herb opens his briefcase and puts the contract on the table and explains what happens from here, as Clara and my family listen, all of us a touch amazed.

With my parents' blessings, I sign a contract with the New York Yankees. I am getting a $2,000 bonus to be a ballplayer. It is February 17, 1990, a Saturday.

My little marble is about to get a lot bigger.

4

Gulf Coast Revelation

GETTING TO THE NEW World isn't easy. My fellow prospect Luis Parra is my traveling companion. We have to change planes in Miami. That means navigating the Miami airport, finding a new gate, and getting there before the plane leaves. Luis is as clueless as I am. It feels as if we've been dropped in the middle of a big city in a foreign country, because we have. People are racing around with manic looks on their faces. Babies are wailing. Announcements are blaring. I've never seen so many people or heard such chaos.

Fortunately, there are enough Spanish-speaking people that, after asking about ten of them for help, we manage to get to the gate for the short hop to Tampa. The flight is memorable only because I discover, two trips into my flying career, that I am terrified being off the ground. I will fly millions of miles in the next twenty-plus years. It never gets better.

We get off the plane and start walking down the concourse of the Tampa airport. It is less hectic but still bewildering. I see all these signs in English that I don't understand.

Bagel? French fries? Home of the Whopper?

What do these things mean?

Baggage claim? Lost and found? Ground transportation?

Can somebody please explain?

Parra and I keep walking. We have one objective: Find a guy in a Yankee hat and Yankee jacket. This is all they tell us: Look for a guy named Chris wearing Yankee stuff. He's sort of a roly-poly guy in his late thirties. You can't miss him.

Actually, we could miss him, very easily. If anybody else is wearing a Yankee hat and jacket, we're in big trouble. They probably wouldn't leave No. 1 draft choices who don't speak English on their own in a strange airport, but we are obscure Panamanian kids who sign for roughly the equivalent of a pound of shrimp. So, no, we aren't going to get the royal treatment.

We're going to get Chris and his Yankee outfit.

Down the escalator we go, near the baggage carousel. Wait.

Look, there's a guy in a Yankee jacket. Maybe that's him, I tell Parra. He looks as if he's waiting for somebody.

We walk over.

Chris? I say.

He extends his hand.

That's me. Welcome to Tampa. You must be Mariano Rivera and Luis Parra. C'mon, we'll get your bags and head over to the complex.

Neither of us has any idea what he is saying. English isn't even our second language. It's not our language at all. Our blank faces tell him as much.

The short trip from the airport to Yankee headquarters blows my mind. The roads are so big…and so paved. The office buildings and stores are all huge and new and look so impressive. The layout of everything is dazzling in size and scope, and then we pull into the Yankee complex and get out of the car, and my awe takes off like a speedboat in the Canal.

I look one way and see the most beautifully manicured ball field I have ever laid eyes on. I look the other way and see another field, just as perfect, and then see two more beyond that, and wonder how it is that baseball fields could look like this (I am guessing the grass is not cut by a kid with a machete).

I am not in El Tamarindo anymore. I am in Hardball Heaven.

There are spotless offices and a spacious clubhouse. There are batting cages and training rooms and more bats and balls and helmets than I knew existed. Chris, who is a clubhouse guy when he isn't an airport driver, hands us our practice gear and uniforms. I also get a glove and a set of spikes, so I can retire the pair with the hole. It's like Christmas in April. We head over to the Bay Harbor Inn, the nearby hotel that belongs to Yankees owner George Steinbrenner; it is where we will be living for the season. I have stayed in a few roadside motels that cost ten or twelve bucks a night traveling around Panama, but those are places where you are lucky if you get a bed. Here, Parra and I have a television and our own bathroom. We have a stockpile of towels and soaps and shampoos. There is room service, too.

What's room service? Parra asks me.

I have no idea.

Luis and I don't venture far from the hotel very often, mostly because of the language barrier. When we go out to eat, if we don't have a Latin server, we point to the photo on the menu that looks good. Iguana dishes are strangely absent.

When we get on the field and start the workouts, I am struck right away by the size of the players, the pitchers especially. They are all big and a bunch of them are thick-bodied. Our top pitcher, a left-handed kid from Duke University named Tim Rumer, is six foot three and over 200 pounds. Russ Springer, from Louisiana State University, is six foot four and about 200 pounds, and even a six-foot right-hander from Clemson, Brian Faw, outweighs me by 30 pounds or so. I watch these guys throw and I figure the radar gun is about to break, they are throwing so hard. Rumer has a curveball that breaks about two feet.

But the more I am out on the field with the Gulf Coast Yankees, the more I know I can compete with them. When we run and field and do drills, I am right there with everybody. And when I am on the mound I discover that, as skinny as I am, and as underwhelming as my 86- or 87-mile-per-hour fastball is, I can do one thing better than just about anybody else:

Put the ball exactly where I want.

With most pitchers in rookie ball, the coaches tell them to just throw strikes, even if they are over the middle of the plate. Once you can do that, you can expand the strike zone and work on fine-tuning your command. But I am not like that. The Lord has blessed me with the gift of control. If I want to throw the ball knee-high on the black, I do it. If I want to paint the black on the other side, I can do that, too. I still have my one-pitch repertoire—fastball—with a pretty lame slider and a mediocre changeup mixed in. I will work on the changeup for years, and it never gets any better. The rookie hitters watch me warm up and probably think, *This is going to be easy.*

Tim Cooper, our third baseman, sometimes catches me in the bullpen. Coop, as we all call him, studied Spanish in high school and becomes my language instructor. I throw my fastball and he smiles, shakes his head, and says, How are guys not whacking these pitches out of the park every time?

My manager is Glenn Sherlock, and my pitching coach is Hoyt Wilhelm, the old knuckleballer. They are both good guys, though I understand little of what they say. They put me in the bullpen to start the year. Wilhelm is doing what he can to help, but basically I know nothing about the nuances of pitching. All around me are guys who have been groomed to do this for a decade or more, and here I am, a guy who got here because one Sunday afternoon the Panama Oeste Cowboys needed somebody to finish a game.

But when I get in the game, I am usually ahead of the hitter,

1–2 or 0–2, by the time the announcer finishes saying my name. It goes that way pretty much the whole year. I pitch a total of 52 innings and give up 17 hits and one earned run. I strike out 58 and walk 7 and have an ERA of 0.17. Tim Rumer is the club's pitching star, one of the best guys in the Gulf Coast League, but with my very average fastball I have quite a run of success.

This doesn't surprise me.

It shocks me.

All around I see guys who are stronger than me and throw harder than me, and I am outperforming nearly all of them. It is almost an out-of-body experience. I get guy after guy out and think the same thing every time:

How on earth am I doing this?

The way everything is falling together is almost incomprehensible. First, I am supposed to be in the Dominican Republic, not Tampa, but the Yankees decided to bring me to extended spring training because I am already twenty. Now, in the first few weeks, they see how raw I am as a pitcher and start talking again about moving me to the Dominican Republic to get in extra work, but Herb intervenes.

Yes, he's raw, but look at the command he has, Herb tells his scouting bosses. Let's let him pitch in games and see what we've got.

It has to be the work of the Lord. I am getting results that are way beyond my physical abilities. I don't fully understand what is going on, but it feels much bigger than me.

Rookie ball is unlike any other level of pro baseball, because it is all so new and different for everybody. For foreign guys like me and American guys who bypass college, it's not just our first time away from home, it's our first time playing this many games—more than sixty—in a season. There is so much to get accustomed to, and performance can be totally skewed. The top pick in the entire big league draft in 1990, Chipper Jones, is in our league. He plays for the Gulf Coast Braves. He hits .229 that year. The premier pitching prospect in the league, Jose Martinez of the Mets, winds up appearing in a total of four big league games. The top reliever, Anthony Bouton of the Gulf Coast Rangers, piles up seventeen saves and two years later is out of baseball altogether. Tim Rumer never pitches in the big leagues. I am the twenty-sixth-rated pitcher in the Gulf Coast League. I do not make the All-Star team. I am as anonymous as you can get. I take home $310 every two weeks, after taxes, and save it to give to my parents when I get back to Panama.

Tim Cooper and I get closer and closer as the season goes on. I even let him cut my hair. He does a good job, and instructs me on ballplayer humor, too. I can't do anything about your face, he says. We travel the Gulf Coast by bus, to Dunedin and Clearwater and Bradenton, and we make up a rule: Coop is only allowed to speak Spanish, and I am only allowed to speak English. Some people go with Berlitz to learn a language. Others go with Rosetta Stone. I go with Tim Cooper, of Chico, California. I start to pick up some words, even some sentences, and I pick up even more when we go out to play pool after dinner. We bet $1 a game, and I take a lot of Coop's money. (I got pretty good at pool hanging out in the clubs in Chorrera.) I learn how to say, This is like taking candy from a baby.

We also go fishing a lot. Behind the Bay Harbor, there's a wooden pier, and we buy some fishing poles and put the lines in the water. If the fish aren't biting off the pier, we'll wade into the Gulf. Mostly we reel in catfish, and then we release them and catch some more. I can't get away from fish no matter where I go.

On a bus trip to Sarasota one day, Coop decides to raise the bar on my English.

Okay, we're going to do a little role play right now, Coop says. You just won Game 7 of the World Series, and Tim McCarver wants to talk to you. You can't call in a translator. That'll kill the moment. You have to be able to speak English, so you might as well start learning now.

Ready?

And Coop channels his best Tim McCarver:

Mariano, could you ever have imagined this when you were growing up in Panama—pitching in the World Series for the Yankees?

Not really. It's amazing. Thanks to the Lord, I was able to get those last outs.

You had to face three strong hitters at the end. What was your approach?

I just want to make good pitches and get ahead.

You used to work on your father's fishing boat, and now you are a world champion. What have you learned along the way?

I think if you have the help of the Lord, you can do anything. You can dream big things.

Coop ends the interview there.

Muy bueno, he says.

Thank you, I say.

The Gulf Coast Yankees are barely a .500 team, but I keep getting people out. With one day left in the season, I have pitched a total of 45 innings—5 innings short of qualifying for the league ERA title. Sherlock consults with Yankee player-development people and asks them if I can start against the Pirates so I can get the innings I need, even though I had pitched a couple of innings the day before. The Yankees okay it. I haven't gone five innings the whole season, but I figure I can do it if I am economical.

It is August 31, 1990, a Friday. The game is at home, in Tampa. I cruise through three scoreless innings, then a fourth. We take a

3–0 lead. I have not given up a hit as I take the mound in the top of the fifth. A Pirate hitter rips a ball toward third base. Coop makes a diving grab on the backhand side, and fires to first to get him. Minutes later in the outfield, Carl Everett, the Yankees' No. 1 draft choice that year, runs down a ball in the gap.

Going into the seventh, the Pirates are still without a hit. They have had one base runner; he got on when our second baseman booted a grounder. I get the first two outs in the seventh and have only one out to go (we're playing a doubleheader; in the minors, that means that the games are shortened to seven innings). All I am thinking about is hitting the glove of my catcher, Mike Figga, and making a good pitch. I don't let my mind go anywhere else. I get the guy on a fastball on the corner and an instant later I am engulfed by teammates.

There may be fifty people in the stands, but this moment — and sharing it with my teammates — is one of the best feelings I've ever had on a ball field. It's the first no-hitter I've ever thrown. By the terms of my contract, it is also supposed to earn me $500 and a watch from the Yankees, but I'm not sure if those bonuses are in play for a seven-inning game.

So I call the head of the whole player-development operation for the Yankees, Mark Newman, who is traveling in Washington, and make my case in my best broken English.

You've had a great season, Mariano. We'll give you your bonuses, happily.

In the clubhouse after the game, the Yankees reward our rousing finish by ordering in wings from Hooters. Speaking in Spanish, Coop says: I think you owe me a cut of the bonus for saving your no-hitter.

Speaking in English, I reply: I no understand.

I fly back to Panama the next day with a profoundly different outlook than I had only five months earlier. I am a pitcher now. A pitcher who wants to compete at the highest level I can. A door has opened to a world of larger possibilities than I have ever imagined. I am not a wannabe mechanic anymore. I am definitely not a fisherman anymore.

I am a professional baseball player.

For the whole off-season, I train with Chico Heron at a gym in Panama City. I get up at 5:00 a.m. and take the same two buses I took to the Yankee tryouts at Juan Demóstenes Arosemena, spending the same 45 cents and 65 cents on fare, only now I don't have to ask for credit. I do this five days a week. I lift and run and go through exercise regimens to build up my strength and overall fitness. I throw to build up my arm strength. I've seen the competition now, and I've seen how long the odds are for a player to get out of rookie ball. We had thirty-three guys on that Gulf Coast Yankee team. Only seven would make it to the majors, and only five would have careers of any substance: Shane Spencer, Carl Everett, Ricky Ledee, Russ Springer, and me.

If I don't make it to the top, it isn't going to be because somebody outworked me.

I move up to Single-A ball in 1991, pitching for the Greensboro Hornets in the South Atlantic League, splitting time between starting and relieving. It makes no difference to me at all. I will rake the mound if they want me to. The bigger challenge for me is off the field. I've gotten off to a good start learning English, thanks to Coop, but unlike Tampa, Greensboro, North Carolina, is a place where almost nobody speaks my native language. It is tremendously isolating. In restaurants and malls and convenience stores, my English shortcomings keep slamming into me.

I try to ask somebody for directions after a game one day.

Excuse me, my English no good, you can tell me how . . .

I stammer and wobble all over the place, and can't manage to say anything. I thought I was way beyond this, but now my English seems to be getting worse. Another time, I ask a clerk in a store a question about merchandise and again come up with nothing. I return to my apartment feeling so alone, more defeated than I have on the field the whole season. I don't know why it hits me in that moment, but it does. I feel like a sardine out of water, tangled in a net with no chance for escape. It feels really bad, completely overwhelming. I start to cry. I go to the bathroom and wash my face and look in the mirror. I turn out the light and go to bed.

I am still crying.

My linguistic pity party doesn't last long. I find Coop the next day.

I need to work on English, Coop. I am not doing good with it. I have to be able to talk when I win the World Series, right?

Coop smiles. We've got a lot of road trips left this year, he says. You are going to be giving speeches by the time we're done.

I don't give too many speeches, and don't give up too many runs, either. My elbow doesn't feel right all season, honestly, but I don't say anything because I don't want anybody to know. No sense jeopardizing anything by speaking up about pain that I can manage. So I just keep pitching. Thanks to the much longer road trips in the South Atlantic League, Coop and I have four- and six- and eight-hour bus rides to speak English and Spanish. The extra hours make all the difference. I get comfortable speaking English at last. I am not lost anymore. I am not alone. Tim Cooper is some teammate. Cuts hair, gives language lessons, saves no-hitters. He and I learn an awful lot on those long trips, and not just language.

If we ever make it to the top, let's make a deal that we're never going to big-league anybody, Coop says. We're never going to act better than anybody or look down on anybody, because that's not what real big leaguers do.

That's right, I say. We don't big-league anybody. We stay humble. We remember where we came from.

What's important is how you treat people. That's what really matters, right? Coop says.

Amen, Coop.

This simple truth becomes a beacon for how to live life for me, in baseball and out of baseball. The Lord doesn't care about wealth or fame or the number of saves somebody has. We are all the children of God, and the Lord cares about the goodness and love in our hearts. That's all.

My faith in what's important helps me appreciate the moment. Players in the minor leagues always curse the marathon bus rides, the fume-filled hours that are supposed to be the dreary essence of life in the bush leagues. Me, I can't see it the same way. Without those bus rides, I don't learn the language I have to learn. I don't reaffirm the values I want to live by.

I finish the year with a 2.75 ERA and more than a strikeout per inning, even though my record stinks (4–9). I remain a complete nobody in the orbit of prospects, but you know what attention I pay to *Baseball America* and all this ranking nonsense?

None.

I don't care what some ranking list says, what arbitrary judgment a computer spits out based on a bunch of data. When they give me the ball, I take it. I pitch. Most of the time I get people out.

Simple is best.

My trip home after the season lasts only four days, because I have to go back for instructional ball. All I want to do is see Clara. We have been together for six years now. She meets me at the airport and I give her a hug and a kiss. I know that it is time. Three years before I signed, Clara and I went for a walk and sat down on a bench at a little park near the water. It was a beautiful, starlit night, and we looked at the sky and decided that if either of us saw a shooting star we would make a wish but had to wish out loud before it disappeared.

Suddenly a star shot across the sky.

To get married to Clara, I said, as fast as I could get the words out. Clara laughed. We both knew we were not getting married at seventeen, but now it is a different time, the right time.

The next night, I invite Clara to go to a Chinese restaurant in Panama City called Don Lee. We take the two buses, the usual involved trip. Don Lee is not fancy, but we like it. And it is all we can afford. It's in the banking district, with the name written in neon in big script. As we approach the restaurant, there is a guy selling roses.

I buy one and give it to Clara.

We sit down at the restaurant.

I love you so much and I missed you so much when I was away, I say.

I love you and missed you, too, Clara says.

We get the menus and the water. I know why we are here but just don't know how to get the words out. I keep looking across the table at Clara. How much do I love this woman? How much do I want to spend my life with her?

The words still have not come. The noodles have, but not the words.

Finally, Clara says, We've been going together all these years. Where is this going?

I smile and grab her hand. I feel foolish that Clara takes the lead, but this is just one of the reasons I love her. Her strength. Her conviction. Her sense of the moment.

Where is this going? I say. I want to get married, Clara. I don't want to be away from you anymore. I will be back in a little over a month. It is crazy, I know. I will be gone, so you will have to arrange everything. All the work, all the planning. But I want to get married and I would love to do it when I come back.

Okay, Clara says. I don't know what took you so long.

I fly back to instructional ball, and Clara takes care of everything—the invitations, the reception, the food, the music, the photographer, you name it. We get married before a judge on November 6, 1991, and then have the public wedding, and the party, November 9. The celebration is held in the Fisherman's Hall in Puerto Caimito. I am a fisherman's boy from a fishing village. You were expecting the Ritz-Carlton? The Fisherman's Hall is a pavilion with a roof and no walls. Clara cooks. My mother cooks. I even cook. We all spend the final days preparing arroz con pollo (chicken with rice), puerco asado (roast pork), empanadas, tamales, all kinds of stuff. We have ceviches (marinated fish) for an appetizer. Clara's cousin is our photographer.

We eat and laugh and dance. It is as simple as it can be, with the smell of fish in the air, and it is the happiest day of my life because it is exactly what a wedding day should be about: a celebration of how blessed we are to each be the other's true love.

5

Worst Cut

IF I HAVE HAD a better year in my life than 1991, I can't remember when. I marry Clara, progress as a pitcher, and learn to speak reasonable English. There is just one problem in the midst of all the good. The pain in my elbow never gets any better. In fact, despite my determined efforts to ignore it and pray for it to disappear, it gets worse. Our trainer, Greg Spratt, and I manage it as best we can. I ice it all the time. I make sure to warm up properly. But the pain never relents, and I just hope the off-season rest will get it to stop barking.

With the wedding behind us, Clara and I start our life together in a puny room inside her mother's house in Puerto Caimito, a space that is a little bigger than a coaching box, with room for a double bed and not much more. Our closet consists of two nails and a broomstick. Fortunately, we have very few clothes. The living is humble even by Puerto Caimito standards, but I have a plan, and that is to save every penny so we can build our own home. We live with her mother, and the broomstick, for four years, even after I make the big leagues.

You do what you need to do.

I spend the winter training with Chico again, a 5:00 a.m. regular on the Puerto Caimito/Chorrera/Panama City bus loop, and even as I put in the work, I am so grateful for this man's loyalty and kindness. He just gives and gives. His reward is seeing me do well. That's it. He takes me places, arranges workouts, helps with mechanics, teaches me how to be a professional—his contributions know no bounds. Whatever I need, Chico Heron is there. You do not forget people like this.

It pays off—all of the work, and all of Chico's help. In the spring of 1992 I get promoted to high Single-A ball, and the Fort Lauderdale Yankees of the Florida State League. It's not Yankee Stadium, but if you keep moving forward, even a level at a time, it usually means you are still in the mix. The way I see it, if I put all my concentration into making every pitch a good one, can I possibly go wrong? I don't have a timetable. My timetable is the next pitch.

One of my teammates in Fort Lauderdale is a kid I'd heard a whole lot about. How could you not have heard about Brien Taylor? He was the number one overall pick in the major league draft in 1991, the Yankees' prize for having their worst record in almost seventy-five years, finishing 67–95, in last place in the American League by a wide margin. Brien signed for a record bonus of $1.55 million, a contract that was negotiated by his mother, Bettie, and the family advisor, Scott Boras, and that instantly made him The Future of the Franchise, and a tourist attraction before he even put on his uniform.

Brien warms up before a Florida State League game, and the scene around the bullpen looks like a mall two days before Christmas, everybody clamoring to see the most famous young left arm in baseball. He is mobbed by fans and autograph seekers everywhere we go. One time he is so swarmed he falls down and almost gets trampled. His No. 19 jersey is actually stolen from our clubhouse, a crime that I don't believe was ever solved. Everybody is caught up in Brien Taylor Mania, even Mark Newman, the Yankees minor league boss, who, after Brien's first start, or maybe his second, compares him to Mozart. I am not even compared to a backup singer for Menudo.

Other than the $1,548,000 difference in our bonuses, Brien and I are separated by...everything. He is a left-handed African American, a high-school kid from eastern North Carolina. I am a right-handed Latino, a twenty-two-year-old from southern Panama. He is a prodigy. I am a project. He grew up on the shores of the Atlantic. I grew up on the shores of the Pacific. *60 Minutes* wants to speak to him for a profile. *60 Minutes* wouldn't know my name even with a program. He has a brand-new Mustang with a souped-up sound system. I don't even know how to drive.

Still, we connect easily. He strikes me as a down-home country kid who would much rather not have any of the fuss that surrounds him. He's fun to be with, a good teammate, somebody who wants to be one of the guys, even though he's obviously different. I find out how different the first time I see him throw in the bullpen, marveling at his silky motion, one that you can't believe is the force behind a ball that hits the catcher's glove like a firecracker. He throws 97, 98 miles per hour, the easiest gas you've ever seen, and has a big hard curveball, too.

I watch and I think: *This is amazing, the weapons this guy has. I have never seen anybody throw a baseball like this. Wow.*

Brien is the top-rated prospect in all of baseball, and in his first pro season, straight out of Beaufort's East Carteret High School, he proves why. He gives up 40 fewer hits than innings pitched, and strikes out 187 batters in just 161.1 innings. His earned run average is 2.57. His stuff is ahead of his command and he is still learning the craft of pitching, but what a baseline to be starting at. He moves up to the Albany-Colonie Yankees and Double-A ball the following year, and now that he's just two rungs on the pro ladder away from the big leagues, The Future is almost here. You can imagine him on the Yankee Stadium mound, blowing away hitters the way he has his whole young life.

Brien's going to show us the way, I think. *There is no stopping The Future now.*

And then, a week before Christmas, 1993, I hear the news. I am home in Panama with Clara. The report on the TV isn't immediately clear to me. All I hear are sketchy details about Brien Taylor and a fight. It honestly doesn't sound like such a big deal. Then other facts start coming in, something about defending his brother and getting involved in a brawl in a trailer park in his hometown, and hurting his shoulder.

His left shoulder.

Tell me this is not true, I think. *Tell me this is not going to have any impact on his big league career.*

Brien winds up having surgery, and rehabs through all of 1994. The Yankees bring him back in 1995, in the Gulf Coast League, wanting to let him break in slowly, but the fluidity, the smoke, the domination that seemed to come so easily, they are gone. He has no idea where the ball is going. A year later, he is much worse, walking almost three guys an inning and putting up an earned run average that could be off a pinball machine.

I never see Brien again.

The whole thing is so horribly sad—to think that the course of his entire life could be altered by a fit of anger and a momentary lapse in judgment. You wonder if what happened in the trailer park had anything to do with Brien's name and fame—if the guy would've come after him if he'd just been a regular person. You wonder why Brien didn't understand in that instant that getting into a fight would not be a good idea. It just makes you realize how it can all crater so quickly, leaving a hole that is beyond repair. And for Brien, the hole just seemed to get deeper, with a conviction years later on federal cocaine-dealing charges that put him in a penitentiary.

I obviously was not in Brien's shoes that night, or any other night, so who am I to judge? I just try to take away what I can from every situation, to always keep learning. Life is hard. Life is humbling. I do all I can to keep it simple and to pray to the Lord for clarity and wisdom, so that His will and His Perfect Goodness will guide me and keep me safe. And if I ever start to falter, it's not too hard to remember Brien Taylor, who effectively traded in his Yankees jersey for a prison uniform, a baseball diamond for the Federal Correctional Institution at Fort Dix, New Jersey.

The Yankees decide that I am a starter in 1992, and I start off well in Fort Lauderdale. The elbow pain is manageable, and if I don't compare to our top pitchers, Brien and Domingo Jean, I am a pretty fair number three starter for the Florida State League. I strike out twelve in one early-season victory and follow it with a complete-game shutout of the Fort Myers Miracle, and get congratulations from my manager, Brian Butterfield, and pitching coach, Mark Shiflett, when I am the league's pitcher of the week in mid-May. My precision is better than ever—I walk five guys the whole season—and I am pitching to an earned run average just over two, but as the year goes on a couple of troubling trends are emerging.

One is that my velocity plummets after I've thrown fifty or sixty pitches. The other is that the slider I am trying to throw seems to aggravate whatever is going on in my elbow. It gets bad enough that the Yankees decide to put me on the disabled list in late July to see if rest alleviates the problem.

I stay optimistic, because that is what I do. I'm in my third productive year of pro baseball. There is no reason to panic. I take a break from throwing for a couple of weeks and return in early August against the Dunedin Blue Jays. The Jays have the most dangerous hitter in the league, Carlos Delgado, a twenty-year-old slugger from Puerto Rico. Carlos is on his way to a thirty–home run, one hundred–RBI season, with a .324 average, in the middle of a lineup that also includes Shawn Green, Derek Bell, and Canadian outfielder Rob Butler, who winds up hitting .358, best in the league.

It's a Friday night in Fort Lauderdale, and I am ready for the challenge of a seriously stacked lineup. I am pitching well, and I move into the fourth inning when the Blue Jays get a man on first. I see him taking a good-sized lead. I fire over to chase him back, but as I do I feel something funny in my elbow. It's hard to describe, but it's not normal.

Definitely not normal.

I catch the return throw and take a moment on the mound. My elbow is throbbing. I turn my sights back to the plate and deliver, and now I feel a hard pop in my elbow, as if something just gave out. Or snapped.

Or ruptured.

I get the ball back from the catcher and pause again on the mound. I look around the park, and at the pockets of fans here and there, maybe a few hundred people in all. They are waiting for the next pitch, and it occurs to me that not one of them—not anybody in the whole park, even in the dugout and bullpen—knows that I am not the same pitcher I was two pitches ago. How could they know? How could they possibly have any clue about what just happened inside my right elbow?

I look the same, but I am not.

I finish the inning and walk to the dugout, my elbow hot and pulsing with pain. I know I am not going to be walking back out there, facing Carlos Delgado or anybody else, any time soon.

I can't pitch, I tell Mark Shiflett. The pain is bad.

The trainer, Darren London, packs my elbow in ice, and I spend the rest of the game on the bench. It is a strange sensation to be out there competing with everything you've got one second, and to be a bystander the next. Something goes pop and, faster than you can say Tommy John, you are damaged goods. You try not to project, but you can't lie to yourself.

You know—absolutely know—this is not good.

Does this mean surgery? How long will I be out? What will I need to do to get better? My head is swirling with questions, but somehow I do not feel any deep anxiety, or anything close to despair. It is the peace and grace of the Lord; it cannot be anything else. Of course I am not happy about the pain and whatever repercussions there will be. Of course I am concerned about my future. But I am not flipping out about it. When the fishing nets were frayed or broken, we fixed them. When the engine on the boat broke, we did all we could to fix it. I come at life from a mechanic's mind-set. If you've got a problem, you find it and you take care of it. That's exactly what I'm going to do with my elbow.

The process isn't always pleasant, but it is simple, and straightforward. You do yourself no good by worrying or projecting, letting thunderheads of gloom set up in your head.

We're going to get your elbow looked at and take good care of it, Darren London says.

Okay, thanks, Darren, I say.

I go back to my apartment and think about calling Clara but decide against it. It wouldn't be fair. All it would do is make her feel terrible that she is not with me. After a bad night of sleep—the elbow is really inflamed and tender—I undergo a series of tests with a Yankee doctor in Miami. The MRIs apparently do not show damage to the ulnar collateral ligament. Then there are more tests, and finally they send me to see Dr. Frank Jobe, the same doctor who would operate on Brien Taylor. He is the king of all elbow-fixers, and the inventor of Tommy John surgery—a term that has become as much a part of the baseball vocabulary as grand-slam home run, or performance-enhancing drugs (PEDs).

If you hang around pitchers for any length of time, I guarantee you will hear a conversation that goes something like this:

You ever have Tommy John?

Yeah, two years ago.

How did it go?

Pretty good. Took a while, but eventually I threw even better. How about you?

Yeah, mine was three years ago.

How did it go?

Same thing. It was a rough road, but I'm all the way back.

Tommy John surgery is a reconstruction of the ulnar collateral ligament in the elbow. Elbows don't like throwing baseballs ninety-plus miles per hour, thousands upon thousands of times, and when the ligament goes, it has to be rebuilt with a ligament from your forearm.

In Los Angeles, Dr. Jobe provides the diagnosis: I have a lot of wear, and I have stuff floating around in my elbow. I am going to require surgery, but I do not need a total reconstruction, just a thorough cleanup. It includes the removal of my funny bone, but at least it doesn't put me in the Tommy John Club. I take in Dr. Jobe's words as I sit in his office and don't say anything at first. I am too busy talking to myself:

This injury is not going to define me. It is not going to stop me. I will have the surgery I need and do whatever I have to do to get back.

Dr. Jobe performs my surgery on August 27, 1992. It's not a day that you'll find commemorated anywhere in the annals of baseball history (though it is the ten-year anniversary of Rickey Henderson breaking the single-season stolen-base record). It's just the day I get my elbow cleaned up—and (I hope) a fresh, pain-free start to my pitching career.

Dr. Jobe does a great job on my elbow, and he also does a great job predicting the future.

This is going to be an up-and-down process, he says. One day you may feel very good, and the next day you won't. That is normal. It's part of the process. Don't get discouraged if you don't progress every day. It takes time for the elbow to fully heal. Just be patient and keep doing your work, and it will be fine.

I am out until the spring of 1993, have a short stay back in the Gulf Coast League, and then join the rotation in Greensboro. I have rust to scrape off and don't have the command I had before, and they naturally have me on a low pitch count, but in ten starts I have an ERA of just over two, and that's nothing to be discouraged about. It is all coming together, in the halting way Dr. Jobe told me it would.

It's all good for me in Greensboro, and there's an added bonus, too — because I make a new friend. He's our shortstop, maybe the only guy on the club who is skinnier than me. He was the Yankees' top draft pick the year after they chose Brien Taylor. His name is Derek Jeter, of Kalamazoo, Michigan. I had met him before, in minor league camp, but this is the first time I get to play with him, and it is some show, because the kid is a year out of high school and all limbs, and you are never sure what he will do. I see him inside-out a ball to right-center field and wind up with a triple. I see him rip doubles down the line and hit in the clutch, and play shortstop like a colt in cleats, chasing down grounders and pop flies and making jump throws from the hole.

Of course, I also see him throw the ball halfway to Winston-Salem, over and over, as if he's still trying to get used to being in a six-foot-three body. But I don't worry about the errors at all. Derek makes fifty-six of them that year in Greensboro, and years later, there are stories about how the Yankees were concerned enough that they considered moving him to center field. If anybody had asked me what I thought that year, I would've been happy to offer my opinion:

Don't even think about moving Derek Jeter. He is going to be fine. He's getting better every day. He wants to be great. You can see it in how hard he works, how passionately he plays. He's quick and has pop in his bat and wants to learn and will do anything he has to do to win.

The only thing you need to do with Derek Jeter is leave him alone.

A month into the off-season, Clara and I are preparing to rejoice in the birth of our first child. It has not been an easy journey by any means. Midway through the year, Clara flew up from Panama to visit me. She was almost five months pregnant. The doctor warned her about staying away from chicken pox because of the impact it could have on the baby. It turned out her flight had almost as many kids with chicken pox as it had motion-discomfort bags.

Clara, predictably, came down with chicken pox shortly after. When she had her next ultrasound, the news was about as bad as it could get. The doctor told us our baby already had a pool of fluid in the back of his head and would most likely be born with a large growth in the area that could ultimately be fatal. He said that because Clara was already exposed to the disease there was nothing we could do.

We were devastated. We prayed constantly about it. Clara connected with a group of Christian Latina women and joined them on a retreat, where there were prayers, and more prayers, for our unborn baby.

Clara rested and took good care of herself. We stayed as positive as we could.

Maybe the doctor is wrong. Maybe the baby will be fine, I told her. You can't lose hope.

The next time she visited the doctor, Clara was close to seven months pregnant. The ultrasound showed that the fluid had dissipated. The baby looked healthy.

I'm thrilled for you, but I have to say, I have no idea how this happened, the doctor said. I don't think I have ever seen a case like this in all my years of practice.

On October 4, 1993, in Panama City, we welcomed Mariano Rivera Jr. into the world. Both mother and child came through it beautifully, and so did the father, who spent most of that day, and many days that followed, thanking the Lord.

6

The Call

THE BUS TRIP FROM Rochester, New York, to Pawtucket, Rhode Island, is seven hours. It seems even longer when you make the trip after getting swept four straight. We pull into Pawtucket late at night, a tired bunch of Columbus Clippers piling into a roadside Comfort Inn. It's the middle of May 1995, and after spending 1994 in Single-A, Double-A, and Triple-A, I am off to a strong start with the Clippers, striking out eleven guys in five and two-thirds innings in my previous start.

We finally win a game to start the series against the PawSox. Tim Rumer gets the victory, and Derek Jeter, hitting .363, knocks a double to put us ahead to stay. Rain postpones the second game of the series. I don't want to spend the whole day in my $45-per-night hotel, so I do what minor leaguers usually do when they are on the road: check out the local sights at the mall. The sights aren't really local at all, since most malls look identical, a Gap here, a Foot Locker there, a food court in the middle. In Rhode Island, I just notice that *everybody* is wearing Boston Red Sox gear.

Late in the afternoon, I'm back in the room when the phone rings.

It is the Clippers' manager, Bill Evers.

Mariano?

Yes. Hi, Bill. What's up?

I have some good news and bad news for you. What do you want first?

The bad news, I guess, I reply.

Okay. The bad news is that you are no longer a pitcher for the Columbus Clippers.

What's the good news?

The good news is that you are now a pitcher for the New York Yankees.

Excuse me?

You better pack. You are going to New York.

I hear his words the first time. They are not sinking in.

Are you serious? I say.

I couldn't be more serious, Evers says. The Yankees want you to get down there as soon as you can. You need to reach out to the traveling secretary to make the arrangements.

Okay, thanks very much.

Don't thank me. You earned this, he says.

I hang up the phone. For a long time, I have imagined what it might feel like to get the call to the big leagues. Now I know.

I stand up on the bed and start bouncing up and down, and keep on bouncing, a Panamanian jumping bean. My poor downstairs neighbor. But he won't have to put up with this for long.

I am going to the big leagues.

Las Grandes Ligas.

When I finally stop bouncing, I get on my knees in the Comfort Inn and thank the Lord. Then I call Clara and my parents to share the news—I can barely remember a word I said—and tell them to let everybody in Puerto Caimito in on it: Pili is a New York Yankee.

I take a short flight down to New York and get a cab to the Stadium. We are playing a weekend series against the Baltimore Orioles. When I get to the players' entrance at the Stadium, the guard stops me.

Can I help you?

I'm Mariano Rivera. I just got called up from Columbus.

Okay, we were expecting you.

Expecting me? Imagine that, I think.

Having never been inside Yankee Stadium or any other big league ballpark, I can't even imagine what it must look like. I catch a glimpse of the field before I walk down the stairs to the clubhouse. Even from a distance it looks too big and too beautiful to fathom. I meander through a corridor and arrive at the clubhouse. When I walk in, I look to the left and see a Rivera nameplate over a locker and a No. 42 uniform hanging inside. I wore 58 in spring training, so I guess that makes it official: This really is a promotion.

The whole weekend I am in a pinch-me state, like a cardboard cutout of every major league rookie. I have the time of my life in batting practice, shagging fly balls in what I've come to learn is the most famous outfield in all of baseball. I wish I could stay out there all night, but there is a game to play. The Orioles rally for four in the ninth against John Wetteland to win the opener, but we take the next game behind Melido Perez and then get a complete-game, four-hit shutout from Sterling Hitchcock to take the series before flying across the country to play the Angels in Anaheim. It is the start of a nine-game, three-city swing. The first game is Tuesday night.

The Yankees' starting pitcher is me.

I am filling in for Jimmy Key, who has just gone on the disabled list.

I am more excited than nervous when I get to the ballpark that afternoon. I've had nine days of rest since my previous start in Rochester, so that should help my shoulder, which hasn't felt great early in the season. No big deal. Just a little cranky. Gene Monahan, the trainer, gives me a good, thorough rubdown. Bill Connors, our pitching coach, goes over the Angels hitters with me, giving me a brief overview of the best way to attack them. He gives me plenty to digest without giving me too much.

I take my time putting on my uniform. I start with the socks and then move on to the gray road pants and matching jersey. The uniform feels comforting and good. I run my hands over it when I am done dressing. I want to be sure it's neat, just the way my school uniform used to be. I head out to the bullpen and look up at the three decks of the Big A as I go. The size and scope of everything is staggering. I am not so much anxious or in awe as I am incredibly alive. Everything slows down. Everything is heightened—the sounds, the smells, the colors. I am minutes away from throwing my first big league pitch.

I am so ready.

I am up against Chuck Finley, a big, hard-throwing left-hander. It's a sparse crowd on a Tuesday night, and as Tony Phillips, the Angels' leadoff man, settles into the box in a deep crouch, I am completely locked in on catcher Mike Stanley's glove. It's as if there is nothing else happening in the entire ballpark, the entire world— as if I am in a sixty-foot, six-inch tube, me on one end and Mike Stanley's glove on the other.

All I need to do is hit that glove. This is how all-encompassing my focus is.

I take a breath.

Throw the best pitch you can, I tell myself.

Keep it simple.

I start into my no-windup motion, rocking back slightly, hands together near the waist before I come forward and push off the rubber with my right foot. I fire a fastball that runs down and away for a ball, but come back with two strikes on fastballs away and strike Phillips out with another fastball he is way late on. Jim Edmonds, the center fielder who is batting second, takes a fastball looking for out number two. Tim Salmon singles to deep short and then Chili Davis, the cleanup hitter, swats a 1–0 pitch the other way for a double to left, and quickly I am in my first jam.

The hitter is J. T. Snow, the Angels' first baseman, a lefty. I get ahead, 0–2, and then challenge him with a high heater that he lofts to center, where Bernie Williams has an easy play.

I pitch a scoreless second and get two outs to start the third before Salmon steps in again and drives a double to right center. I pitch carefully to Chili Davis, remembering his first at-bat, and wind up walking him, and then Snow hits a weak grounder that goes for an infield hit. Now the bases are loaded and Greg Myers, the catcher, is at the plate. I get ahead, 1–2, but he bloops a ball into left and two runs score. I get out with no further damage, and walk off needing no reminders that the walk to Davis is what complicated my life and helped put us in a two-run hole.

The trouble starts much sooner in the bottom of the fourth, with two singles to start the inning, bringing Edmonds up. I've struck him out twice, but he battled me the second time and seemed totally dialed in on my four-seam fastball. I fall behind, 2–1, and then leave a pitch over the plate, and he crushes it over the right-center-field fence. Now it's 5–0, and on a night when Finley is making our hitters look like they're swinging with straws, this is not good. One walk later my debut is history, with a terrible line (three and a third innings, eight hits, five runs, three walks, and five strikeouts) and a dispiriting walk to the dugout. We go on to lose, 10–0, and Finley strikes out fifteen, but if there's anything I can take from this, it's that I know I can get these guys out. It may sound strange after I've been roughed up that way, but a couple of better pitches in better locations and the whole thing plays out differently.

I wish my start had been better. I wish the outcome were different. But I'm not devastated, and I am ready to make a better showing the next time out.

You did some really good things out there, Bill says. We'll keep working. You are going to be fine.

Five days later, Sunday of Memorial Day weekend in Oakland, I am back out there again against Tony La Russa's A's. Paul O'Neill belts a long double, Bernie Williams homers, and we put up four runs in the first two innings and I protect it well, pitching one-run ball into the sixth. Bob Wickman bails me out of some minor trouble, and when John Wetteland strikes out the side in the ninth, the Yankees have their thirteenth victory of the season and I have the first big league victory of my life. Catcher Jim Leyritz shakes Wetteland's hand after Stan Javier strikes out to end it, and then manager Buck Showalter shakes his hand, and I get in line and do the same. I am so happy to contribute to a victory that I forget to ask for the game ball. As far as I know everybody else forgets about it, too. We pack up and head for the airport and a flight to Seattle. I never give the game ball much thought after that. I just want to get another ball to throw and help the Yankees win.

I make two more starts, against the A's and the Mariners, and neither one is memorable. I give up a monstrous grand slam to Geronimo Berroa in the first and a three-run homer to Edgar Martinez in the second. I don't make it out of the third inning against the Mariners, the Yankees fall into last place, and after the game Buck Showalter calls me into his office.

I have about three weeks of big league service, but even I know it's not good when you get called into the manager's office, especially when your ERA is 10.20.

We're sending you back to Columbus, Buck says. You showed some good things and you shouldn't be discouraged. Just keep working on it and you will be back.

As I am leaving the office, Derek, who was called up two weeks after me, is summoned in. He is hitting .234 in thirteen games, filling in for the injured Tony Fernandez. Derek gets the same news I do. Back to the bushes. The date is June 11. The two of us have known nothing but advancement. Going in reverse is not what we have in mind. I know my shoulder is not right, but still...

How can it not sting when your team tells you that you're not good enough?

Derek and I share a very quiet cab ride over the George Washington Bridge, and then a very quiet meal. At a booth in a Bennigan's in Fort Lee, New Jersey, across the road from our hotel, we try to figure out what went wrong. It's not the Last Supper, but we're not exactly laughing it up, either.

As much as I know I can compete at the big league level, and as much as I believe that I will be back, I am fully aware that second chances are not guaranteed.

I feel like it's my fault you got sent down, I tell Derek. If I had pitched better today maybe this wouldn't have happened—to either of us.

It's not your fault, Derek says. What happened to me has nothing to do with the way you pitched. We just have to keep working hard. If we do that and play the way we can for the Clippers, we'll be back.

You're right. That's how we have to think, I say.

We head back to the hotel and catch a flight the next morning to Charlotte, where we join the Clippers. My shoulder still feels sore, and they decide to put me on the disabled list for two weeks to see if the rest helps.

My first start back after the time off comes on a damp Monday night in Cooper Stadium in Columbus. I am pitching the second game of a twi-night doubleheader against the Rochester Red Wings. Even as I warm up I can tell that my shoulder feels better than it has all year. I am almost pain-free, throwing freely.

The rest has helped. Big-time.

I smoke through the Red Wings in the first inning. In the dugout, my catcher, Jorge Posada, sits down next to me.

What did you eat today?

Why?

Because I've never seen you throw this hard. The ball is flying out of your hand.

I don't know. I feel good, I reply.

I wind up throwing a rain-shortened, five-inning no-hitter. I walk one guy, and Jorge throws him out stealing, so I face the minimum fifteen batters.

This guy is going back to the big leagues and he is never coming back, Jorge says to a couple of our teammates.

Jorge tells me later that I was at 96 miles per hour all night and might've touched 97 or 98. It is a major jump that stuns people in the Yankee organization. Years later, I find out that Gene Michael, the Yankees general manager, got bulletins that night about how hard I was throwing.

Michael wanted to know, Was the gun working right? Do we know if this is accurate?

He checked with a scout who was at the game, and the scout confirmed it; his gun had 96 on it, too. Michael apparently was in the middle of talks with the Tigers to acquire David Wells. The Tigers were interested in me.

Once Michael confirmed the accuracy of the radar readings, I was no longer in that deal, or any other deal.

The night after my abbreviated no-hitter, Jorge and I and some of the other Clippers go to our regular dinner spot, Applebee's. I have filet mignon and a loaded baked potato and vegetables.

Do you have any idea how you could go from throwing 88 to 90 to 96? I've never seen anything like it, Jorge says.

My shoulder is healthy, but there is only one answer. And it has nothing to do with increased filet mignon consumption. It is a gift from the Lord. I have known for a long time that He is using me for His own purposes, that He wants my pitching to help spread the good news about the Gospel of Jesus.

What else could it be? It makes no sense otherwise.

I never pitch for the Columbus Clippers again.

On July 3, Bill Evers tells me I am going back up. I don't jump up and down on the bed this time. I just get on a plane. Actually, several planes. I'm up at 4:30 to board a flight to Boston (the Clippers are playing at Pawtucket again) and then on to Chicago. By the time I get to my hotel it is evening. I unpack my most precious possession—the red-leather Bible that was a gift from Clara. It has notes in the margins, and verses underlined and passages highlighted. It has been well-thumbed, I can tell you that. The Bible can't tell you the story of my walk with the Lord, but it can tell you everything about how I try to live, and why the love of the Lord is the foundation of my whole life. For me, the Bible is not just the word of God, but a life road map that is packed with wisdom that you cannot beat even if you spent the next hundred years reading spiritual books and self-help books.

It is the best kind of wisdom: Simple wisdom. This sort of wisdom, from the twenty-third chapter of Matthew, verse twelve:

Whoever exalts himself will be humbled, and whoever humbles himself will be exalted.

My journey with the Lord begins with the help of my cousin Vidal Ovalle, in Puerto Caimito. I am eighteen years old at the time. Vidal and I see each other every day of our lives. We chase iguanas together and are on the fishing boat together. When I begin to see a striking change in him, I ask him about it.

I have come to know the Lord, he says. He shares Bible stories with me. I can feel his passion, and his peace and happiness. I have known him his whole life, and it's as if he is a different person now. It is not a fake. When we are out at sea, we talk about the Bible. Vidal is the first one to really teach me about the Bible, and what it means to know Jesus, and to know what he did for us, dying on the cross to forgive our sins. I listen, and I read the Bible, but I am taking spiritual baby steps, not quite ready to surrender. It isn't until almost five years later that the Lord becomes the center of my life. You hear sometimes of people having a Great Awakening, a conversion experience full of white light or full-body trembling or the voice of God, or even all three. For me, it is much more understated.

I am in a small cement church near the center of Puerto Caimito, not far from the dock where my father keeps his boat. I am deep in prayer in a folding chair, thanking the Lord for His blessings, seeking His forgiveness for my shortcomings. The service is coming to a close.

Does anyone who hasn't done so yet want to accept the Lord as their personal Savior? the pastor asks.

I hadn't thought about this beforehand. I never asked myself: Is today going to be the day? I reflect on the pastor's question. I wait a moment or two. I can feel my heart opening, being tender to the word of God. I can feel the Holy Spirit descending on me, very gently, touching my heart:

Come to me, my son, the Holy Spirit is saying.

I raise my hand.

Please come forward, the pastor says.

Somewhere deep inside me, there's an epic Flesh vs. Spirit showdown for my soul.

Flesh: You realize that if you do this you will never have fun again, don't you?

Spirit: This is about much more than fun. This is about having God's grace and peace and mercy, now and always.

Flesh: You are about to lose all your friends, because they won't have anything to do with you.

Spirit: If my friends don't want to be with me anymore, maybe they aren't the friends I want to have, anyway.

Flesh: Your life is going to turn into one long, grim prayer session where all you talk about is your horrible sins.

Spirit: My life is going to overflow with lightness and hope, and the joy of living with the Lord.

I walk forward. I am not nervous or hesitant at all. I am excited. I can feel the Holy Spirit with me, lifting me, propelling me, telling me: Accept Jesus Christ as your Savior, and you will have power and peace that you won't even believe.

The pastor asks again if I am ready.

Yes, I am, I reply.

Soon he leads us in prayer, and already I can feel a burden being lifted. It is the burden of feeling you have to do it by yourself, of feeling alone and overwhelmed by your own limitations. I stand in the front of this tiny church in my tiny village and realize that the Lord is giving me a chance to be a different person, to free me from my sins, to be joyous and to be free.

The Bible says, Come as dirty as you are. Don't clean yourself up or fix yourself up. Come with all your anxieties, all of your imperfections. The Lord will give you peace. He will take care of everything. All you have to do is want Him, and seek Him with a pure heart. He will take care of everything. You can't do it. I can't do it. But the Lord can.

Everything is in the hands of the Lord. All our days are in the hands of the Lord. I woke up today. You woke up today. Today is the day we have been given. I thank God for that. I do not take it for granted. Today is all we have. This exact moment is all we have. It is the way I want to pitch, and it is the way I want to live. Put everything we have into living this moment the best way we can live it. Again, it is simple. Simple is best.

*   *   *

I am starting the next day against the White Sox, the second best-hitting team in the American League. From the moment I walk in Comiskey Park that day, I feel completely at peace. I feel no pressure, just want to go out there and be me, and play the game I love. Already I am learning that when you tell yourself, *I have to do this and that, I must prove myself right now,* all it does is make it harder for you to perform your best. I have the Lord with me, no matter what happens. I lose the urgency, and all it does is change everything.

I can't say that I know I am throwing that much harder than I was in my previous call-up, but I can tell by how hitters are swinging that I am bringing it, and they are not expecting it. I cruise through four innings with one hit—a Frank Thomas single—and five strikeouts. Paul O'Neill belts a homer off of Alex Fernandez to give me a 1–0 lead, and a Luis Polonia sacrifice fly makes it 2–0 after five.

After six innings, I have given up only two hits, both to Thomas, and then I strike out the side in the seventh, getting Ron Karkovice and Warren Newson for the third time apiece.

With the lead now 3–0 in the eighth, I am still coming at them hard. I get Ozzie Guillen to bounce out and Lance Johnson to pop out and Dave Martinez to strike out. It is my eleventh strikeout of the night. When I get into the dugout, Buck Showalter comes over and pats me on the back.

Great job, Mariano. You were tremendous. I'm going to give the ball to Wetteland for the ninth.

Thank you, I say.

If there is any revelation for me against the White Sox, it is that all I have to do is be me. Not do anything more. Somebody tells me later that a few of the Sox hitters complained because the scouting reports they got on me were all wrong. The reports said I threw in the mid- to high eighties, not the mid-nineties.

Well, they are a few weeks out of date.

I stay with the big club the rest of the season, and we clinch the first American League wild-card berth by winning eleven of our last twelve games, and draw the Seattle Mariners in the American League Division Series. It's an emotionally charged time around the Yankees, a joyful time, and I can tell that even though I just arrived. This isn't just the first postseason series for the Yankees in fourteen years, it's the first playoff series ever for the great Don Mattingly, and everybody is thrilled for him. I have only known Donnie for a few months, but it's plenty long enough for me to have deep admiration for his humility and his work ethic, for the way he carries himself. He is a man who does everything the right way, and treats people the right way.

He is a man you want to be like.

We win Game 1 at the Stadium behind David Cone, before a taut Game 2 is tied after nine and moves into extra innings with the score tied at four. Before the top of the twelfth, a call goes to the bullpen.

Get Rivera up.

I start getting loose. I feel good. I like the way the ball is coming out of my hand.

Ken Griffey Jr. hits a home run off John Wetteland to give the Mariners a 5–4 lead. When Wetteland walks the next hitter, Buck calls for me. I run in from the bullpen, across the outfield, for the biggest pitching test of my life. I am a fisherman's son from Puerto Caimito, about to dive into the hottest cauldron I could ever imagine. And I can't wait. I love the stakes, love that so much is riding on every pitch, love that the Stadium is as charged as a 60,000-seat electrical socket.

Maybe it's the training on my father's fishing boat, I don't know. On the boat, if we didn't catch fish, we wouldn't make any money. We had to come through. We had to find a way.

The playoffs feel the same way to me.

I strike out Jay Buhner, the former Yankee, to end the threat.

In the bottom of the twelfth, we are down to our final out when Ruben Sierra rips a double to left to tie the game, and now it's up to me to hold it. I have an easy thirteenth inning and strike out the side in the fourteenth. I get Griffey on a flyout to center, retiring eight straight batters, before giving up singles in the fifteenth to Edgar Martinez and Buhner. I strike out Doug Strange but now fall behind Tino Martinez, 3–0, with two men on. I throw a fastball and he has the green light. He hits a fly ball to center.

Threat extinguished.

My first postseason outing concludes with three and a third innings of scoreless relief.

Minutes later, with one man on and one man out in the bottom of the fifteenth, Jim Leyritz steps up to the plate. He rocks a two-run homer into the right-center-field bleachers, and as I watch its flight in the dugout and listen to the building roar all around me, I think only one thing:

This is the loudest noise I've ever heard in my life.

It almost feels as if the Stadium is lifting off of River Avenue. We are up two games to none, and I get the victory. It is hard to even comprehend where I am, and what I am doing.

The Lord's blessings only get richer every day.

The series moves to Seattle, and the Mariners take the third and fourth games. In the eighth inning of Game 5, after the last of David Cone's amazing 147 pitches, a ball four forces in a run to tie it. Buck gives me the ball. The bases are loaded and Mike Blowers is at the plate.

Four months earlier, I was a Columbus Clipper who had washed out in his first big league audition. Now I have the outcome of an entire postseason series hanging on my every pitch. The pressure is immense, but I feel none of it. This is no time to think about how fast, or how far, I've come. I have a hitter to get out. I lock in on Mike Stanley's glove. I am back in the tube.

I strike Mike Blowers out on three pitches.

We wind up losing in the eleventh inning, when Edgar Martinez belts a two-run double down the left-field line off of Jack McDowell. It is a brutal ending, an ending I never see coming. My insides go cold watching the Mariners celebrate right in front of us. I was sure that we were winning this series, that it would be us doing the dancing. But along with the sting, there is also a resolve that borders on defiance:

We will learn from this. We will be back. We will prevail.

With the passage of a little time, it's impossible for me not to feel heartened by what happens in 1995. I don't know where the Lord's grace and mercy will take me from here, but I know it will be rich, and know that I am not alone. After all, I begin the year as a question mark with a shaky history of injury, a Triple-A pitcher all the way. I finish it with five and a third scoreless innings and eight strikeouts in postseason competition for the New York Yankees, in *las Grandes Ligas,* in the greatest city in the world, playing a game I learned on a beach. It's all part of the Lord's plan, and I am loving it.

7

Relief and Belief

I HAVE A NEW pitching home in 1996, and I spend the next 1,096 appearances of my career there. It's called the bullpen. I guess if you put me against a wall and force me to answer, I'd say I slightly prefer starting, but whatever the club needs, I will do my best.

It's a season of major transition for the Yankees. We have a new manager, Joe Torre. A new ace in twenty-four-year-old Andy Pettitte. A new shortstop in twenty-one-year-old Derek Jeter, as well as a new first baseman, former Mariner Tino Martinez, and a new catcher—a smart, solid guy named Joe Girardi. You never know how it's all going to piece together, and I guess George Steinbrenner isn't so sure himself, which is why the Yankees are in talks with the Mariners about trading me for their shortstop, Felix Fermin. Steinbrenner apparently has questions about whether Derek is ready to take over and wants Fermin as an insurance policy. I have no clue the talks are going on, and don't want to know. Some players obsess about this stuff, and want to be on top of every last trade rumor and bit of speculation. But I am the exact opposite. To me, such rumors can only be a distraction, and in my worldview as a pitcher, distractions are the enemy.

If it's not going to help me get people out, why even bother paying attention?

My main focus in the spring is making a strong first impression on the new manager. I have never heard of Joe Torre, know nothing of his playing career, his MVP award, his Brooklyn boyhood, or his previous managerial stops. Buck Showalter, my previous skipper, has seen me for years in the Yankee system, and I knew he was a big supporter of mine. When the Yankees decide to let Buck go and bring in Mr. T—it's what I call him even now—I get fired up for keen competition to win a bullpen spot. There is a boatload of relievers in camp. I am just one of the deckhands. Just because I did well in the playoffs the year before, I take nothing for granted, in spring training or that year.

In my first outing of the regular season, I throw two scoreless innings with two strikeouts against the Rangers and feel as good as I ever have on the mound. It's almost embarrassing, but I still basically have a repertoire of one pitch, my years in the laboratory—trying to develop a trustworthy slider and serviceable changeup—having yielded no breakthrough. So my arsenal consists of a four-seam fastball.

When I want to mix it up, I throw a...four-seam fastball.

I bet I don't throw even ten sliders the whole season. It doesn't seem to matter. I have easy heat with late movement, and usually can put it exactly where I want.

Six weeks into 1996, I have an ERA of 0.83. I throw fifteen straight no-hit innings at one point. During a midseason hot streak in which we win eight of nine, I strike out three Red Sox—Troy O'Leary, Lee Tinsley, and Jeff Frye—on twelve pitches, and I get the hold for Wetteland. Soon there is a lot of clamoring that I should be named to Mike Hargrove's All-Star staff. Hargrove passes on me, and if Yankee fans get all worked up about it, I do not. It simply doesn't bother me. It's another gift the Lord has seen fit to grant me. I'm just not wired that way.

All I want to do is get back to Panama for the All-Star break to see Clara, who is pregnant with our second son, Jafet.

I finish the year pretty much the way I start it, with a 2.09 ERA and 130 strikeouts in 107 innings; I even finish third in the Cy Young voting for the league's best pitcher. We win the American League East and draw the Rangers in the division series. The Rangers win Game 1 at the Stadium, 6–2, so it makes the second game even more important, if we want to avoid going to Texas having to sweep.

Andy goes into the seventh and then I get the ball from Mr. T. We are down, 4–2. I strike out Ivan (Pudge) Rodriguez on three fastballs and then get Rusty Greer to ground out. I face eight Rangers in all, and get all eight of them, including Juan Gonzalez, the league's Most Valuable Player that year and a guy who already has two homers and four RBIs in the game, and three homers for the series. Gonzalez is in one of those zones hitters get into — when the ball looks as big as a cantaloupe, and they don't *think,* they *know,* that they can hit anything. Pitchers get in zones, too, though. And I am in one, a place where you are completely committed to every pitch you throw, and you know you can put it exactly where you want. Gonzalez hit a homer off me the year before, so I know just how dangerous he can be. Unlike most sluggers against me, he also almost always makes contact; I would strike him out only one time in twenty-four career at-bats. He is a very good low fastball hitter, so I try to keep the ball up and away from the middle of the plate. I get him to ground out to short to lead off the eighth.

We wind up tying the game in the eighth on Cecil Fielder's soft single, and winning it in the twelfth after Derek smacks a leadoff hit and scores on an errant throw.

We have been a resilient team all season, never quitting, always fighting back, and we demonstrate it again in Game 3, in Texas, when we're down a run in the ninth and score twice on a long sac fly from Bernie Williams, who is almost as hot as Gonzalez, and Mariano Duncan's single. Wetteland closes it out, and one game later, I throw two more scoreless innings as we take a 5–4 lead into the ninth. Bernie hits his second homer of the game, and in the bottom of the ninth, Wetteland whiffs Dean Palmer to close the series out.

We move into the ALCS against the Baltimore Orioles, and right away we have to come back again. In Game 1, we fall behind by two runs and don't get even until Derek hits an opposite-field home run off Armando Benitez in the bottom of the eighth, a Yankee Stadium special and a Jeffrey Maier special, too. No, it wasn't a legitimate home run, and yes, the eleven-year-old kid interferes with it, and the Orioles have every right to argue, but what can you do? You keep fighting, that's all. I get Mike Devereaux to ground out to get out of a jam in the tenth, and then strike out the tough Roberto Alomar to end the eleventh, and then three minutes later, Bernie wraps a 1–1 pitch from Randy Myers around the left-field foul pole to seal a 5–4 victory.

The Orioles square the series at one by taking Game 2, and then we head to Camden Yards, where Jimmy Key pitches a masterpiece in Game 3. Then, in Game 4, our bullpen — David Weathers, Graeme Lloyd, me, and Wetteland — throws six shutout innings after Kenny Rogers is cuffed around early. We go up, 3–1. I don't do it the easy way, though; I load the bases on three singles, and then strike out Brady Anderson and Chris Hoiles, going up the ladder and getting them to chase high fastballs, then getting Todd Zeile to pop up. Andy finishes off the Orioles in Game 5 by pitching three-hit ball over eight innings, and Jim Leyritz, Fielder, and Darryl Strawberry all homer in a six-run third off of Scott Erickson to put us into the World Series against the Atlanta Braves.

*   *   *

You'd think that being in my first World Series would bring a whole new level of pressure, but that is not the case at all. The way the year went, we expected to be in the Series. If we had fallen short, that would've been crushing, so it was almost as if the pressure felt greater in the two rounds of American League playoffs.

You never would know that by the way the Series begins, though, with the Braves playing the role of tractor and the Yankees playing the role of dirt clump. We lose two games at home by a combined score of 16–1, mostly because Andruw Jones, a nineteen-year-old kid from Curaçao (practically a Central American neighbor), crushes two homers in Game 1, and the Braves' starting rotation—one of the best ever—is as good as everybody says. John Smoltz shuts us down in the first game, Greg Maddux in the second. I am in awe watching these guys, especially Maddux. He is a master craftsman, whittling here and whittling there, carving us up before we even know it. He throws eighty-two pitches in eight innings. He goes to a three-ball count on only two batters the whole game. In the fourth inning, he sets down the heart of our order on six pitches. He does what great artists in every line of work do.

He makes it look easy.

The Series switches to Atlanta, and we win Game 3 behind David Cone (I give up my first postseason run), but we are in big trouble with only five outs to go in Game 4, down 6–3—five outs from being down three games to one, and having to face Smoltz and Tom Glavine in the next two games. I am getting loose in the bullpen as the eighth inning begins, with Charlie Hayes leading off against Mark Wohlers, one of the most dominant, and one of the hardest-throwing, closers in the game.

Hayes hits a swinging bunt that teeters along the third-base line and somehow stays fair. Then Darryl Strawberry rips a line drive to left and we have two runners on. I keep throwing to Mike Borzello, the bullpen catcher, as Mariano Duncan hits what looks to be an automatic double-play ball to Rafael Belliard, the Braves' shortstop.

Belliard bobbles it and only gets one. It brings up Leyritz, a tremendous fastball hitter who likes to be in the batter's box in clutch situations. He'd hit that huge homer against the Mariners the previous October, and homered in the clinching game against the Orioles. Leyritz has never faced Wohlers before.

What's Wohlers got? Leyritz asks Chris Chambliss, the hitting coach.

He's got a one-hundred-mile-per-hour fastball, Chambliss says.

Leyritz steps in, using one of Strawberry's bats. On Wohlers's first pitch, Leyritz is right on the fastball, then takes a slider for a ball. On the 1–1 pitch, Wohlers throws another slider, up and over the plate, and Leyritz extends and drives it deep to left. Andruw Jones climbs the left-field wall, but the ball is beyond his reach. The game is tied, and as Leyritz fist-pumps his way around the bases, I know it's on me to make sure it stays tied.

I pitch a scoreless eighth, and get one out in the ninth. Graeme Lloyd picks me up, getting Fred McGriff to hit into a double play, and we go on to win in ten.

In Game 5, Andy outduels Smoltz in a game neither deserves to lose, and the 1–0 victory takes us back to Yankee Stadium with a 3–2 lead. We finally get to Maddux with three runs in the third, and we still have a 3–1 lead when I come in. It's the seventh inning, and I am not changing anything now. I am throwing heat and throwing it in the best locations I can, and I plow through two innings, retiring six straight after walking Terry Pendleton to open the seventh, and then leave it to Wetteland. He gives up three singles and a run and the Braves have the tying run on second when Wetteland gets Mark Lemke to pop a foul ball behind third, where Charlie Hayes catches it.

The Series is ours.

From the top step of the dugout, I sprint to the mound and get there almost before Charlie comes down from his jump. It's the Yankees' first World Series title in eighteen years, and my first World Series title ever, and for three guys from Columbus — Derek, Andy, and me — to play such important roles makes it that much sweeter. To be in that pile and celebrate after we had to come back again to beat a team as good as the Braves is an indescribable feeling.

After the season ends, the Yankees decide I am ready to close games and let Wetteland, a free agent, sign with the Rangers. I minimize the difference in the roles publicly, insisting I feel no added pressure, but the truth is that I *do* feel pressure. I want to prove that the Yankees did the right thing; I want to show everybody that I can do it. I want not only to be as good as John Wetteland. I want to be better than him.

The '97 season does not start well. We win only five of our first fifteen games. I blow three of the first six save opportunities I have. Through the first nine innings of the season, I give up fourteen hits and four runs.

The most recent slipup comes against the Angels at the Stadium, and the guy who gets me is Jim Leyritz, of all people. Traded about six weeks after his homer against Wohlers, Leyritz whacks a two-run double down the left-field line. After the game, Mr. T calls me into his office. Mel Stottlemyre, the pitching coach, is with him. I have a pretty good idea that they don't want to talk about the stock market. I know I haven't been doing the job. I know that if it keeps up this way, they are going to have to make a change.

I'm sorry I've blown so many games. I am not sure what's wrong. I feel good but I am not getting the results, I tell them.

Mr. T says, Mo, do you know what you need to do? You need to be Mariano Rivera. That's all. Nothing more, nothing less. It looks to us like you're trying to be perfect.

You've gotten away from what has made you so successful, Mel says. By trying to do too much, you are taking away some of your aggressiveness and hurting your command.

You are our closer. You are our guy, and we want you to be our guy, and that is not going to change, okay? Mr. T says.

I feel an immediate sense of relief. I look both of them in the eye, first Mr. T and then Mel.

Thank you, I say. Knowing you still have faith in me means so much.

One of the great ironies about sports is that trying too hard to succeed is about the surest way to bring on failure. Joe and Mel are exactly right. I still have the same arm, the same stuff, but pushing myself to be better or faster than I was before is only hurting me. You have to get out of your own way sometimes and just let your body do what it does naturally.

As I walk out of Mr. T's office, I feel about 10,000 tons lighter. I make a vow to myself to remember what he and Mel told me. And I devise my own little trick to help: I am not going to even think about what inning it is. Whether it's the seventh or eighth inning, the way it was a year ago, or the ninth inning, the way it is this year, I still have a ball, the hitter still has a bat, and my only job is still to get him out, one pitch at a time.

I've had a great deal of success since the end of 1995 in getting big league hitters out. So why change anything? Why focus differently? That's what I need to keep in mind.

The payoff from the meeting is immediate. I stop trying to be Wetteland and stop demanding perfection, and run off twelve straight saves. I am getting completely comfortable with the new role now, and by the time we head into Tiger Stadium for a three-game series in late June, the insecurities are behind me.

Who had any idea what would be ahead of me?

*   *   *

I am playing catch with Ramiro Mendoza, my fellow pitcher and fellow Panamanian, a couple of hours before the game. We are in front of our dugout. Our catch is no different from hundreds of other games of catch I've had. As I get loose, I start to throw a bit harder. I am feeling good. I catch Ramiro's throw and, heating up now, I fire it back to him.

My throw seems to surprise him. He has to move his glove at the last moment to catch it.

Hey, stop playing around, Ramiro says.

What are you talking about? I'm not playing around.

I'm talking about the ball you just threw. It almost hit me.

I just threw a normal ball, I say.

Well, it didn't look normal to me.

We keep playing catch. I throw the ball to him again and the same thing happens. It breaks about a foot right when it is on top of him, and again he almost misses it completely.

That's what I'm talking about, he says. Stop doing that.

I promise in the name of the Lord I am not doing anything, I reply.

I make several more throws to Ramiro and every one of them has the same wicked movement at the end.

You better go find somebody else to catch you, he says, finally. I don't want to get hurt.

He's serious. Our game of catch is over.

I have no idea what just happened, and no idea why the ball is moving this way. I am not aware of doing a single thing different. I head to the bullpen, which is on the field at old Tiger Stadium, and throw to Mike Borzello. My ball—what I think is my regular four-seam fastball—is doing the same thing that it did with Ramiro.

Whoa! Where did that come from? Borzi says. He's sure something is wrong with the baseball—that it has a scuff that's making it move this way. He throws it aside and gets a new ball.

The same thing happens. Borzi holds up his hands.

What's going on? What are you doing? he asks.

I don't know. I am just throwing my regular four-seam fastball, I say, showing him my grip.

We talk again after the game, and agree to go back in the bull-pen early the next day and try to figure this out. The pitch keeps cutting, hard and late. Now I'm getting concerned.

Borzi, this isn't good. We've got to straighten this pitch because I have almost no command of it at all.

Mel Stottlemyre joins the conversation and closely observes me throwing. We look at my grip, my arm angle, everything. We cannot get me to throw this pitch straight.

For two weeks, maybe three, we work to do just that. We fiddle with my grip and release point. It's as if the ball has a mind of its own, because it keeps moving late, on a horizontal plane, boring in on left-handed hitters and away from righties. As we tinker, I continue to pitch in games, and the more I throw this new pitch, the more I begin to get command of it. I am starting to throw it for strikes.

I am starting to come to the realization that it's absurd to try to throw the ball straight.

Whoever heard of a pitcher trying to get less movement on the ball? The whole thing is crazy.

And this is how my cut fastball, or cutter, is born. It is as if it is dropped straight from the heavens, as if I were out on my father's boat and a million pounds of fish just swam into our nets, the radar gone a deep, deep red.

How can I explain it any other way than as one more incredible gift from the Lord?

I do not spend years searching for this pitch. I do not ask for it, or pray for it. All of a sudden it is there, a devastating baseball weapon. It is not a pitch I had yesterday. But it is a pitch I have today and that I would have until the end. I am throwing the ball across the seams with what feels like the littlest bit more pressure on the ball from my middle finger, and my fastball now has this wicked tail on it. How does this happen? Why does this happen? Why not somebody else? I don't know the answers, except to say that the Lord must've had a plan, because He always has a plan. And it is some plan.

All it does is change my whole career.

By midseason, I have 27 saves and a 1.96 ERA and Mr. T names me to the All-Star team. The game is played at Jacobs Field in Cleveland. I come into the ninth with a 3–1 lead, thanks to a two-run homer by the Indians' Sandy Alomar, the hometown hero, and a solo blast from Edgar Martinez. I am very happy to have Edgar on my team. He hits me better than any man on earth. Just owns me, so much so that I feel like throwing a party for him when he retires (with an average of .312 against all pitchers and a .579 average against me).

I start the ninth by striking out Charles Johnson, then get Mark Grace to ground out and Moises Alou to line out, getting in and getting out, my favorite kind of save.

We fly home the next day on a plane the Yankees charter for us—Mr. T, his coaching staff, Paul O'Neill, Bernie, my father, Clara, and I—a whole bunch of people. It's a propeller plane, and looks as if it might go back to Mr. T's playing days. Oh, boy. Jet engines are bad enough. Now I have to look at blades that I imagine are powered by rubber bands?

Not good.

I keep hoping and praying that my fear of flying will pass, but it never does. Not on this flight or the hundreds that follow it. On all those countless Yankee charters to all corners of the United States, I sit in Row 29, in the middle seat, with my red leather Bible in my hand and Christian music in my earphones. My teammates? They are unmerciful. Mike Harkey, our bullpen coach in my last years, is a prime offender, walking down the aisle and motioning for me to take off my headphones, as if he has important news to share.

Hey, Mo, I just spoke with the pilot, and he said it might be a rough flight, so you may want to buckle up a little tighter.

Clara is even more afraid of flying than I am. And here she is next to me on this vintage prop plane, the two of us almost as white as Casper. Twenty minutes out of Cleveland, the sky turns black and the plane starts rolling around like an amusement-park ride at thirty thousand feet, swooping up, plunging down, bouncing sideways. I am a mess. Clara and I are saying our prayers, clutching each other, asking the Lord to get us all safely on the ground.

We are flying into Westchester County Airport, just north of the city, and the only merciful thing about this trip is that it is short. As we make our descent, things finally calm down and I begin to feel better. We are almost down now. I close my eyes, just waiting and waiting to feel the ground beneath the wheels, so I can exhale once and for all. An instant later we hit with a hard thud, a tire blowing out, the plane careening, bouncing down the runway before coming to a stop.

Are you okay? I say to Clara.

She looks very pale, but she nods.

Thank you, Lord, for getting us here safely, Clara says.

I can barely unlock my fingers from the armrest. I feel as if we've circumnavigated the globe, not flown in from Cleveland. When we get inside the terminal, I find out that almost all the commercial airliners are grounded because of the weather. We are the only ones who flew.

The second half of the season is a whole lot better than that flight. We are one of the best teams in baseball after the break, going 48–29, and win eight of our last nine. We win 96 games, finish two games behind the Orioles, and earn a division series matchup against . . . Cleveland. It opens at Yankee Stadium, and the traffic is still clogged on the Major Deegan by the time the Indians score five times in the first against David Cone, who can't find the strike zone. A walk, a hit-by-pitch, a wild pitch, three singles, and Sandy Alomar Jr.'s three-run homer make for a big mess. But, just as in our championship run the year before, we never stop coming at you.

Ramiro Mendoza pitches three and a third superb innings in relief of Cone, and we start our charge. Tino Martinez homers, and we scratch out another run and then, after chasing Orel Hershiser in the fifth, Tim Raines, Derek, and O'Neill pound out consecutive home runs to put us up, 8–6, in the sixth. Jeff Nelson holds them into the eighth, then I get four outs, striking Matt Williams out looking to end it.

Tino, who had a monster regular season (44 home runs, 141 RBIs, .296), keeps it going in Game 2, drilling a two-run double in a three-run first. With Andy going, I figure it is going to hold up, but the Indians score five times with two outs in the fourth, and by the time Williams takes Andy deep for a two-run shot an inning later, the Indians are on their way to a 7–5 victory.

In these tight best-of-five series, the third game is always pivotal, and it couldn't go any better as the series shifts to Cleveland, thanks to a grand slam from Paul O'Neill and a Maddux-like performance from David Wells. We cruise, 6–1, and, now just a victory away from the ALCS, we get a solid start from Dwight Gooden and take a 2–1 lead into the eighth. Mike Stanton strikes out David Justice looking, and then Mr. T gives the ball to me to get the last five outs. I get Matt Williams on a flyout. The next hitter is Alomar Jr.

I fall behind, 2–0. I don't want to put the tying run at first, so there's no way I am going to walk him. But I'm not giving in, either, by just throwing something down the middle to get a strike. Alomar stands a long way from the plate, bent a bit at the waist, with a slightly closed stance. Joe Girardi sets up away. I am looking to hit the outside corner, low. I come set and fire a cutter. The ball is out over the plate, almost shoulder height. I miss my spot badly. The pitch is ball three.

I am surprised when Alomar swings.

I am shocked when he hits it into the first row in the right-field seats.

The game is tied and the place erupts. I put my head down for a moment and pick up the rosin bag. The Indians go on to win in the bottom of the ninth and then take Game 5 to end our reign as world champions much sooner than any of us expected.

Giving up that homer is the greatest failure of my young career. I know Joe and Mel are concerned about how I am going to handle it. Mark Wohlers is never the same pitcher after the Leyritz home run. Other relievers have responded similarly after giving up huge home runs. But almost the minute the ball sails over Paul O'Neill's glove, I know that not only is this not going to break me, it is going to make me better.

I learn from that pitch. If you watch the replays closely, you can see I don't finish correctly, and leave my release point too high. I'm not sure if I gave Sandy a hundred more pitches in the same spot that he would hit another one out, but the point is that I have to finish that pitch properly, have to be so focused, have to be so completely consistent with my mechanics that I do not miss my spot by so much.

The Lord has blessed me with an ability to pour all my energy into places where it can do me good. I have a strong mind, one that is not easily distracted or deterred or discouraged. I cannot bring Sandy Alomar's ball back. I can't change the outcome of the division series. But I do know that I hate the feeling that I have when I walk off the mound that night in Jacobs Field. And I am going to do all I can to make sure it doesn't happen again.

8

Shades of '27

You NEVER KNOW WHEN the peace of the Lord will make a difference in your life. I find this out early one Sunday morning in the off-season. Clara and I go to visit a house in Westchester County that we are interested in buying. It is a handsome home in a nice area. A friend of ours from church goes with us, just in case we begin negotiating and need an interpreter to go over fine points. It's an 8:00 a.m. appointment, and it's such an early hour that we don't dress up for it; I am in sweatpants and a T-shirt, and Clara is dressed the same way.

We ring the doorbell and a woman opens the door. She looks aghast at the sight of us.

Good morning, we are here for our appointment, our friend says.

The woman looks us up and down. She doesn't seem happy.

Okay, she says brusquely. Please take your shoes off. There is somebody else coming at 8:30, so you are going to have to look at the house quickly.

The look on her face, and her manner, suggest that she thinks we are drug dealers, or maybe gardeners who are playing a joke.

She gives us a ninety-second tour of the house. Two minutes, tops. I am not kidding. It lasts as long as it takes the Yankee Stadium ground crew to do their YMCA routine.

We do have other people coming, so thank you very much, she says.

We'd like to see the master bedroom and the closets, our friend says.

The woman seems incredulous now, and beyond annoyed. There is no way she wants gardeners in her master bedroom, peeking at her shoe collection.

She pulls our friend aside.

Can you explain to me what is going on? Who are these people, and why are they here?

Ma'am, our friend says, the man who is with me is Mariano Rivera of the New York Yankees. The woman is his wife, Clara. They are serious buyers and are very interested in this home.

The woman now looks much more aghast than she did before.

Oh my God, I am so sorry. I had no idea. I am so very sorry. She goes and gets her husband, a local official. Suddenly, she wants us to sit down for pastries and coffee. She doesn't care at all about the 8:30 appointment.

You will never guess who is here... it's Mariano Rivera of the Yankees and his wife, she tells her husband.

I shake hands with the man. I thank him for showing us the house. We have a nice talk. I know exactly what just happened. I know that the homeowners basically profiled Clara and me not only as people who couldn't possibly have the means to buy their home but who really were unfit to even be in it.

It is only the Lord's grace that allows me to look beyond the incident, and to recognize that there is no malice or insult intended. A rush to judgment, surely, but no malice.

The Lord teaches us not to judge people by appearances, and not to close the door on anyone. We are all God's children, after all. It should not make any difference whether I work with a baseball or a machete, whether I am a fisherman's son or a New York Yankee. I could've walked out of that house that day. I could've let the flash of anger I felt get the better of me. But I do not. I am far from perfect. So I forgive, just as the Lord forgives me.

And it all works out. Clara and I wind up buying the house.

I start 1998 with a blown save and a trip to the disabled list in my first appearance, thanks to a strained groin muscle. We lose four of our first five games and get outscored 35–15 in the process.

Not much more goes wrong the rest of the year.

We finish the first half with a record of 61–20. In the second half we slump and go 53–28. We hit .288 as a team, score the most runs in the league, and have the best ERA in the league (3.82) — almost a full run better than the league average. I wind up with 36 saves and a 1.91 ERA, and a total of 36 strikeouts — the lowest total for any full year of my career. This is quite by design. Mel Stottlemyre is concerned that striking out too many guys is running up my pitch count, and that it could contribute to my getting tired at the end of the year. In 1997, for example, when I basically strike out a batter an inning, I throw 1,212 pitches. A year later, with maybe even better results, I throw more than three hundred fewer pitches (910).

Would Sandy Alomar Jr. have hit that homer if my arm had been a little fresher? Would my cut fastball have had a little more bite on it? The Lord knows that, but you don't and I don't. Still, it makes complete sense.

Why not save the wear on your arm? Mel says.

Sounds good to me, I say.

With my cutter getting better and better, I am getting more broken bats, though not as many strikeouts as with the straight fastball. When I first came up, especially in 1996, I'd throw a fastball at the thighs, a fastball at the waist, and then a fastball at the chest—going up the ladder, as they say—and guys would swing and miss and chase the high one. But hitters adjust. When they realize they can't touch the 96- or 97-mile-per-hour fastball up in the zone, they lay off. So you find another way to beat them. And for me, that way is the hard, late movement of the cut fastball.

We wrap up the regular season with a record of 114–48, or 22 games ahead of the second-place Red Sox.

There are wacky numbers all over baseball that year, especially in the home run department. Mark McGwire and Sammy Sosa have their celebrated chase for the home run record. They wind up with 70 and 66, respectively, and a slew of other guys aren't that far behind. Ken Griffey Jr. hits 56. Greg Vaughn hits 50. Andres Galarraga hits 44 and barely makes the top five in the National League. I don't think anything of it at the time, but then I am totally naive when it comes to steroids. I'm not saying that everybody among the home run leaders is dirty, though I'm sure a number of them are. I'm just saying that I could've stepped on a pack of syringes and not known what was going on. Not only have I never taken any steroids, I've never seen anybody else take them, either. Not once has anyone pulled me aside and said, Mo, you should try this because it helped me and it could help you.

I know there are people who may have huge doubts about this; my name has been whispered in this context because of my dramatic velocity increase in 1995. Believe me, I understand the cynicism, especially after so many star athletes, from Ben Johnson to Lance Armstrong to Mark McGwire, have turned out to be chemically enhanced—all of them after denying everything up and down. All I can tell you is the truth as it relates to me—I have never cheated, and never would cheat, because I love and respect the game too much for that.

Look at all the years of terrible publicity and disgrace these things have brought. When the issue gets all the way to the United

States Congress, and you have players bobbing and weaving or pretending they don't speak English, well, that's pretty bad.

If I could erase one thing from recent baseball history, it would be performance-enhancing drugs. I'd do whatever I could to make sure everybody played the right way—played honestly. I understand that there are players who are desperate to make it and feel as though getting some chemical help is the only thing that can get them there. I get that people want to fulfill their dreams, but do it the right way. If you have the ability to be a big league ballplayer, great. If you don't have the ability, and you've done all you can to get the most out of yourself, don't turn around and do something that hurts the game.

When it comes down to it, we all make choices. Steroids are there on the streets. They are there right now. You can go get them and have the stuff in your bloodstream before you finish this chapter, if that is your choice. Nobody is putting a gun to your head to do this. You know where it will take you. You will bulk up and get more bat speed and hit the ball harder, farther. If you are a pitcher, you are going to add some muscle to your fastball.

You also know that even if your choice never becomes public, it's something you have with you forever, no matter how much you deny it, or how good your counsel is, or how brilliant your excuses are. And the strong odds are that somehow, some way, you are going to get caught. Maybe not this year, maybe not even next year, but eventually it's going to happen.

And when it does, your name will be *barro*—mud. You will be on the front pages and the sports pages and get more time on *SportsCenter* than the anchormen. Reporters will follow you and ask for comments from your manager and teammates. People will rip you and your kids will be teased and humiliated, and it will be a *lio enorme*—a huge mess.

Knowing all this, if you still go ahead and take performance-enhancing drugs, you know what I think? I think you have problems. I think you have big problems. I think you are in complete denial, or reckless, or so sure that you are untouchable because you are a rich, famous ballplayer that your troubles probably are just beginning.

Taking PEDs is cheating, plain and simple. It robs the game of integrity and legitimacy. If you get caught, you have to pay up. You should accept your punishment and shut up. You should be fully accountable and not hide behind your agent and some slick statement in which you offer some vague apology and don't even say what you are apologizing for.

And if you are my teammate and you turn out to be a drug user? I am not going to coddle you or look the other way, I promise you. But I am also not going to abandon you. I will be there for you when you need it the most. I may believe you cheated and made a bad mistake, but I am not going to bail on you. If a brother or sister messes up, are you going to turn your back on them? I look at my teammates as family. So as much as I may abhor the behavior, I'm not going to rebuke them, as if I am some high moral authority. In the Sermon on the Mount, in Matthew 7:1–5, Jesus says:

Judge not, that you be not judged. For with what judgment you judge, you will be judged; and with the measure you use, it will be measured back to you. And why do you look at the speck in your brother's eye, but do not consider the plank in your own eye?

I look at it very simply: We are all human, and we all make mistakes. Some worse than others, some far harder to forgive. But who am I to judge?

When you spend 152 consecutive days in first place, it usually means there's not a red-hot pennant race going on. But you still have to take care of business every single day. As I approach my thirtieth birthday, I understand more than ever that preparing properly is everything.

I am a person who likes order and finds comfort in routine. Never is this more true than on game days. After I shag flies and batting practice is done, I grab a little something to eat, usually chicken or pasta, though I can't lie... every now and again we order in from Popeyes. (An amusing image, I know—a delivery kid showing up with fried chicken at the Yankee Stadium security gate saying, I have an order for Rivera...) Once nourished, I am in the hot tub before the first inning starts, usually around 6:50 p.m., if we are playing at night. I submerge myself up to the neck and get my body good and loose. After fifteen minutes or so, I towel off and go to a massage room, where I do some stretching and have the massage therapist work on my legs and anywhere there might be tightness, a process that takes about thirty minutes. Then I get dressed (very methodically) and go to the trainer's room, typically at the start of the fourth inning, and Gene Monahan begins by stretching my arm and legs some more. Then, depending on how I feel, he might put steam heat on my shoulder and rub my arm down with some hot stuff. All the while, I am paying close attention to the game on TV. I am studying the opposing hitters' at-bats, looking for tendencies or possible weaknesses.

This time with Geno is probably my favorite part of the day, outside of being on the mound. It's measured, purposeful. It is unhurried. I am in touch with my body. I am in touch with Geno. We talk about our families and our days and what's going on in the world. We are honest and connected. It brings closure to my preparation. By the time I leave his training table, I can almost feel my adrenaline starting to surge. I head for the bullpen in the middle or the end of the sixth, and I get ready to compete.

On a Sunday in early August at the Stadium, I stick to the routine religiously, throw a scoreless inning against the Royals for my thirtieth save, and lower my ERA to 1.25. It raises our record to

84–29, and by the time our nine-game winning streak is over, we are 89–29.

We get there by taking care of business, and being prepared.

With the way we've dominated all year, we're obviously huge favorites to win it all, a status that can bring its own pressure. The Rangers are our first-round opponent, and their loaded lineup scores one run in three games. Juan Gonzalez, who almost beat us by himself two years earlier, hits .084. Will Clark and Rusty Greer both hit .091, and Pudge Rodriguez hits .100. John Wetteland, my former mentor, only gets in one game. I pitch in all three games, save two, and give up one hit, and now it's on to a rematch with the Indians.

After we take the opener behind David Wells, the Indians win two straight, and now we're looking at the biggest game of our season. A loss and we're in a 3–1 hole, staring down an elimination game in Jacobs Field. Orlando Hernandez (El Duque), making his first postseason start, is brilliant, throwing three-hit ball over seven innings in a 4–0 victory to tie the series at two games apiece.

In Game 5, Wells is superb for the second time in the series, striking out eleven and pitching into the eighth. I come on with one out and a 5–3 lead, and the tying runs on board. So here I am again in an eighth inning at Jacobs Field, in Year 1 A.A. (After Alomar). At the plate is the Indians' left fielder, switch-hitter Mark Whiten, who had been on our side in this series the year before. Hard Hittin' is what Whiten likes to be called. He's a guy with a lot of power. It's the biggest at-bat of the game, if not the series. The count goes to 2–2, and all I'm focused on is finishing the pitch well, coming in hard on him with a cut fastball. From the set, I bring a hard cutter that does just what I want, busting him on the hands. Whiten hits a weak grounder to second that turns into a double play to end the threat.

An inning later, I close it up with two quick outs on Jim Thome and Brian Giles, then strike out Enrique Wilson to put us one game away from the World Series.

David Cone, a twenty-game winner, starts well in Game 6, and Scott Brosius clobbers a three-run homer and we jump to a 6–0 lead. A party atmosphere is building in the Stadium, but Thome hits a grand slam and the Indians get within one, and it's only because Mendoza, the guy who won't play catch with me, gives us three brilliant innings of relief, and Derek hits a two-run triple, that we add some breathing room.

I come in for the ninth with an 8–5 lead. Nine pitches later, I grab Omar Vizquel's comebacker and toss to Tino and we're heading back to the Series. The guys mob me, and the joy I feel is deep. I am not big on redemption. It's not as if I go out there consciously thinking I have to make up for the Alomar home run. All I want to do is throw good pitches and get outs.

I am convinced that being fully committed to the moment, without any worries about the past or projections into the future, is the best attribute a closer can have. You wonder why the shelf life of so many short relievers is, well, so short? Why guys can be unhittable for a year or two and then disappear? It's because it takes a ton of concentration, and self-belief, to stay in the moment this way and not let the highs and lows mess with your psyche. The Lord has given me a strong arm but an even stronger mind. It is the key to everything, allowing me to not succumb to doubt or weakness when I fail. Twelve months After Alomar, I pitch in four of the five games against the Indians, and give up no hits in five and two-thirds innings. I strike out five. I have an ERA of 0.00. In nine innings across two playoff series, I have given up one single.

I am ready for the San Diego Padres, and the World Series, and ready for an interesting family subplot, too. My cousin and former teammate Ruben Rivera is now a Padre. Ruben is four years younger than me, a strong, fast, power-hitting center fielder, a player with the sort of physique and skills that make scouts feel faint. A Panamanian Mickey Mantle? More than a few baseball people think he has that kind of ability. In 1995, he is not just one of the hottest Yankee prospects in years; he is one of the top prospects in all of baseball. He makes some nice contributions with his bat and glove when the Yankees call him up in 1996, a year after me, and then it all begins to unravel.

You can be an All-Star for a long time. You have that in you, I used to tell Ruben. You just need to focus more and decide if this is what you really want.

It is what I want, Ruben would reply. I work hard.

I know you work hard, but there's more to it than that. You also have to take care of yourself. You have to make good decisions. You have to realize you are only going to get one chance at this.

Ruben is one of those young guys who just seem to be a little too taken with the fame and the adulation that come with being a gifted big league player. He parties a little too much, stays out too late, never quite shows the patience he needs to let his talent take hold. He wants to be a star yesterday. He wants to swing at every pitch, whether it's a strike or not. He wants it all, now, and when it doesn't happen on his timetable, he gets frustrated. As the years pass, the frustration only grows. Ruben would wind up moving ten times in his big league career (he signed with the Yankees three different times). He hit 23 homers and stole 18 bases as a full-time player for the Padres in 1999. He also batted just .195 and struck out 143 times. I always wanted him to find a stable situation in the big leagues so that he could relax and let his gifts shine, but the stability never really happened for him until he got to Mexico, where he has played for the last seven years and, at the age of forty, is still one of the league's top sluggers.

I want all the best for Ruben as the Series starts, but only after we win four games.

David Wells gets the ball to start a third straight postseason series for us, but this time is outpitched by Padres ace Kevin Brown, who takes a 5–2 lead into the bottom of the seventh. When Brown gives up a hit and a walk to start the eighth, Bruce Bochy, the Padres' manager, calls for reliever Donne Wall, who immediately gives up a three-run homer to Chuck Knoblauch. Soon Wall leaves and Mark Langston arrives, and before the inning is over, Tino hits a grand slam and we have a seven-run inning. This is how it has gone all year. Production comes from everywhere. We have a No. 9 hitter, Scott Brosius, with 19 homers and 98 RBIs. We have Jorge Posada, a switch-hitting catcher in his first full year, hitting 17 homers and knocking in 63 runs, also at the bottom of the order. We have no 30–home run guys, but we do have eight guys who hit 17 or more, and five guys who drive in over 80 runs. The balance is incredible.

I come on in the eighth and get a four-out save, and the Padres' problems deepen when we score seven more times in the first three innings of Game 2. With our Cuban rookie, Orlando Hernandez, on the mound, that is a massive deficit to overcome, and we're half-way home after a 9–3 victory.

Our confidence is so unshakeable at this point that even when Sterling Hitchcock, the former Yankee, shuts us down through six and takes a 3–0 lead into the seventh, I sit on a bullpen bench and think:

We have them just where we want them.

All season we've fought back. All season we've had different guys come through in the biggest moments. So I am not surprised when Brosius, who's been crushing the ball the whole Series, belts a homer to lead off the seventh, or when Shane Spencer follows with a double. Hitchcock is done, we creep one run closer, and, one inning later, Brosius steps in against Trevor Hoffman, one of the best closers in the business, and sends another ball over the wall, this time with two men on.

Now we're up, 5–3, and after a few hairy moments, I finish off a 5–4 victory by striking out Andy Sheets with the tying run at third. With a sweep one victory away, Andy outpitches Brown and throws seven and one-third superb innings, leaving with a 3–0 lead and two guys on. Jeff Nelson comes in and strikes out Vaughn, and then Mr. T calls for me. I run in from the pen, and am not thinking about dogpiles or Champagne showers or anything else. I am thinking:

Get an out.

Ken Caminiti singles to load the bases, and who should come up but Jim Leyritz. He seems to be following us around. Leyritz can crush anybody's fastball if it's not well located. On a 1–2 pitch, I throw a cutter, a little up and away. Leyritz swings. It is not the contact he is looking for, his short fly to center an easy play for Bernie, who grabs it with a basket catch.

My cousin leads off the ninth, and singles up the middle in the only at-bat he ever has against me, but he is not on first long. Carlos Hernandez, the catcher, hits into a 6-4-3 double play, and now I am looking in at Mark Sweeney, a left-handed pinch hitter. I pump in two fastballs, and then come with a cutter away that he bounces to Brosius, who throws across to Tino, and now the dogpile is *all* I am thinking of. Joe Girardi arrives first and hugs me as I raise my arms straight overhead, thanking the Lord. Soon I am engulfed by Brosius, World Series MVP, and everybody else. My postseason ends with six saves and 13.1 scoreless innings. It is the first time in my life I've gotten the last out of a season. It's a feeling I could get used to.

9

Spirit and Summit

THIS IS NO MIDSUMMER night's dream. It is real. The Holy Spirit is speaking to me. Not in a regular voice, as if Clara were talking to me in the kitchen. But it is definitely the Holy Spirit.

It's a hot Friday night at Yankee Stadium in July of 1999, the Atlanta Braves are in town, and it is a strange game from the start. The pitching matchup is Greg Maddux vs. El Duque. Who would ever guess Maddux would give up nine hits and five runs, and Duque would give up eight hits and six runs—and they'd both be gone before the game was half over?

Derek, in the middle of the best year of his life, hits his fifteenth homer and knocks three hits, raising his average to .377. Ramiro Mendoza is sensational in relief and gets us to the ninth with three-plus innings of scoreless ball. I run in from the bullpen, accompanied by the guitar riffs of Metallica's "Enter Sandman," the new entrance song the Yankees have picked for me. I have no advance notice about it and honestly don't pay the song much mind. Ever since we played the San Diego Padres in the '98 World Series and the Yankees noticed how San Diego fans got all fired up by Trevor Hoffman's entrance song, "Hell's Bells," by AC/DC, they have been trying to find the right introduction for me. (I might've gone with "Onward Christian Soldiers," but I don't think that would've flown.) For a while they try Guns N' Roses' "Welcome to the Jungle," which the fans seem to like. Then one day a Stadium operations worker named Mike Luzzi cues up "Sandman," and the fans go berserk. So the search is over. I am not consulted and don't need to be. If the fans like it, let's go with it.

I am done with my warm-ups, and am standing on the back of the mound, head bowed, ball in my right hand, about to say my customary prayer:

Lord, please keep me safe. Keep my teammates safe, and every-body safe. I pray that You will protect me and give me the strength I need. Amen.

I am concentrating deeply and can feel my heart opening up. Suddenly I feel the overpowering presence of the Holy Spirit. My English isn't good enough to describe what this feels like. Neither is my Spanish. You just have this supercharged sense of the Spirit in your heart, pouring into your soul.

I am the One who has put you here, the Spirit says.

I stop. I turn around and look up at the fifty thousand people surrounding me. I know what I just heard, and know that I am the only one who heard it. The tone of the voice is joyful, but it is also admonishing. I am at a point in the season and in my career at which I feel very much in charge of what I am doing on the mound. I don't express this outwardly, but I am so full of confidence and vigor that it's as if I am the one calling all the shots. In this moment, the Lord has apparently decided that I've gotten a bit too big for my closer's britches, and that I need to be reminded that He is the one who is all-powerful, not me.

As I stand on the Yankee Stadium mound before all these people, I am flooded with emotions. I am chastened and humbled, profoundly shaken by this sudden spiritual wake-up call.

I am sorry that I have gotten carried away with my own sense of importance. I am sorrier still that I have ventured off on my own, to a degree, instead of seeking the Lord's will. The Lord has indeed put me here. Without Him I am nothing. The only reason I am here, and able to do what I do, is because He gives me strength.

It is time to pitch now.

Oh boy, I am thinking. *I really don't know how this is going to go.*

I am going to do my best, but in this instant I probably have as much doubt about my ability to focus on the task at hand as I ever have in my professional career. Maybe this is part of the lesson that the Lord wants to teach me—I don't know.

I get Bret Boone on a fly ball to right, and for a moment I think that maybe I can steady myself after all.

The thought does not last for long.

I bounce a pitch badly to Chipper Jones, then walk him on another ball way out of the strike zone. On my first pitch to Brian Jordan, he rips a hit-and-run single to right field. After I fall behind Ryan Klesko, Mel comes out to visit to get me to relax and throw the strikes that I almost always throw. I nod. I act as if everything is okay.

It is not okay.

Klesko laces a single. That blows the save. Two batters later, Andruw Jones takes me over the wall in left center. That blows the game.

It is about as bad an outing as I've ever had as a closer.

I don't say a word about what happened to any of my teammates, but I know I have learned an important lesson. I am a human being, and human beings get complacent. We lose our way sometimes. The Lord decides that this hot summer night is the time to help me find my way again.

Is it a coincidence the way the rest of the season goes? That I give up one run for the rest of the year? That I finish the season with streaks of thirty and two-thirds scoreless innings and twenty-two consecutive saves? I have no idea. All I can tell you is that I spend the next three months in a zone of profound humility and as much concentration and confidence as I've ever had in my life.

We win sixteen fewer games than we did the year before, but our record of 98–64 is still the best in the league, putting us in the division series against the Rangers for the third time in four years. The Rangers are a very good club, but, let's face it, there is a part of them that seems to wilt like a flower in the Texas heat at the very sight of us. We sweep three straight games again, and for the second straight year, their loaded lineup manages a single run against us in the three games. I strike out Rafael Palmeiro and Tom Goodwin and pop up Todd Zeile to save Game 2, and throw two more scoreless innings to finish the series and put us into the ALCS against the Red Sox — the matchup everybody seems to want.

Ever since he arrives on his boat from Cuba, El Duque keeps proving what a big-game pitcher he is, and here he is again, going eight strong innings in Game 1, which is tied at three when I come on to start the ninth. I get six outs and allow one hit in two innings, taking it into the bottom of the tenth, when Bernie Williams socks a Rod Beck pitch over the fence a few minutes after midnight.

It's a rousing way to start, and we don't let up. Chuck Knoblauch has an RBI double and Paul O'Neill an RBI single late in Game 2, then Ramiro strands the bases loaded with two immense outs in the eighth, before I get the save in a wobbly ninth, striking out Damon Buford with Nomar Garciaparra, the tying run, on third.

We head to Boston with a 2–0 lead, and though the Red Sox emphatically get one back with a 13–1 victory in which Pedro Martinez is brilliant and Roger Clemens, longtime Sox ace turned Public Enemy No. 1, has the worst postseason start of his life, the slippage stops there. Andy is dominant in Game 3, and Ricky Ledee hits a grand slam off Beck in the ninth inning, and we win, 9–2 — and before you can bake a batch of beans, we are dancing on the Fenway infield after Duque rides again to lift us to a 6–1 victory in Game 5.

It puts us up against the Braves in another World Series, and wouldn't you know it, the Game 1 matchup is El Duque and Greg Maddux, the same guys who were on the mound when the Holy Spirit visited me in the Bronx three months earlier. I do not hear voices this time. I just marvel at the contrast between these pitchers, and how they go about their craft. Here you have Duque, with his spring-loaded leg kick and gyrations, and arm angles he seems to invent as he goes, throwing all kinds of nasty stuff. There you have Maddux, as steady as a metronome, commanding the ball with flawless, brutally efficient mechanics. Unlike in the regular-season game, they are both in peak form, and eventually it is a 1–1 game in the eighth. It stays tight until Paul O'Neill comes up that inning.

This World Series isn't especially dramatic—another four-game sweep—and is without epic games and highlight-film moments. People remember how I break three of Ryan Klesko's bats in one trip to the plate in the final moments of the Series, and how Chipper Jones is laughing about it in the dugout. For me, though, this is a World Series that is all about Paul O'Neill.

Paulie got to the Yankees in 1993, and the team immediately started winning. In fact, the Yankees haven't had a losing season since his arrival. It would be silly to say that the turnaround was all about him, but it would be even sillier to say that it was a complete coincidence.

The first time I meet Paulie is in spring training. Right away you notice not just his strength and size (a broad-shouldered and muscular six foot four) but his intensity and serious sense of purpose. He never says much, and he never hot dogs about anything. He does his work and wants to win. He's a guy who once hit .359, and yet he just wants to be one of the guys in the lineup.

I admire that about him from the beginning. You learn early on in the big leagues that some guys play to the cameras, and some guys wish the cameras weren't there at all. Paulie is in the latter group. He loathes talking about himself, even after he goes 4 for 4 or saves the game with a nice catch. He also doesn't like getting attention after he heaves a helmet over a called strike, or batters one more watercooler into extinction. Paulie is unbelievably hard on himself, a perfectionist to the core. Early in 1999, we have a game at home against the Angels, and Paulie goes 1 for 5 and strikes out three times. The last time, he's caught looking by Troy Percival with a guy on in the bottom of the ninth, the tying run at the plate. When umpire Greg Kosc punches him out, Paulie heads back to the dugout, and the next thing you know there's an airborne watercooler on its way to the field. His temper can definitely cloud his judgment; once, he swings at a pitch and is so disgusted with the contact that he flings the bat away in a rage. The ball goes over the right-field wall. We give him a good going-over for that one.

You can always count on this guy, though. Paulie has a long-running feud with Lou Piniella, the Mariners' manager, dating to their years together in Cincinnati. Lou loves to get into Paulie's head and publicly calls him a baby for whining every time somebody pitches him inside. Maybe this is all gamesmanship; I don't know, because I never get into that stuff. There isn't one time in all my years of pitching when I either work an umpire or beef about a call so I might get the next one, or try to intimidate a hitter by telling him he better get ready to move his feet.

It's not just that I think it's unsportsmanlike; it's just not the way I want to do business. I have a ball in my hand, and I believe I have all I need to get the hitter out without any of the extracurricular stuff.

In any case, all it does is make Paulie even more determined. He hit three homers in five games in the 1995 division series against the Mariners, and hits .417 with a couple more homers in the ALCS in 2001, the year Piniella's Mariners won a record 116 games.

That's what I love about this guy; he is always there when the team needs him most. In June of 1999, we have a nasty little bean-ball game against the Indians. Wil Cordero homers off Clemens and later gets hit by our reliever Jason Grimsley. Not long after, Derek gets drilled by the Indians' reliever Steve Reed. Derek isn't even done glaring at Reed before Paulie rips a Reed pitch over the wall in right to lock the game away.

Nice job of taking justice into your own hands, I say to Paulie afterward.

He smiles.

It's the best way to get even with a pitcher, he says.

Paulie is there with the glove, too, never more than in Game 5 of the 1996 World Series, as Wetteland tries to protect Andy's 1–0 lead in the bottom of the ninth. The Braves have runners at first and third and pinch hitter Luis Polonia at the plate, and after six foul balls, Polonia drives a ball to deep right center.

I am sure that this ball is in the gap and that the game is over, the Braves taking a 3–2 lead. But Paulie runs and runs and chases it down near the warning track—never mind that he has a bad hamstring. His catch saves the game, and very possibly the World Series. Again, in 1998, with two on in the first inning of Game 2 against the Padres, he makes a leaping grab at the wall to rob Wally Joyner and sets us on our way.

Three years later, back in the Series again, it is not an easy time for the Yankees. A season that begins with Mr. T taking a leave of absence to get cancer treatment continues with the death of Scott Brosius's father and then Luis Sojo's father. Luis misses the first two games of the Series after his father passes.

Paul's father, Charles O'Neill, is home in Ohio fighting a seri-ous heart condition. I know it weighs on Paulie all year, and even more so in the postseason, when his father's condition worsens. I get so much comfort when I see him out there in right field—a man who you know is going to give all he has to help you get an out—that I wish somehow that I could comfort him.

Paulie's father dies in the early hours of the morning before Game 4 against the Braves in 1999. When Mr. T posts the lineup and I see O'Neill in the usual No. 3 hole, between Derek and Bernie, I am not surprised at all. I look at Paulie as he sits at his locker in the back of the clubhouse before the game, wondering what this loss must feel like for him. I want to pray with him and console him, but now is not the time. That comes five hours later, after I break Klesko's bats and get Keith Lockhart to fly out to left to finish off the sweep.

As the guys all converge on me in the center of the Stadium diamond, Paulie is the last one to arrive, the joy and grief and everything seeming to hit him all at once as he hugs Mr. T and begins to cry. He leaves the field in tears and walks into the dugout. As Mr. T said, Paulie is going through the highest of highs and the lowest of lows, all on the same day. Nothing prepares you for that. In the clubhouse chaos, with the Champagne spraying everywhere, I walk over to Paulie at his locker.

I am so sorry about your father, I say. I don't know why the Lord wanted him to come home today, but I am sure he's very proud of you.

Thank you, Mo, he says. He was watching, guarantee you that, and he's happier than anybody that we did it.

I face forty-three batters in three postseason series that year, and none of them scores. The last run I gave up was almost three months and forty innings ago, on a double by Tampa Bay catcher John Flaherty. I finish the season with more saves (45) than hits allowed (43). I am named World Series MVP, and back in Puerto

Caimito and all over Panama, family and friends are telling me I'm the talk of the Canal Zone, and everywhere else. Fame is fine, but it is not what I seek. What I seek is the light and love of the Lord, for as He reminded me on that hot July night on the pitcher's mound in the Bronx, He is the one who has put me here.

There is nothing like a ticker-tape parade in New York City. You ride through that canyon of skyscrapers, with millions of pieces of confetti swirling and almost as many fans cheering, and the out-pouring is a humbling spectacle. All this love, all this adulation — it's remarkable to bask in it, and to share in people's happiness. Maybe my most enduring memory of that 1999 celebration comes at the City Hall ceremony. Mr. T has the microphone and summons Jorge Posada to join him.

Tell them what we say at the end of our meetings, Jorgie, Mr. T says.

Grind it out! Jorgie hollers as he turns his fist, smiling as he does.

There isn't a better grinder-outer on those championship teams than Jorgie Posada, let me tell you that. Nobody works harder, either. A second baseman when he was drafted, Jorgie spends countless hours, over the years, refining his footwork, his pitch-blocking, his throwing mechanics — and it all pays off in 2000, when Joe Girardi is gone and Jorgie gets more of the workload than ever. He puts up an All-Star season, hitting 28 homers with 86 runs batted in and a .287 average; with his 107 walks, he posts the highest on-base percentage (.417) on the club. He strikes out more than anybody, too (151 times), but I cut him slack on that because he is such a total gamer.

Jorgie is emotional and unyielding at times, with a will as thick as his catcher's physique. You want him on your side, for sure. We're in St. Petersburg at the start of July 2000 to play the Rays, and we are in a tailspin, having lost 4 of 5 and 7 of 9, our record just two games over .500 (38–36). Duque is pitching well, but he and the Rays are barking at each other after Randy Winn steps out just as Duque is about to throw a pitch. Jorge calms Duque down—an ironic scene, because often Jorge would motivate Duque by riling him up (something like putting quarters into a jukebox)—and later Tino clears the bases with a three-run double. In the bottom of the seventh, the Rays' Bobby Smith goes down on strikes against Jeff Nelson, and as Jorgie pops out to fire the ball to Brosius, Smith bumps him slightly with the barrel of his bat.

Jorge jabs the ball into Smith's side and then they're at it, bodies tumbling, Smith's helmet flying, revealing the best blond Afro this side of Randy Levine. Jorge and Smith are both ejected (and later suspended), and even though I never ask Jorgie if he had an ulterior motive by getting into it with Smith, he knows how to rouse the troops. The game means so much that Mr. T has me come in to close even though we have a five-run lead. We win seven of our next eight and climb back into first place, staying there the rest of the year.

When you go through such long seasons with guys, ups and downs are inevitable, and more than anybody else on the team I feel for Chuck Knoblauch. I think people forget what a huge factor he proved to be in our championship runs in 1998 and 1999. For almost a decade he's been one of the top leadoff men in baseball. He hit .341 and .333 in back-to-back years with the Twins, and the year before we traded for him, he hit .291 with ten triples and sixty-two steals—the kind of player whose speed and energy can change a whole game. He also won a Gold Glove as the league's top defensive second baseman, which is why it's so hard to see him suffering the way he is with his throwing. Chuck, simply put, has the yips—the term baseball people use for players who suddenly, inexplicably, lose the ability to execute a simple skill they've demonstrated mastery of their entire career. It can be a pitcher who loses the strike zone and never relocates it, a catcher who can't throw the ball back to the pitcher, a pitcher who can't throw to first, or, in Chuck's case, a second baseman who can't make a twenty-five-foot throw to the first baseman right next door. Chuck is fine when he has to make a diving play, then scramble to his feet and throw. The yips come when he has time to think about it. I've never been on a team with a player who has had the yips until now, and it's just hor-rific to watch. To see a guy who is a phenomenal athlete and com-petitor get invaded by these demons, and have a runaway mind grind him into mulch — it's so sad. And probably the worst part — beyond even the embarrassment and humiliation — is the way it sucks every bit of fun out of playing the game.

Chuck had one error in his Gold Glove year, thirteen the fol-lowing year, and twenty-six the year after that. His problems seem to be on the wane as the season begins, but then they flare up again in a 12–3 loss to the White Sox at Yankee Stadium. Chuck makes errors on two routine throws to Tino, missing badly, and then, on a perfect double-play ball, gets the shovel feed from Derek and throws the ball about twenty feet up the line from where Tino is stretching toward him. The fans boo him unmercifully. At the end of the inning, he runs into the dugout, talks to Mr. T, and in an instant he is not only gone from the dugout; he is gone from the Stadium.

When a teammate is going through something like this, not just a slump or rough patch but a psychological disorder, you don't know what to say or do. You feel helpless. You just try to stay positive and let him know you are there.

Chuck toughs it out, and it sure looks as if he is getting better toward the end of the year, but by then our issues go way beyond the yips. When Roger defeats the Blue Jays and I get my 34th save on September 13, we are 25 games over .500 (84–59). At which point we sink faster than my father's rusty old anchor.

We lose eight of our next nine, and fifteen of our last eighteen. In one three-game stretch, we give up thirty-five runs. In our last seven games—all losses—we are outscored, 68–15. That's hard for an expansion team to do, never mind a two-time defending World Series champion.

So we limp into the division series against the Oakland A's, and have a question to answer: Are we the club that has won twenty-two of its last twenty-five postseason games, and captured three of the last four World Series?

Or are we the club that hasn't pitched, fielded, or hit in the clutch for more than two weeks?

When Roger gives up four runs in six innings and we lose Game 1 in Oakland, I can't deny the obvious: We are up against it in a way we haven't been since 1997. We either show up and play hard for nine innings in Game 2 or we're just not made of the same championship fiber we once were. Could it be that the Mets, who are on their way to the National League pennant, are going to be the New York team that gets a parade this fall?

Not many managers have better instincts than Mr. T, so when he makes lineup changes for the second game, I don't think of it as panic; I think of it as a smart manager playing a strong hunch. Against the Padres in 1998, Mr. T had a feeling about Ricky Ledee, who was rarely used during the season, and Ledee wound up getting six hits in three games. He had a feeling that Ramiro Mendoza should be the long man in the postseason, and it worked spectacularly. Knoblauch, now a designated hitter (DH) because of his throwing issues, sits down; Glenallen Hill takes over. Paulie, struggling with a bad hip, moves down in the order, and Jorge moves up to the second spot, right behind Derek. Hill and Luis Sojo, our second baseman now, deliver big hits, and Jorgie is on base three times. Andy pitches brilliantly, taking a shutout through seven and two-thirds, and then Mr. T calls for me, and I get four groundouts to complete a 4–0 victory, even the series, and remind us what it feels like to win.

Back at Yankee Stadium, Duque outduels Tim Hudson, and I get the last six outs without giving up a hit, and the 4–2 victory in Game 3 puts us a game away from the ALCS. I would've bet money that, after losing Game 1, Roger would lock the A's up in Game 4; and if I had, I would've lost it. Roger gets spanked around, giving up a three-run homer in the first to a Panamanian DH, Olmedo Saenz, and the A's go on to an 11–1 rout, and we all go back to Oakland, where we blow out to a six-run lead in the first and then hold on, as I get Eric Chavez on a pop-up to put us up against Piniella and his Mariners in the ALCS.

The Mariners are the club that I came of age against five years earlier, of course, establishing myself for the first time as a pitcher who was capable of dominating. Once you have that breakthrough, it changes not only how other teams perceive you but how you perceive yourself. I always knew I could be effective, but when I walk off the mound after striking out Mike Blowers with the season on the line, I can't say that it isn't a powerful affirmation.

On our way to a triumph in six games, the ALCS against the Mariners produces one of the truly great pitching performances that I have ever seen, delivered by Roger Clemens in Game 4, when he throws a one-hitter and strikes out fifteen. The hit — a double by Al Martin — doesn't come until the seventh inning. Roger then responds by striking out Alex Rodriguez, Edgar Martinez, and Mike Cameron. He doesn't just overpower the Mariners; he dices them up with his location, and competes the hardest when he needs it most. Clemens's heroics give us a three-games-to-one lead, before we close it out in Game 6, when David Justice, the series MVP, rips a massive homer to power a six-run seventh that gives us a 9–4 lead. It's 9–5 when I come on to close in the eighth, and I give up two more runs to make it 9–7. In the ninth, I get two outs on five pitches before Alex Rodriguez gets on with an infield hit. This isn't good.

Because the next hitter is Edgar Martinez, Mo-killer.

I fire strike one and then come at him again, trying to stay in so he can't smack the ball the other way, something he is very good at. The cutter comes in at him and breaks hard, breaks late. Edgar swings but hits it weakly, a grounder to short. Derek scoops it up and throws over to Tino.

What do you know?

I actually got Edgar Martinez out.

An instant later, Jorge is rushing to hug me, and Derek races in and rams me with a boyish body check.

Edgar Martinez can't hit you, Derek says.

The crowd chants, "We want the Mets." They will get the Mets, and so will we, in the first Subway Series since 1956.

10

New York, New York

THE DEPTH AND INTENSITY of the intra-city rivalry between fans of the Yankees and the Mets is still new to me. It's not as if I've grown up with it, after all. Half the fishermen on our boat are not wearing Met hats and the other half are not wearing Yankee hats, and none of us spend our days debating who is better, Keith Hernandez or Don Mattingly.

But it doesn't take me long to find out that this is going to be a very different World Series than the previous three. Nothing changes with the goal—win four games—and nothing changes with my get-in-and-get-out approach. I'm not someone who is going to get caught up in the hysteria and Super Bowl–style craziness.

But:

To be in a Series that requires no flights (a good thing) and lets me sleep in my own bed and wake up with my family every day (an even better thing), and that is being covered by about ten million reporters and is drawing out every second of old Yankee–Dodger film clips ever recorded, well, it's just not the same. I feel that, too.

Despite our dismal playing down the stretch, we show signs of getting back to winning baseball in the first two rounds of the play-offs. You may get us down. You may knock us around. You may think we're on our way out. But you better know we are going to fight back and keep on fighting for as long as it takes.

I am all legs, and full of pride, the day I graduate from Victoriana Chacón Elementary School—and shake hands with Puerto Caimito mayor Eugenio Castañón.

For most of my childhood, my dream was to be the Pelé of Panama. Here I am at eighteen—right before I gave up the sport of soccer due to a serious eye injury.

Clara and me on our wedding day, November 9, 1991. Marrying her was the best decision I've ever made.

Getaway day: Clara and I are off to Panama City for a two-day honeymoon before I have to leave to play instructional league ball.

On the day I leave Panama for the first time—and get on a plane for the first time—I put on a brave face, but don't be fooled. Here I am at the Panama City airport with my father and mother. That's my cousin Alberto hiding in the back. (Clara took the photo.)

Walking through Tocumen International Airport in Panama City with my plane ticket in hand, I am heading off for another season, not letting anybody know how terrified I am of flying.

I had a good year in 1992 as a starter for the Fort Lauderdale Yankees in Single-A ball—until an elbow surgery made me much more suspect than prospect.

Scott Brosius *(left)* and Jorge Posada tackle me after we sweep the Braves in 1999 to capture our third World Series title in four years. *(Jamie Squire / Getty Images)*

Saluting the fans after I pick up save number 602, passing Trevor Hoffman to become baseball's all-time leader. *(Rob Tringali / Getty Images)*

Another cutter is about to be launched. *(Ronald C. Modra / Sports Imagery / Getty Images)*

The last out is always the hardest one to get. Here I celebrate getting Mark Sweeney and completing our sweep of the Padres in 1998. *(Vincent Laforet / Getty Images)*

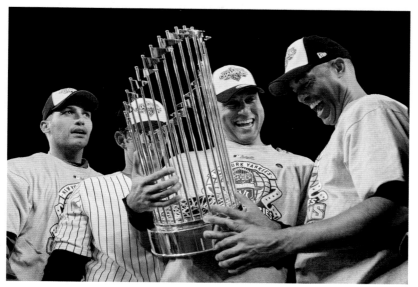

Winning never gets old. *(Pool / Getty Images)*

Having consistent, repeatable mechanics is a tremendous asset for a pitcher. Here I repeat mine in one of the last pitches of my career. *(Jim McIsaac / Getty Images)*

About one second after my old friends Andy Pettitte and Derek Jeter came to get me with two outs in the ninth of my final game, I was sobbing in Andy's arms. I had held in my emotions for a long, long time. I was ready to let them go. *(Al Bello / Getty Images)*

Walking off the mound for the final time on September 26, 2013—with the fans standing and cheering and the Tampa Bay Rays *(background)* and the Yankees both standing, too—was one of the most powerful and emotional moments of my life. *(Jim McIsaac / Getty Images)*

And beyond that, you better know we are not ever going to get complacent and think that there's no doubt we're going to win because we're the New York Yankees. All the credit must go to Mr. T and his staff for that. They have created this culture of deep belief in ourselves, but no arrogance. That is such a fine line you can't even see it, but we walk it. You know how many times I've gone out to the mound thinking, *This guy has no shot, because I am Mariano Rivera?*

Never.

The guy with the bat in his hand is a professional. He is a big league hitter, whether his name is Mike Piazza or Bubba Trammell or Benny Agbayani. He is trying just as hard to get a hit as I am trying to get him out. I respect that. I respect every competitor, from Edgar Martinez to the guy who has never hit a fair ball off of me.

The Series begins at Yankee Stadium, with the Mets sending out someone else I respect—Al Leiter. He is a winner and a battler, a world champion for the Marlins in 1997 who pitched six gritty innings in a Game 7. Leiter and Andy match zeroes through five innings, and then Timo Perez, a fleet outfielder whose energy and pop have been a big piece of the Mets' run late in the year, singles up the middle.

I am still in the clubhouse, watching on TV, having just gotten a rubdown from Geno. I am about ready to head to the bullpen when, with two outs, Todd Zeile crushes a line drive to deep left. It looks as if it's going out, but the ball hits the top of the wall, missing going over by the width of a fishhook.

It drops on the warning track. David Justice, our left fielder, picks it up and hits the cutoff man, Derek, who takes the throw near the left-field line, spins, and, off the wrong foot, crossing into foul territory, fires a one-hop strike to Jorge, who blocks the plate and slaps the tag on Perez.

You see that, Geno? I say. What a relay! What a play! I shout out loud. All right!

It's just a perfect throw by Derek, all the more so because he is off balance and on the move. It is a terrible play by Perez, who is so sure the ball is gone that he is running half speed as he rounds second. If he's running even three-quarter speed, he scores standing up.

In the bottom of the inning, Justice hits a two-run double and we have just nine outs to get, but the Mets don't stay down, taking a 3–2 lead on a two-run single by pinch hitter Trammell and, with Jeff Nelson on in relief of Andy, a well-placed roller down the third-base line by Edgardo Alfonzo.

Out in the pen now, I wait for the phone to ring. The message is always the same:

Get Mo going.

It rings a moment later. Tony Cloninger, the bullpen coach at the time, answers.

Mo, Tony says.

That is all I need to hear. I start warming up with my weighted three-pound ball, windmilling my arm around as I bend at the waist. Then I follow my usual routine with bullpen catcher Mike Borzello. I start with three easy tosses to Mike as he stands behind the plate, then motion for him to get down, and throw a half dozen or so pitches to the glove side, another half dozen to the other side, then come back to the glove side. In fifteen to eighteen pitches, I am loose, and then I just watch the game.

I enter in the top of the ninth. Jay Payton, leading off, flies out to deep right center, and then I nick Todd Pratt and give up a double to Kurt Abbott and have myself in a bit of a mess. Perez steps up. I need either a strikeout or a grounder right to somebody, with the infield in. On a 1–2 pitch, I come inside hard with the cutter and Perez taps it to second for the second out. Then I get Alfonzo, a very tough hitter, swinging.

Now it's our last chance to tie or win the game, against the Mets closer, Armando Benitez, and he's looking for three outs. Jorge fights him through seven pitches before hitting a long fly to center. Paulie steps in and tries to change recent history. He is thirty-seven years old, has a bad hip, and has been slumping, but if there's one guy who is going to battle to the end to get something going, it's Paulie. Benitez jumps ahead, 1–2. A massive man with a massive fastball, Benitez keeps pumping in high-ninety heaters, and Paulie just keeps getting a piece, fighting them off with short, defensive swings. After two fouls, Benitez misses for 2–2, and misses again to run the count to 3–2. Now the pressure is even. Paulie spoils another strike, and another, and the crowd is starting to roar and Benitez is getting exasperated.

On the tenth pitch of the at-bat, Benitez fires and misses outside and Paulie throws away the bat and takes his hard-won walk. It's as good an at-bat as I've ever seen. The Stadium is rocking. Pinch-hitting for Brosius, Luis Polonia hits a single to right, and Jose Vizcaino goes the other way, knocking a single to left, but too shallow for Paulie to score. Knoblauch hits a fly ball to left, a sacrifice fly that sends O'Neill home to tie the game.

I strike out Piazza and Zeile and get Robin Ventura to fly out to take care of the tenth, and then Mike Stanton throws two strong innings and Game 1 moves into the bottom of the twelfth. It's approaching one in the morning, and the game is more than four and a half hours old.

This is just the kind of game we find a way to grind out and win, I think.

I pick my spots when I decide to be vocal in the dugout. I usually only do it in the biggest moments, the most important games. Games such as this.

Now's the time, I say, walking up and down the dugout. Let's win this right now.

With one out, Tino singles and Jorge doubles off Mets reliever Turk Wendell. The Mets walk Paulie to load the bases and get a force at the plate. Luis Sojo pops up, and now it's Vizcaino's turn. He already has two hits, another of Mr. T's hunches that works brilliantly. (Mr. T likes Jose's career numbers against Leiter and gives him the start, even though Sojo has been playing second almost every game.)

On Wendell's first pitch, Vizcaino swings and serves a line drive into left. Here comes Tino, and there goes Vizcaino, leaping his way around first. It is 1:04 on a Sunday morning. We pour onto the field and mob Viz. It's a game that we win on a relay throw, a ten-pitch walk, and three hits from a Dominican journeyman on his seventh team.

He fits right in. He knows how to win.

It's the bottom of the first inning, about nineteen hours after Viz's game-winner, and I am in a hot tub in the Yankees trainer's room. There is no TV in there, but I know that Mike Piazza is the third man up against Roger, and it is the most anticipated heavyweight showdown since Ali and Frazier, if you believe the media buzz. I don't believe it much of the time, but I *am* curious to see what happens. When we played the Mets in early June, Piazza hit a grand slam against Clemens. When we played the Mets in early July, Clemens hit Piazza in the head with a fastball. I can't say what Clemens's intentions are. I never talk to him about it, though I do know Piazza has had a lot of success against him. Only Clemens and the Lord know what was in his mind the day he beaned Mike Piazza. I never hit anybody in the head in my whole career, and I never would. Not intentionally. You can talk all you want about keeping hitters honest and instilling fear that could ultimately help you win, but you never do something that endangers somebody's well-being, or their livelihood or even their life. Good ol' country hard-ball? To me, it's more like good ol' country cowardice, throwing a baseball at 98 miles per hour at somebody's head. This man with the bat is somebody's son. He is probably somebody's husband and somebody's father. You can't deny that or ignore that. I compete as hard as anybody, but you do it within the confines of fair play, and headhunting is not fair play.

By the time I am out of the tub, I find out I missed all the excitement, so I immediately catch a replay: Clemens quickly gets two strikes on Piazza. He throws a ball and then comes inside with a fastball, and as Piazza swings, his bat splinters, the barrel bouncing right out to the mound. Unaware the ball is foul, Piazza starts running toward first, and Clemens picks up the bat barrel and flings it sidearm, and hard, toward Piazza on the first-base line. The bat skims along the ground and kicks up, and its jagged edge misses Piazza by a foot or two.

What's your problem? Piazza says as he takes a step toward the mound. I have no idea what's going on, or why Roger would do that, but it's mind-boggling to me that you could be so emotionally wound up that you snap that way. Roger is an insanely intense competitor. I never ask him about what's going through his mind then, mostly because everybody else is doing it for me.

Mike Hampton, the Mets starter, is wild early, helping us score two in the first, before Brosius leads off the second with a shot into the seats in left. Before we tack on three more runs later, I run into George Steinbrenner in the clubhouse. I'm over thirty years old, but he has always called me Kid, and isn't stopping now.

I call him Mr. George.

Kid, you want a hot dog? I'll get you a hot dog.

No thanks, Mr. George. I'm good.

You sure?

I'm sure, thanks.

Hey, Kid, we going to win this Series? What do you think?

We are going to win, and I am so sure I will make you a bet, Mr. George. If I am right and we win, you'll fly my wife and kids and me to Panama on your private jet. If I am wrong, I will take you out to dinner at the restaurant of your choice.

You got a bet, Kid, Mr. George says.

Mr. George disappears and I head for the bullpen. Roger pitches eight shutout innings and leaves with a 6–0 lead. The game seems about as safe as it can be, until it isn't. Nelson gives up a two-run homer to Piazza and a single. Then I come in and Clay Bellinger, our left-field defensive replacement, saves my tail by going back to the left-field fence and making a superb, poised catch of a long Todd Zeile drive. Agbayani singles, but then I get Lenny Harris on a fielder's choice and have two strikes left to close it out, and two guys on, when Payton, the Mets center fielder, takes an outside cutter the other way and hits it into the seats in right.

Suddenly, the score is 6–5, and the growing panic in the Stadium is palpable. Kurt Abbott steps up. He doubled off me in Game 1. Here's what I am thinking:

This game needs to end now.

I hate messy innings, and this has turned into a big mess. I get ahead, 0–2, and fire the next cutter just where I want it, on the inner half and up. Abbott takes, and Charlie Reliford, the home plate umpire, rings him up. Abbott has a brief fit as Jorge comes out to shake my hand. Fifty-six thousand fans start to breathe again. I face 309 more hitters in my postseason career, and never give up another home run after Payton's.

After a travel day to allow us to go over the Triborough Bridge into Queens, the Mets, losers of two agonizing one-run games, return home to Shea Stadium, their bowl by the bay with the LaGuardia Airport traffic overhead. I'm surprised at how many Yankee fans have found their way into Shea, but it doesn't stop the Mets from knocking El Duque around in Game 3 and taking a 4–2 victory behind Rick Reed, even though Duque strikes out six Mets in the first two innings, and twelve overall.

We're not getting a lot of production from our leadoff guys (they are 0 for 12 in the three games), so Mr. T decides to move Derek up to the top spot for Game 4. Bobby Jones is the Mets starter, and on his first pitch of the game, Derek drives it over the left-center-field wall at Shea Stadium. It's a single run that feels like ten, for the way it fires us up and coldcocks the Mets. It is Derek Jeter at his best, providing just what we need, when we need it. Jones steadies himself after giving up two more runs, and when Piazza buries a Denny Neagle pitch for a two-run homer, the Mets are within a run at 3–2. Piazza comes up again in the fifth with two out and nobody on. Neagle is one out away from completing the five innings you need to get the win. Mr. T comes and gets him, and brings in David Cone, and Neagle is so incensed that he won't even look at Mr. T. Cone is thirty-seven, an ace turned forgotten man, coming off the worst year of his tremendous career, a year-long struggle that ended with a 4–14 record and 6.91 ERA. He hasn't thrown a single pitch in this World Series.

It's another Mr. T hunch…that David can find a way to get Piazza. David gets ahead, 1–2, and comes right at Piazza with a sharp slider. Piazza swings and pops up to second.

In the clubhouse with Geno, I can only marvel at our manager's instincts yet again.

Both bullpens pitch flawlessly and now it's on me in the eighth and ninth. Paulie makes a fine grab of a sinking liner by Alfonzo to lead off the eighth, and then I get Piazza to ground out, before Zeile singles. I get out of it by popping up Ventura, and record two quick outs in the ninth, too.

Next up is Matt Franco, who had a game-winning hit against me the year before. On the first pitch, a strike, Jorge and I can tell Franco is waiting for the cutter in on the hands, edging farther from the plate to give him more room to turn on it.

Jorge catches my attention and points to his eyes, as if to say:

You see that?

I do see it. I nod. I buzz a fastball on the outside corner, and Franco never moves. Strike two. I know he's sitting on the cutter in. Jorge knows it, too. I buzz another fastball on the outside corner. Franco never moves again.

Game over.

In four games, we have fifteen runs, and the Mets have fourteen. Every game pivots on one or two plays, or one or two pitches. I like the way the pivots have been going, and now it's time to finish things up in Game 5, Leiter vs. Andy, a rematch of Game 1.

Bernie, in an 0-for-16 slump in the Series, rips a homer to start the second, and after the Mets answer with two runs in the bottom of the inning, Derek takes two tight fastballs from Leiter and then pounds his second homer in two games. It's 2–2, and Andy and Leiter are competing their left arms off, matching zeroes and guts. Mike Stanton comes on for a 1-2-3 eighth, and Leiter comes back out for the ninth and gets two quick strikeouts.

With Leiter nearing one hundred forty pitches, Jorge, the guy with the best eye on the team, keeps fighting pitches off, battling the way Paulie did in the ninth inning of Game 1. After a nine-pitch drama, Jorge walks. Brosius drills a single to left. Luis Sojo, a huge factor the whole Series, swings at the first pitch and hits about a ten-hopper through the middle. Jorgie barely beats Payton's throw, and when he slides, the ball careens away and Brosius scores, too.

We're up 4–2 now, three outs away. As I throw my warm-up pitches, I am thinking about making the first pitch I throw as good as it can be.

The pinch hitter is Darryl Hamilton. He takes strike one, fouls off strike two, and swings through a high cutter for strike three.

Next up is Agbayani, the left fielder. I try to work him away but miss my spots and walk him on four straight. Bad thing to do, putting the tying run at the plate, but it's done. I let it go. I shift all my focus to Alfonzo, get ahead, 1–2, and fire a cutter away. He lofts a ball to right that Paulie catches easily.

It is now down to Mike Piazza, one of the most dangerous hitters in baseball. Derek and Sojo trot in to the mound for a quick visit. Sojo stands back a bit. Derek does the talking.

You want to be careful here. You know what he can do. Move the ball around and go after him hard, Derek says.

He slaps me on the leg with his glove and returns to short. I blow on my right hand. I look in at Jorge's glove, alone in that tube again. I am not overthinking this. I am going to throw the best pitch I can.

I am going to keep it simple.

Piazza has tremendous opposite-field power. I want to stay in on him. My first pitch is a cutter, in. Strike one. Jorge sets up inside again, calling for the ball a little higher. I come set and deliver, a cutter not quite as in as I want, a few inches out over the plate. Piazza takes a rip and hits the ball pretty well, a fly to center. I turn and watch Bernie's body language as he is easing back, completely in control. A few steps in front of the track, he makes the catch, and at exactly midnight on October 27, 2000, Bernie goes down on a knee, bowing his head in momentary prayer. Now both my arms are in the air and I am jumping up and down, up and down, until Tino arrives for a hug, until the whole team pours onto the field, and the tension and high-stakes stress of big-time competition evaporate faster than a puddle in the Panamanian sun, and the joy is everywhere you look, flowing long before the Champagne is.

The day after the Series is over, I get a phone call from Mr. George's assistant.

Good morning, she says. Mr. Steinbrenner asked me to call. Are you ready to make the arrangements for your trip to Panama?

11

The Day the World Changed

It's the bottom of the eighth in Baltimore and the tying run is at the plate, an iron man in the twentieth and last season of a legendary career. We are a month into the 2001 season. It's a hot night, my favorite weather to pitch in. Cal Ripken Jr. and the Orioles are down, 7–5. I am ahead in the count, 1–2, just a few pitches into my outing but feeling very strong. I check the runner at second, Delino DeShields, and bring a hard cutter, 93 miles per hour, in on Cal. It looks as if it might hit him, or at least graze his No. 8 uniform. He leans back to get out of the way, just as the pitch makes a left turn, veering sharply toward the inside corner.

Charlie Reliford, the home plate umpire, yanks up his right arm. Cal drops his bat and walks away, shaking his head. I walk off the Camden Yards mound, registering no emotion, though I know it's one of those nights when the cutter is breaking like a Wiffle ball, when the ball feels almost perfect as it comes out of my hand.

You got no chance when it moves that much, Derek tells a reporter later.

We spend most of the season dominating the American League East, and when we take three straight against the Red Sox at Yankee Stadium in early September, our lead is up to thirteen games. The series is scheduled to conclude on a Monday night, with Roger Clemens trying to extend his record to 20–1 against his old team.

A huge crowd and a postseason atmosphere are expected, but a drenching rain makes the field unplayable and the game is rained out.

The date is September 10.

By morning the rain has gone, leaving behind a hint of autumn chill and a spectacularly blue sky. It's a school day, so I am up early with the boys. I am brushing my teeth when my mother-in-law, who is staying with us, calls for us and sounds alarmed.

Clara! Pili! Come quick! Look at what's on TV!

I hustle downstairs into the kitchen and listen to a bizarre report about a plane flying into the World Trade Center. It's a few minutes past 8:45. Information is scarce. One of the towers is on fire, smoke billowing out of the top. I wonder how this could've happened, and if the workers in the building will be able to get out. Then a second plane hits the other tower and now things become much clearer.

This is a terrorist attack.

More tragic reports follow, about the plane that hit the Pentagon and Flight 93 crashing in the Pennsylvania countryside. The images are too horrific to comprehend, the evil behind the attack even more so. I pray for the victims and their families. I pray for all of us, for the country. The city grieves and we grieve along with it. All ball games are canceled for a week.

I stay close to home and watch the horrific cleanup process unfold. I pray constantly, and just want to stay near Clara and the boys. When the games resume we have to fly to Chicago, but because it's the Yankee charter, it's not any more traumatic a flight for me than usual. It's the same plane we always take, transporting us to the next game. (When I fly commercially to Panama after the season, that's when I am a total mess.)

We pick up the season on September 18 in Comiskey Park, winning, 11–3, then return for our first game in New York since the attacks. Roger visits a New York firehouse in the afternoon and starts the game at night. It's a powerful night of tribute and memorials to the victims and the first responders. The Stadium almost feels as if it's a church; the whole night seems more like a vigil than our 150th game of the season. Tampa beats us, 4–0, but with the Red Sox loss we clinch the AL East title for the fifth time in six years. The corks remain in the Champagne bottles. We are the New York Yankees. Our city is hurting in a big way, and so are we. It is no time to celebrate.

Even though we win 95 games in 2001, we aren't close to being the premier team in the American League. The Seattle Mariners are even better than we were in 1998, finishing with a record of 116–46, a feat so ridiculous that the Oakland A's win 102 games—and wind up fourteen games out of first.

We might be three-time defending World Series champions, but we are only the third-best team in our league. If anybody doubts that, they are not paying attention. We draw Oakland in the division series. In Game 1, at Yankee Stadium, Mark Mulder outpitches Roger, and the A's get two homers from Terrence Long and one from Jason Giambi and win, 5–3. Tim Hudson shuts us down in Game 2, and the A's win, 2–0, to go up 2–0. Now we fly west, one defeat away from 2002, our season riding on the right arm of Mike Mussina. The A's have won seventeen straight games at home. Barry Zito, a twenty-two-year-old left-hander, is aiming to make it eighteen. The game is scoreless through four. With one out in the fifth, Jorge drives a 1–0 pitch over the wall in left to give us a 1–0 lead. I watch in wonder as my friend circles the bases.

I have no idea how he can possibly be playing at the level he is—or how he's even able to focus on baseball at all.

Jorge's two-year-old son, Jorge IV, has a serious medical condition called craniosynostosis, in which the pieces of an infant's skull fuse prematurely, with potentially devastating consequences for brain and neurological development. The condition gets more acute almost by the day. Little Jorge has eight hours of surgery on September 10, and two more hours of surgery a few weeks later. It seems as if this baby is being operated on constantly, and somehow Jorge is able to perform as well as he ever has on the field, putting together a tremendous season, an All-Star season, hitting .277 with 22 home runs and 95 runs batted in and doing a great job handling the pitching staff on top of it.

You are as strong mentally as anybody I know, I tell him. I am praying for little Jorge, and praying that one day he'll look at you and know how lucky he is to have you as a father.

Meanwhile, Mussina keeps the zeroes going and sets down Johnny Damon, Miguel Tejada, and Jason Giambi in the sixth. He gets two quick outs, retiring Jermaine Dye and Eric Chavez, in the bottom of the seventh. Jeremy Giambi singles to right and it brings up Terrence Long, who drills a 2–2 pitch inside the first-base line, past a diving Tino. The ball caroms into the right-field corner. Shane Spencer retrieves it and comes up throwing, but misses both cutoff men, Alfonso Soriano and Tino. It is all happening right before my eyes, since the visiting bullpen is wedged along the first-base line, all of us crammed onto a bench that looks as if it were lifted from a bus station. Giambi rounds third and looks as if he will score easily to tie the game. Spencer's throw bounds toward home, along the first-base line, in no-man's-land.

That's when I see Derek running this way, across the infield, toward us.

Toward the first-base line.

Where is he going? I think. *This play has nothing to do with him.*

Derek keeps sprinting toward the line. Closing in on the ball.

Now I know what he's doing.

He is almost at the line now, maybe fifteen or twenty feet from home plate. Still running hard, he bends down and scoops up the rolling ball. He shovels it backhand toward Jorge.

Giambi is coming in standing up. I have no idea why.

Jorge gets the flip and makes a swipe tag on Giambi, an instant before he touches home.

Jeremy Giambi is out. Our 1–0 lead is intact. Derek Jeter pumps his fist. Mussina pumps his fist. I feel like running out of the bullpen and pumping my fist. Half the dugout, it seems, is charging out on the field, a spontaneous burst of emotion for a player who never stops thinking or hustling.

It is the greatest instinctive play I have ever seen.

With six outs to get, I come on in the bottom of the eighth and get through it with no major difficulty, and then have to face the heart of the order in the ninth, starting with Jason Giambi, the American League's reigning MVP, and Jeremy's big—and I mean very big—brother. Giambi bounces a 1–0 pitch to second for one out, and after a Jermaine Dye double, I strike out Eric Chavez and up steps Jeremy, the man who doesn't slide. On a 1–1 pitch, another Giambi grounds to second, and we are still alive.

In Game 4, we get heroic pitching and hitting from Duque and Bernie, who has three hits and five RBIs, and after a 9–2 victory, we fly three thousand miles back to New York to play Game 5 the next day, a Monday. Before a single pitch is thrown, I'm struck by how different the city feels than it did before September 11. It's hard to describe. It just feels as if everything is heightened—more vivid; more urgent, somehow; infused with an attitude that seems to be saying:

We've got this day and we are going for it.

There's always emotion and energy pulsing through the Stadium.

But now it seems packed with even more meaning, as if our mission is not only to win one more World Series, but to do it for the city.

Neither Roger nor Mark Mulder has his best stuff, and we take a 5–3 lead through six on a Derek sacrifice fly and a David Justice homer. After Ramiro hurls a 1-2-3 seventh it's on me to get the last six outs. Jason Giambi singles off me to start the eighth, and then I get Eric Chavez on a fielder's choice, bringing up Terrence Long, who pops up a 1–1 pitch toward the seats behind third, and now here comes Derek again, racing behind the bag and leaning over the railing and then making a phenomenal catch even as he goes head over heels into the seats. Somehow he holds on to the ball, and then I get Ron Gant on a groundout to third to finish the eighth.

In the ninth, Olmedo Saenz bounces out to second, and then I strike out Greg Myers, the Oakland catcher, on three pitches. Pinch hitter Eric Byrnes steps in, and the Stadium crowd is on its feet as Byrnes crouches into a slightly open stance. The count goes to 2–2. Jorge sets up inside. I fire a fastball and Byrnes swings through it, and without even thinking about it, I jump up and do a complete 360. I have no idea where that comes from; I don't remember ever doing it before, and I never did it again. Jorge pumps his fist and jumps up and runs out to shake my hand, wrapping an arm around me, touching my neck. Mr. T escorts New York mayor Rudolph Giuliani, who has done so much to help the city heal after the attacks, onto the field. It's a night super-saturated with emotion: We've come back to win three straight against a great team, somehow embodying the city's resilient spirit. Now it is on to face the mighty Mariners, who have their own anxious moments, falling behind the Indians, two games to one, before pulling it out.

The first two games are in Seattle, and we are ready. We know how good the Mariners are, and we respect what they have done this season, but we are as confident as ever that we can get by them.

Andy is our Game 1 guy, and he answers another big-game start with another big-time effort, giving up only three hits and a run and striking out seven. All night he is throwing his curveball exactly where he wants to. Knoblauch's single gets us going in the second, and when Jorge pounds a ball from Mariners starter Aaron Sele off the wall in right in the top of the fourth, he hustles all the way and challenges Ichiro's rocket launcher of an arm. Ichiro's throw is outstanding, but Jorge somehow gets under the tag. Paulie drills a two-run homer off Sele, and Andy protects a 3–1 lead right through the eighth.

In the ninth, Alfonso Soriano drives a ball off reliever Jose Paniagua he is sure is going out. He raises his bat and stands at the plate to admire his hit. The ball hits the wall, and Sori winds up at first, and Mr. T is furious. Sori is a gifted young hitter, but he may not know yet that admiring home runs, not running, taking a page out of Mannyball, is not how we do things. As if to atone for his lapse, he steals second and then scores on a David Justice single and pushes the lead to 4–1.

I come on for the ninth, and with one out, Ichiro, a guy who handles the bat as if it is a magic wand, drops a double down the left-field line. He isn't just the league batting champion (.350), a guy who had 242 hits, he is on his way to being the American League MVP, a brilliant all-around player. I am an out away from closing it after getting Stan Javier on a comebacker, but as I field the ball, I tweak my ankle, which has been bothering me on and off for a month or more. On my first pitch to Bret Boone, I throw a wild pitch that allows Ichiro to go to third. On my third pitch, I throw another one wild, and Ichiro scores. I do not throw another wild pitch in the postseason for the rest of my career, but that does me no good now. Boone walks, and it's obvious my mechanics are off. I have walked just four batters since the All-Star break, and now I get to face Edgar as the potential tying run.

I get ahead with a strike and then throw a cutter away and

Edgar goes for it, hitting a grounder to first. Tino digs it out and I run to cover, and Game 1 is ours.

Mussina, who was so sensational in the flip-play game against Oakland, isn't quite as sharp in Game 2 but competes hard from start to finish. He gets an early 3–0 lead thanks to a Brosius two-run double, but the Mariners are doing what our hitters do: They are making Moose work. In the bottom of the second, Dan Wilson fouls off seven straight pitches before singling, one batter after Javier works a nine-pitch at-bat for a walk. Moose gets out of it, but Javier drives a two-run homer in the fourth and now it's a one-run game. Moose grinds through six, finishing by striking out Edgar and Cameron and popping up John Olerud. For me as a pitcher, I don't think there's anything better than seeing a guy compete so hard and get such good results—even when his stuff is not quite what he wants it to be.

Ramiro takes over in the seventh, and with a man on and two out, Mr. T makes a brave call, ordering Ramiro to walk Ichiro. You are not supposed to put the potential winning run on base—ever—but Ichiro is just too dangerous to worry about what the book says. Mark McLemore taps out to second, so the strategy works just the way Mr. T hoped it would.

I enter with one out in the eighth and Edgar on first. I get Olerud on a force-out and strike out Cameron, and then throw a fastball by David Bell to finish the ninth, and we fly back east, halfway to the World Series.

Duque doesn't have it and the bullpen gets rocked in Game 3, and the Mariners win, 14–3. The visiting team has now won all three games. If we can stop the trend, we can avoid a return trip to Safeco Field. We've got Roger, who struck out fifteen Mariners the last time they saw him in the playoffs, and they've got Paul Abbott, who won seventeen games during the season but had a disastrous start against the Indians in the division series and can be all over the place with his control.

Abbott, a rangy guy, is as erratic as advertised. He walks eight guys in five innings. He throws 49 strikes, 48 balls, but somehow gets every out he needs to and doesn't allow us a single hit in five innings.

Limited by a bad hamstring, Roger goes five and gives up only one hit, and the bullpens take over and it's still 0–0 into the eighth. Ramiro gets the first two outs, finishing up his third inning of work without giving up a single hit, before Bret Boone hits an 0–1 changeup into the seats. The Mariners have a 1–0 lead—and need just six outs to tie the series at two games apiece.

Arthur Rhodes, a left-hander, comes out of the Mariners' pen for the bottom of the eighth. He is a guy who, for whatever reason, is good against the rest of the league and not very good against the New York Yankees. With one out and a full count to Bernie, Rhodes throws a fastball, his best pitch, out over the plate. Bernie stays back and swings and hits a high fly to right that drops into the seats, just beyond the glove of a leaping Ichiro. The game is tied. The next pitcher to enter the game is me, not on hand to save a game. Just keep it tied.

Olerud grounds out to first on my first pitch. Javier pushes a bunt toward second and is out on my second pitch. Cameron pops a foul fly to first on my third pitch. I am on the mound for about ninety seconds, maybe less. I am surprised that Cameron doesn't take a pitch or two, just because one of those unwritten rules in baseball says that you are not supposed to let a pitcher have a three-pitch inning.

I am not complaining.

Kazuhiro Sasaki, the Mariners' closer, comes on for the bottom of the ninth. Shane Spencer grounds out to third to start the inning, and Brosius smacks a hard ball up the middle that McLemore stops, but he can't get the ball to first in time. Up steps Soriano. Sasaki throws a splitter down. Soriano is a free swinger, but doesn't offer. Sasaki doesn't want to get behind, and certainly doesn't want to push the winning run into scoring position. He throws a fastball, a little over waist-high, directly over the middle of the plate. Soriano, coiled in a closed stance, jumps on it and drives it far to right center. Mike Cameron climbs the wall but has no shot, and our star rookie, who breaks into the big leagues with eighteen homers and seventy-three RBIs, has put us a game away from the World Series. The Stadium is going berserk. It seems to get louder every time somebody produces another round of late-inning heroics.

Game 5 is the next day, and our philosophy is: Why wait? You do not want to give a club that won 116 games any reason for hope. Aaron Sele, another pitcher who seems to have a miserable time against us, whether he's wearing a Rangers or a Mariners uniform, throws two scoreless innings and then we break out, scoring four times in the third, the big hit a two-run homer by Bernie. Paulie homers off Sele an inning later, and with Andy cruising, there seems to be no danger at all, and especially not after we pile on four more runs against the Mariners bullpen. The crowd starts chanting "Overrated" at the Mariners and "No Game 6" at their manager, Lou Piniella, who had guaranteed that the series would return to Seattle.

I don't like this kind of taunting and never have. I know fans are happy, but what is the point of mocking anybody? How does that make you feel better? It certainly doesn't help give us an emotional edge...so in my book, why do it? But I don't give sermons on the subject; I just want to savor this moment—and get back to the World Series so we can try to bring home a fourth straight title.

I'm not sure why, but Mr. T brings me in to close it out with a nine-run lead (12–3). On my twelfth pitch, Mike Cameron hits a soft liner to right, and Spencer, who comes on for Paulie in the late innings, runs it down and closes things out. Soon the whole team is on the mound, pinstripes everywhere, all of us taking turns hugging each other. In consecutive series, we've beaten the two best teams in the game this season.

There are four more games to win.

The Series opens in Phoenix, in a ballpark with a swimming pool in center field. We don't go for a dip, and we don't hit a lick, either. Bernie stays on fire with an RBI double off of Curt Schilling in the top of the first, and it's a great way to get going, since the consensus is that if Schilling and Randy Johnson can pitch like a latter-day version of Koufax and Drysdale, we are going to be in deep trouble.

After Bernie's hit, our bats go utterly silent. Brosius doubles in the second and Jorge singles in the fourth, and that is the sum total of the Yankee offense for the night. Schilling goes seven innings and strikes out eight and will win his fourth game against no defeats in the postseason (the Diamondbacks beat the Cardinals and then the Braves to win the National League pennant). Mussina, who has been our best starter for the last month, gets taken deep by Craig Counsell and Luis Gonzalez and we are on our way to a 9–1 spanking.

Now it's Johnson against Andy in Game 2, and here's the bad news: Johnson is even more dominant than Schilling was. He gives up no runs and three hits, and goes the distance with eleven strikeouts. Matt Williams socks a three-run homer off Andy and the score is 4–0. It might as well be 40–0 for the way Johnson is pitching.

We fly back to New York, putting our season—and a fourth straight World Series title—in the hands of Roger. Jorge gives us an early lead with a homer off of Brian Anderson, the Diamondbacks lefty starter, in the second. Roger dodges a bases-loaded jam early and escapes again in the sixth when Shane Spencer makes a sprawling catch of a searing Matt Williams liner to save two runs. Brosius hits a single to give us a 2–1 lead in the sixth and Roger finishes strong, with two punch-outs in the seventh in a 1-2-3 inning, and then gives the ball to me.

I haven't pitched in eight days, but I warm up well and feel strong and sharp. I get Counsell on a bunt try, then strike out Steve Finley and Gonzalez, and I get two more strikeouts in the ninth, before Williams bounces out to end it. It's a huge win for us, with Schilling set to go again in Game 4.

Schilling is just as good as he was in Game 1, but Duque is right there with him. Tied at one, the game goes into the eighth, Mike Stanton on the mound. Gonzalez singles, and Erubiel Durazo, the DH, pounds a double, and the Diamondbacks go up, 3–1, and call for their closer, a South Korean submarine pitcher, Byung-Hyun Kim. Kim has been untouchable in the playoffs, with his heavy sinker and his nasty delivery. He goes to full counts on Spencer, Brosius, and Sori in the bottom of the eighth and strikes out all three.

Ramiro plows through a clean ninth, and now we're down to our last three outs. Derek tries to bunt his way on; Williams, the third baseman, throws him out. After Paulie singles to left, Bernie goes down swinging on three pitches and now it's on Tino. We are one out from being down three games to one, with Randy Johnson and probably Schilling to contend with. We have a pulse, but it's faint. Kim checks Paulie and delivers, belt-high to the outside part of the plate. If Tino tries to pull it, it's a ground ball to second, or maybe a weak pop-up to right center.

Tino doesn't try to pull it. He brings the barrel around and mashes the pitch right over Kim's head, a rising line drive just a few steps to the right of center. Finley races back and looks like Spider-Man trying to climb the wall, but this ball is gone and this game is tied.

I get three quick groundouts in the top of the tenth and will be going out for the eleventh if necessary. Brosius leads off and rips a line drive to left that swerves foul by maybe ten feet, then gets a good swing on a ball he skies to right for the first out. Sori also has a good hack or two before flying out to left. Next up is Derek, who has but one hit in the four games and is batting .067 in the Series. The clock strikes midnight and the Stadium scoreboard says "Welcome to November." With the whole season pushed back a week after September 11, this is the first time baseball has ever been played in November in the big leagues. Derek goes down 0–2 but works the count and fouls off one ball, then another, and another, clearly looking to knock a ball to right with his trademark inside-out swing.

With the count full, Kim delivers again and Derek inside-outs it again, driving the ball down the line in right, a ball that keeps going and going...right into the right-field stands. Jeter gives his right-angle fist pump—another trademark—and the Stadium is quaking as we pour out of the dugout for the party at home plate.

It's November 1 and the World Series is tied. I drive home to sleep in my own bed. It's hard to beat this.

Mussina gets a second shot at Arizona in Game 5, and he is back on form. He has six strikeouts and allows just one hit through four innings, though we're not touching Miguel Batista, the veteran right-hander starting for Arizona, either. In the fifth, Finley leads off by driving a 1–2 pitch over the wall for the game's first run, and three batters later, catcher Rod Barajas does the same thing.

Batista seems to be getting stronger as the game goes on. I head to the bullpen in the bottom of the sixth.

We sure like to do things the hard way in this World Series, I think.

Mussina stays aggressive, and when he pops Williams up with two on to get out of the top of the eighth, a splendid night's work is done. We put two on in the eighth but don't score, and Ramiro takes over for the ninth. As I begin to warm up in the bullpen, I hear the fans in the bleachers and right-field seats chanting, "Paul O'Neill! Paul O'Neill!" They have been cheering him all night, knowing that if we don't pull it out this is likely going to be his last game at the Stadium, since he seems headed for retirement. The chant is engulfing us in the pen. I get goose bumps listening to it. Paulie doesn't know what to do. He keeps spitting in his glove and tries to pretend nothing is going on. I'm thrilled for him that he is getting this kind of send-off, because he deserves nothing less.

Ramiro sets down three Diamondbacks in the top of the ninth, and we are exactly where we were a night earlier: down two, with Byung-Hyun Kim on the mound. Jorge leads off with a double down the line, but Spencer grounds out and Knoblauch strikes out, and now it's Scott Brosius's turn. He takes a ball. Kim looks at Jorge, then gets set. He submarines the 1–0 pitch and Brosius swings and the sound is good and off the ball goes, deep into the left-field seats. Now it is Scott Brosius's right fist in the air.

You can't make this stuff up.

For the second straight night, we are down two, down to our last at-bat, and we hit a game-tying two-run homer. As Brosius rounds the bases, Kim is crouched on the mound, like a catcher. In the TV close-up he looks as if he might cry. Bob Brenly, the Diamondbacks manager, comes out to take him from the game in favor of Mike Morgan.

I cruise through an easy tenth, but Morgan is cruising through us, too, retiring seven straight. In the eleventh, I give up two singles, and after a sacrifice, we walk Finley to load the bases. With Johnson looming in Game 6, I know exactly how huge this moment is. I come at Reggie Sanders hard, go up 0–2, and get him on a liner to second.

Now the hitter is Mark Grace. Again I go up 0–2, and that makes all the difference. I can make him try to hit my pitch, and I do, getting him to bounce to third for an inning-ending force.

The game keeps going, Sterling Hitchcock (he got traded back to the Yankees from the Padres in midseason) relieving me and pitching a scoreless twelfth, and Albie Lopez coming on for Arizona. Knoblauch greets him with a single up the middle, and Brosius bunts him to second. Soriano comes up and, on a 2–1 pitch, serves a ball into right for a single, and here comes Knoblauch with the winning run. We win our third straight one-run game and protect our home court. All we need is one more, and a fourth straight world championship is ours.

12

Trophy

WE ARE BACK IN the desert for Game 6, and the night turns out to be as pleasant as sitting on a cactus. Going back to 1996, Andy has proven himself to be as big a gamer as you will find, but he doesn't have it tonight, and neither do we. The Diamondbacks score one in the first, three in the second, eight in the third, and three in the fourth. Randy Johnson is on the mound. It's pretty clear we are not going to tie or win this game with another ninth-inning home run.

The final score is 15–2, and the Diamondbacks have twenty-two hits, two more than we had in the first four games of the Series. Ten of the hits come against our long reliever, Jay Witasick, in one and a third innings. I feel for Jay. It's his only appearance in the Series, and his job is to take the beating and try to save the other arms in the bullpen. The whole night is about as ugly as it can be, but it only counts for one loss, so here's how I look at it:

Now it's a best-of-one World Series.

The matchup for Game 7 is right out of a movie script...two of the best pitchers in the game...two jumbo right-handers...Curt Schilling and Roger Clemens. Their combined record for the year is 42–9.

I don't think this will be a blowout.

Mr. T isn't sure what he's going to say to us in the locker room before the game. He has already said so much to us, told us how proud he was of us and how he'd never forget this team and its makeup.

I think I'll let you have the floor, Mr. T says to Gene Monahan. The guys in this room don't respect anybody more than you.

Geno laughs when Mr. T tells him this, because he doesn't think he's serious.

When he told me he *was* serious, I just about crapped in my pants, Geno says.

It is an inspired idea by Mr. T. Geno is so much more than a trainer to us—somebody who helps our bodies heal and nurtures us through the physical grind of the season. He is also as kind and generous a man as you will ever meet. All he wants to do is give and serve. To make you feel comfortable, feel better. He is a special man.

We come off the field after batting practice. Everybody is at the lockers. Mr. T goes to the center of the room.

Geno, you got the floor, he says.

Geno looks aghast for a minute. His face is saying, *Oh my Lord, now what do I do?*

He has been with the Yankees for forty years. The spotlight is never, ever what he wants. But he has it now, and he's running with it:

No matter what happens tonight, guys, you have had some year, Geno says. From Day One of spring training, through 9/11, through two tough series...you've played with such heart. You've played with class and you've been winners—you've been true Yankees. And I've never been prouder to be part of a club, because of what you guys bring every day. Whatever happens out there tonight, you guys are going to walk into this clubhouse and you are going to be the same champions you've been all year. Nothing will change that.

The room is completely silent after Geno finishes, except for the sound of bench coach Don Zimmer crying. A lot of us feel like crying.

Now I want to say a few things.

This is our game to win, I say. We just need to trust. Trust in our heart, trust in each other. My heart, it comes from the Lord. We are blessed to be here again, to be with each other. Whatever happens, I am going to trust the Lord.

My point is not that the Lord wants me to save the game, or that the Lord is on the side of the Yankees and not the Diamond-backs. It is that the Lord is always there for us. His grace and mercy are infinite. They are there for us to the end of the age. So really there is nothing to fear, no result that isn't part of the plan, for we are in the arms of the Lord. That belief is what frees me to live, and pitch, in the moment.

Roger and Schilling both come out in top form. Roger strikes out eight guys in the first four innings, and Schilling is even sharper, allowing one hit and striking out eight through six.

Finley leads off the bottom of the sixth for the D-Backs with a looping single to center, then Danny Bautista, the right fielder, smokes a fastball to the wall in left center. Finley scores the first run of the night, before a brilliant relay throw from Derek nails Bautista as he goes for a triple. Roger gets out and we go to the seventh, and Derek leads off with a single to right. Paulie follows with a single up the middle, and with one out, Tino drives a hard single to right to score Derek and tie the game. Spencer almost gets us two more runs, but Finley runs down his drive to right center for the final out.

The game moves into the eighth. Sori is leading off and falls behind, 0–2. He fouls off two pitches and then Schilling delivers a low splitter and Sori is all over it, golfing it over the left-center-field fence. It's the first time we have the lead in Bank One Ballpark since the first inning of the first game. Moments after Sori's ball lands, the bullpen phone rings.

Mo, you got the eighth, bullpen coach Rich Monteleone says.

Miguel Batista and then Randy Johnson get the final two outs in relief of Schilling, and I come on for the bottom of the eighth. Luis Gonzalez is leading off. I go to the back of the mound and hold the ball in my right hand, and close my eyes and pray:

Dear Lord, please keep me safe and keep my teammates safe, and allow me to use Your blessings and Your strength to do my job. Thank You for all the ways You have blessed me. Amen.

I strike out Gonzalez on a cutter right under his hands, then get Williams to chase a fastball up for another strikeout. Finley drives a single to right and then I get Bautista to chase a cutter up and out of the zone to strike out the side.

Johnson sets down Bernie, Tino, and Jorge in order and now it is time. There are three outs left in the season. Three outs separating us from another championship, not just a fourth World Series in a row, but a championship for the city of New York. I am thinking only about hitting Jorge's glove, taking care of business, one cut fastball at a time.

Get three quick outs and let's get out of here.

I have as powerful a sense as I have ever had that we are going to win this game. This is my fifty-second postseason appearance. I have converted twenty-three straight save opportunities and have the lowest ERA of any pitcher in World Series history. I am not overconfident. I just know in my heart that we as a team are going to finish the job, because we do that as well as any club I've ever seen.

My warm-up pitches feel good. All I am thinking about is throwing the best pitch I can . . . spending the inning in the tunnel with Jorge and his glove.

The first hitter, veteran first baseman Mark Grace, fights off a 1–0 pitch and hits a broken-bat looper into center for a single. David Dellucci pinch-runs for him, extra speed that is important with the next hitter, catcher Damian Miller, surely bunting. Miller squares and taps his bunt almost straight back to me, an easy force at second. I pounce on it and fire to Derek at second, but my throw sails to the right, into center field. It is the second error of my Yankee career.

It is an easy play. I just blow it.

I get back on the rubber. Bank One Ballpark, as quiet as a funeral parlor just a minute earlier, is suddenly throbbing with sound and excitement. Mr. T comes out of the dugout. The infielders converge on the mound.

Let's just get an out—make sure we get one, he says. I hear him, but my mind is elsewhere.

I am going to smother this bunt. I am going to be all over it. I've just made a terrible play on a bunt and now I am going to make amends.

As the pinch hitter, Jay Bell, steps into the box, I am almost ready to charge the plate before I throw. Bell has the reputation of being a very good bunter, but if I have anything to do with it, these runners will not be advancing.

Bell squares and bunts the first pitch, hard, slightly to the third-base side. It's not a good bunt, and I am on it, catching it, spinning and firing to Scott Brosius at third for the force. Scott comes off the bag and holds the ball. Bell may not even be halfway down the line. I am waiting for Scott to throw it across to Tino at first. It is a guaranteed double play, leaving us with two out and a man at second.

But he never throws the ball. Scott is an aggressive, heads-up ballplayer, an excellent third baseman and a total gamer. Does he have Joe's words—"Make sure we get one"—in mind when he holds the ball? I don't know. I can't worry about it now. The inning is not going the way I expect it to. I can't worry about that, either. I can't start letting negative thoughts seep in. I never deliver a pitch thinking that something bad is going to happen. The Lord has blessed me so much with that ability.

There are runners at first and second, with one out. There is a batter to get out. That's all that I am focused on—Tony Womack, the Diamondbacks slap-hitting shortstop. Womack settles into the left-hander's batter's box. If I throw my best cutter, I know I can saw him off, get either a strikeout or a broken bat. I throw a cutter up for a ball, and then another, to fall behind, 2–0. My command is not what I want it to be. I am not hitting the spots I want to hit. I battle back to 2–2 and fire another cutter at Womack, but it's not inside enough, and he hits the ball into right field, a double that ties the game and puts runners at second and third.

The crowd is in a full frenzy now, smelling victory, and I'm sure it's sweeter still that it's coming against the mighty Yankees and their supposedly invincible closer.

I never think in such terms. I am not going to give in, or give up. Ever.

The next hitter is Craig Counsell, another left-hander. On an 0–1 pitch, my cutter bores in on him. He starts to swing and stops and the ball hits him on the right hand. Now the bases are loaded.

I take a deep breath.

Now it's Luis Gonzalez again, the Diamondbacks' best hitter. In two previous at-bats in the Series I have struck him out and got him to hit a weak grounder. He has an exaggerated, wide-open left-handed stance. Mr. T has ordered the infield in to get the run at the plate, not wanting to risk a weak grounder that could end the World Series. Gonzalez hasn't made good contact off of me, so he shortens up, choking up an inch or two on the bat. Later I find out it is the first time he has choked up all year.

Make a good pitch, get an out—these are my thoughts. I am calm. Focused. I am sure that I am going to get him.

Gonzalez fouls off my first cutter, and then I come to my set position and fire another one, a good one, a pitch that veers hard into his hands. Gonzalez swings. He breaks his bat. The ball pops into the air, toward shortstop. I see its trajectory and know it is heading for the edge of the grass behind Derek.

I know it is trouble.

In his normal position, Derek backpedals a few steps and makes the play. But he is not in his normal position.

The ball plops a foot or two beyond the infield dirt. Jay Bell races home.

There are no more pitches to make.

The Arizona Diamondbacks are world champions.

I walk off the field just as the Diamondbacks are pouring onto it. I am in something close to shock. Never could I have envisioned this ending.

I walk into the dugout, down the steps, up into the clubhouse. Jorge comes by and gives me a pat on the back. I get a lot of pats on the back. I don't remember if anybody says anything to me.

I sit at my locker for a long time afterward. I don't know what happened, I tell Mr. T. I knew we were winning that game. I knew it. I don't understand it. I lost the game. We lost the game. But look at how it happened. Look at all the things that occurred that were so different, so bizarre.

There has to be an answer for why this happened. I just don't know what the answer is.

I don't know what the answer is, either, Mr. T says.

I talk to the press, answer all the questions, take the blame. Yes, I threw the pitches I wanted. No, I don't remember the last time I threw away a bunt like that. Yes, I got Gonzalez to hit my pitch, but he fought it off and was able to make contact. I speak softly. I do not throw anything or kick anything. But I am hurting more than I have ever hurt after a game. I have done my best, sure. But my best is not good enough. I have let the team down. That is what hurts. My teammates are all counting on me and I do not come through.

I just don't know why. There must be a reason, and I have no idea what it is.

After I shower and change, I find Clara outside the clubhouse. I give her a kiss and a hug. She rubs my back. It is what Clara always does to comfort me. She rubs my back gently, tenderly. It is more comforting to me than any words can be. I take her hand and we walk to the bus. I have tears in my eyes. The guys on the team are there for me, I know that, but they are giving me space. We get to the airport and get on the charter, and Clara and I sit in my row, 29. I have my Bible and I have Clara. I don't say anything and she doesn't, either. She just rubs my back. The tears do not stop. They don't stop for the whole trip across the country.

Clara is right next to me, as she has been since I was a boy. Even in my sorrow and hurt, I am so thankful for my wife and her tender, loving heart, so thankful for the love the Lord has surrounded me with. We land in New York and we drive to our home in Westchester, still barely saying a word. It is about five o'clock in the morning.

I walk upstairs to the master bedroom. As I approach the room, I see something on the floor right in front of the doorway. I bend down and pick it up. It is a small trophy, probably eight inches high, with a wooden base and the golden likeness of a ballplayer above it. It is a Little League trophy. It belongs to our oldest son, Mariano Jr., who has just turned eight.

I hold it close, not smiling but feeling something much deeper.

13

Plans

As much as I am committed to living in the present, I have a hard time with the ending of the 2001 World Series. I search for an answer as to why it unfolded the way it did. I don't believe that things happen randomly, for no reason. I *do* believe that the Lord is in charge and has Infinite Wisdom, even if we may not understand it in that moment.

Eight days later, on a Tuesday morning, I get my answer.

I stop by the Stadium to pick up some stuff. Mr. T is there. I haven't seen him since the Series ended.

Well, Mo, I guess we know why it happened the way it did now, don't we? Mr. T says.

What do you mean? How do we know?

You didn't hear? About the plane crash, I mean? And then he tells me about American Airlines Flight 587, from John F. Kennedy Airport in New York to Santo Domingo. It crashed that morning and all 260 people on board died.

Oh, no. Oh my Lord. That's terrible, I say.

Yes, it is . . . such a tragic loss of life, he says.

It does not take me long to connect the dots. A dear friend and teammate of mine, Enrique Wilson, was booked on that flight, along with his wife and their two kids. When we didn't win, there was no parade, no post-Series celebration to stick around for. So Enrique and his family took an earlier flight. Our losing had saved his life, his family's lives. Please understand that I'm not suggesting the Lord cared about Enrique Wilson and his family and didn't care about the people who did die that day. And I am certainly not saying Enrique's life is more important than the lives that ended in the tragedy. I am simply saying that for whatever reason the Lord had His own play that day, and in effect said to Enrique that it was not his time to join Him.

So there you go. Losing a game instead of losing a friend? I will take that trade a million times out of a million. As painful as it was to lose, it's just another reminder for me that we are not the ones in charge—and that just because we may pray for something, that doesn't mean it automatically comes to fruition.

Prayer is not like a vending machine, where you put in your quarters (or words) and then wait for the product to be delivered. It's not as if I can say to the Lord, "I pray for this World Series victory," or "I pray for a clean bill of health on my next checkup," and then just sit back and wait for Him to deliver it. I very rarely pray for specific outcomes. When my agent is negotiating a contract for me, I never get down on my hands and knees and ask the Lord to make me wealthy. I don't pray for a new car or a good MRI result, or a strikeout in a big spot. For me, the most meaningful prayers are when I ask for God's wisdom.

So, no, my faith that we would win Game 7 is not realized. But in another way, a much more important way, it is realized. Because we are humans and we are so limited, sometimes we ask for the wrong thing, or don't look beyond ourselves. But God knows what is ahead. He always has a plan for us, and in November of 2001, that plan did not include a ticker-tape parade for the New York Yankees, and it did not include a heroic moment for me.

*　　*　　*

It is a raw Saturday in April in the first week of the 2002 season, and we are playing the Tampa Bay Devil Rays (that is still their name then) at the Stadium. I am at my locker in the clubhouse, starting to get dressed, thinking about how beautiful my uniform is, and how much I cherish wearing it.

For me, putting on the Yankee uniform every day is a process full of rapture. You hear guys who get traded to, or sign with, the Yankees talk about how great it feels to be putting on the pinstripes. For me, the thrill never wears off. It is about the history of the uniform, the dignity and the championships, the way it stands for something enduring, for excellence. Maybe it's because I am from a fishing village that is one stop from the end of the earth that wearing a Yankee uniform means so much. I just know I never take it for granted, for even one day. It's so easy to get caught up in the problems and complications and sadness that life can confront us with, but by opening my heart to the Lord, I am filled with lightness, with appreciation for the gifts He has given me, with the ability to pay attention to what is good and not what is not good.

And when I am getting changed into my Yankee uniform, it is all good.

I am extremely methodical about how I put the uniform on. I begin with one sock, then the other. I move on to the undershirt. I carefully take the pants from the hanger and slip them on, and follow with the jersey. I take my time doing all of this. I want to savor it, and I do, day after day, year after year. Posada likes to tease me that I am so fanatical about my uniform that I probably try to get the pinstripes of the pants and shirt to line up. I don't really do that, but he's not far wrong.

I want to honor the Yankee uniform for as long as I am wearing it.

The uniform may be timeless, but there is more change around the Yankees this season than any year since I arrived. Paul O'Neill retires after the Series, and so does Scott Brosius. Tino Martinez is now a Cardinal, and Chuck Knoblauch is a Royal and retires himself after 2002, his rapid and mysterious decline ending his career prematurely. Jason Giambi, our big free-agent signing, is now our first baseman, and David Wells is back and we've also added Robin Ventura and Steve Karsay and Rondell White. It is another stellar season, with 103 victories, but it's also the most frustrating season of my career, as I make three separate trips to the disabled list and pitch in the fewest games (45) of any year since 1995, when I was up and down from Columbus. A groin strain sidelines me in June, and shoulder tightness comes along later. The idleness is not easy. I can't shag batting practice fly balls. I can't do my job. I take pride in being someone my teammates can count on. I rest and get treatment, but I am not a good patient. I am not very good at being patient, either.

You can just ask Clara about that.

For someone who may seem outwardly serene and composed, I have moments when my buttons get pushed and I lose it, the hottest buttons being traffic and rude people. One time Clara and I stop in a little neighborhood pizzeria. The place is in New Rochelle, a city about fourteen miles northeast of Yankee Stadium. We have been going there for years. It's a modest roadside storefront, sandwiched between a dry cleaner and a liquor store, with no frills and great pie. It's a place where I can just hang out and be with the guys and not have it turn into a mass autograph session or photo op. You like these kinds of places when you are in the public eye. I try hard to be accommodating and treat all people with respect, but sometimes you don't want to be on display, and that's how it is at our pizza place.

It's early afternoon when Clara and I walk in, and there's one other customer in there, a stocky Latin fellow, in his mid-thirties probably. He doesn't seem to know who I am until the guys in the shop greet me.

Then he pipes up.

Hey, give me some tickets.

The guy looks as if he's been drinking or is under the influence of something. His words are slurred.

I don't say anything. I just laugh and kind of look away.

C'mon, man, give me some tickets. You guys make all this money. You can afford it. I want some tickets.

Now my temperature is rising. I am not laughing anymore. To me, patience and keeping one's temper in check are fruits of the Holy Spirit. The fruits are eluding me at this moment.

Leave him alone. He is our friend. Don't treat him with such disrespect, one of the countermen says.

The guy is not letting up. He takes a step toward me. I look at Clara, and she doesn't say anything, and doesn't have to. She is calm, steady.

Her look says: *Take it easy. Let it go. Turn the other cheek.*

I pause for a minute. I don't like the way you are talking to me, I tell the guy.

Now he raises his voice, steps closer.

Too bad, you cheap so-and-so, he says, calling me as bad a name as there is, and now I have had it. My blood is boiling and I'm ready to hit this guy, and hit him hard. Clara grabs me and says, Pili, no. The countermen order the guy to leave the store, escorting him out.

He curses again and is on his way. All I can think of as I try to settle down is thank God my wife was there, because if I had been alone I would've belted the guy.

I'm sorry that happened, one of the countermen says. He had no right to do that. He must've been drunk.

It's okay. It's not your fault.

I look at Clara and she still has the same expression on her face: *You don't have to react. The guy is just looking for trouble. Don't let it get to you.*

She is completely right, of course, and that is what I have to work on, and I do work on it, every day. If somebody cuts you off when you are driving or flips you off, what do you do? Flip him back? Curse him or chase him? To me the little daily encounters are more challenging than bigger things, and how you react in those situations when nobody is watching is more telling than anything.

I pray to the Lord all the time to help me be more patient—to not overreact. Sometimes it can be dangerous. One time, Clara and I are driving on Interstate 95, heading to Baltimore. Cars are flying on the interstate, as usual, when all of a sudden a guy blows past me and swerves into our lane—crazy stuff. I lean on the horn, and the guy slams on his brakes as if he is daring me to ram into him. He speeds up and I speed up with him.

Pili, no, Clara says again. Let him go.

I am not in listening mode. I am in retaliation mode, being a reckless fool, again turning away from the Spirit. I pull alongside the guy and start to creep over toward his lane. I am going to teach him, show him who he is messing with, swap a little paint to set him straight. The same person who is not fazed by thirty-seven thousand people riding him in Fenway Park is losing his mind over a macho motorist, endangering himself and his wife in the process.

How idiotic is that?

Stop it! Stop it now! Clara says. This is crazy. She is right, of course. She finally gets through to me, gets me to calm down. It takes much longer than it should have.

I am an imperfect man on an imperfect journey, but I am trying to be better. Next time I am in that situation, I hope I just let the guy drive away.

I'm doing more watching and waiting this season than I want, by far, but another first-place finish in the American League East earns us a best-of-five division series against the Angels. They are the best-hitting team in baseball (.282), a young club that won 99 one year after winning just 75. We have been crushing home runs all year (223 in all), and Game 1, at Yankee Stadium, brings no change. Derek, Giambi, Rondell White, and Bernie all homer, and even though Roger and Ramiro get slapped around a bit, I get the save in an 8–5 victory on thirteen pitches, retiring Tim Salmon and Garret Anderson to finish.

We rally from an early 4–0 deficit in Game 2 to go up, 5–4, but then the Angels get late homers from Troy Glaus and Garret Anderson to take the game, 8–6. The series shifts to Anaheim, and we jump out to a 6–1 lead after two and a half innings, but here come the Angels again, getting three more hits, including a homer from Adam Kennedy and a homer and four RBIs from Tim Salmon, and rolling to a 9–6 victory.

We are one game away from getting bounced out of the playoffs earlier than we have in our entire championship era.

By the time the Angels put on a parade worthy of Disneyland in a seven-hit, eight-run fifth inning against David Wells, we are basically done. The final score is 9–5. The Angels hit .376 for the series and come from behind in all three victories. They are fearless and relentless, and their bullpen dominates ours. Though I cannot fathom the result, how it happens is a bit familiar. Their grittiness reminds me of exactly the way we played when we were winning championships. You can win all the games you want in the regular season, but when your postseason ends in four games it is impossible to feel good about the year.

*   *   *

Our third son is named Jaziel, which means "strength of God." He is born seven weeks after our season ends, a Caesarean section delivery by Dr. Maritza Cruz, Clara's obstetrician. Jaziel weighs almost nine pounds, and all goes fine for him, but Clara has severe hemorrhaging that requires another surgical procedure. I am in the delivery room with her when Dr. Cruz realizes the extent of the bleeding. It is terrifying to see my wife this way, a strong woman suddenly so vulnerable.

I told you I don't often pray for results, but I was praying for them then:

Dear Lord, please look after my wife and our baby. Please help them through this. Please give Dr. Cruz the skill and poise to take care of the problem and give Clara's body the strength she needs to get through it. Amen.

It is six hours before the hemorrhaging is under control. Dr. Cruz, a person of deep faith herself, tells us later she could feel the Lord's presence in the operating room. She says for Clara to recover from the blood loss as quickly as she does is a miracle.

Our first off-season as a family of five passes in a snap, and it is almost time to go to spring training. It's a wintry Sunday morning, and I am more nervous than a rookie at his first camp. But not because of baseball. I am about to talk about the Lord in front of four thousand people at the Brooklyn Tabernacle. Jim Cymbala, the pastor, has read about my faith and invites me to share it in testimony before the congregation.

I have no idea what to say. A friend suggests Scripture from Psalms that says, *The steps of a good man are ordered by the Lord.*

Why don't you preach about that?

So I do. I talk about how sometimes we venture onto a path that is not ordered by the Lord, and that's when we fail. It is when we are separated from the Lord that trouble and stress arrive. I speak about my journey, and how the grace of the Lord helps me cope with adversity and shows me the way, every day of my life.

I am here today because the Lord ordered my steps, I say.

The thing is, we can't ever know those steps in advance, which is hardly more evident than in the 2003 season, when all kinds of unforeseen things happen. On opening day, Derek slams into the shin guards of the Toronto Blue Jay catcher at third base; he will miss six weeks. I miss the first twenty-five games of the season when the groin problem resurfaces on the last pitch of one of my last spring training outings. We still start off with a record of 23–6 but then go 11–17 in May. We finish tied with the Braves for the best record in baseball (101–61), and yet we lose eleven out of twelve in our own ballpark at one point, and somehow get no-hit by six Houston Astros pitchers—the first time a Yankee team has been no-hit since 1958.

Who ever heard of getting no-hit by six pitchers?

But by the time October arrives, I have a much better feeling about things. We take the Twins out in four games in the division series, and I retire all twelve batters I face. Now it is time for the Yankees and the Red Sox, best-of-seven for the American League pennant. The Red Sox, who have played us tough all year, are convinced that this is the year they finally bring the mighty Yankees down, and they go out and take Game 1, behind Tim Wakefield and the home run bats of David Ortiz, Manny Ramirez, and Todd Walker. Andy gets us even in Game 2, pitching into the seventh, before giving way to Jose Contreras (subject of a hot Yankee–Red Sox bidding war in the off-season) and me in a 6–2 triumph, sending us up to Fenway for a Game 3 matchup of Roger Clemens and Pedro Martinez. It is supposed to be Roger's last game in Fenway, and even as he warms up, there's this buzz in the park you'd feel at a heavyweight prizefight.

Manny Ramirez hits a two-run single to give Pedro a lead in the bottom of the first, but in the third Derek drives a hanging curveball onto Lansdowne Street, clear over the Green Monster, and we're rallying again in the fourth when Hideki Matsui, playing in his first Yankee–Red Sox postseason series, rifles a double to right.

Karim Garcia, our right fielder, steps in. He already has an RBI single off of Pedro. Pedro's first pitch is a fastball behind Garcia's head, hitting him in the upper back. Garcia is furious; he glares at Pedro and curses him out. Pedro curses right back. Our bench is up. So is the Red Sox bench. One play later, on a 6-4-3 double-play ball, Garcia overruns second and takes out Walker, the Sox second baseman. It's a dirty play, and Walker is rightfully steamed. Now Garcia is jawing at Pedro as he heads off, both benches are up on the steps, and nobody is giving Pedro more of an earful than Jorge.

They don't like each other, and in the playoffs, the emotions burn even hotter. Pedro stares and points at Jorge, and then points to his head, twice. I am watching on the clubhouse TV screen and am angry and disgusted at Pedro's antics. He's too good a pitcher to act like such a punk. First he headhunts Garcia, and now he inflames things even more by supposedly threatening to drill Jorge in the head.

If somebody rubs two sticks together this whole place could explode, I think.

The sticks get rubbed a few minutes later, in the bottom of the fourth. Roger throws a high fastball, slightly inside, to Manny Ramirez. The pitch isn't close to hitting him, but Manny brandishes his bat and starts hollering and walking out toward Roger, and now the benches empty. While everybody else heads for the mound, Don Zimmer, our rotund, seventy-two-year-old bench coach, takes off for the Sox dugout—Pedro Martinez is standing in front of it. Pedro sees Zimmer coming at him like a round little bull. Zimmer raises his left arm and Pedro steps back as if he were a matador, shoving Zimmer to the ground. Zim's hat falls off and he suffers a little cut, and everybody is gathering around him to make sure he's okay.

How much lower can Pedro go? I wonder.

Zim is totally wrong to bull-rush Pedro, but you can't throw an old man on the ground. You find a better way, that's all. The drama continues, and it boils over once more when a fight breaks out in our bullpen. It involves a Fenway groundskeeper, Jeff Nelson, and Garcia, who hops the fence to get in on it.

I don't let this mayhem get into my head at all. I am calm and I am positive, even though I haven't done well against the Red Sox this year; I've blown two saves and they have sixteen hits against me in just over ten innings. I can't tell you why, but I can tell you that as much as I love the intimacy of Fenway, the mound is one of my least favorite in the league. Maybe it's because the clay is on the soft side, so by the time I get out there, often after two hundred fifty or so pitches have been thrown, it is pretty roughed up and doesn't have the hard landing spots I prefer. But none of that matters. You compete where you have to compete. The mound is soft?

Deal with it, Mo.

I run in from the pen and start warming up with Jorge. We have been together for nine years now, and he isn't just a close friend, he's a soul mate, a guy I am in total sync with. He knows what I like, how I think, that I want to keep things simple. He knows I will never shake my head if I want to change a pitch or a location. All I will do is keep on looking in. If I keep looking in, then he knows I want to throw something else.

But who is kidding whom? I throw the cutter about 90 percent of the time. For most pitchers, a catcher puts down one finger for a fastball, two for a curve, three for a slider, and so on. With me, one is a cutter, and two is a two-seam fastball. If there is a runner on second base, four is a cutter and two is a two-seamer. If Jorge waggles his fingers as he puts them down, it means he wants it up in the zone.

That's the sum total of our signs.

Jorge puts down one finger almost exclusively at the end of Game 3. I face six Red Sox hitters and retire them all, requiring just nineteen pitches. We win, 4–3, and take a 2–1 lead in the series, but this is Red Sox–Yankees. I have a feeling this is going the distance, and that is exactly what happens. We win Games 2, 3, and 5. The Red Sox win games 1, 4, and 6.

Game 7 is at the Stadium, Pedro vs. Roger, Part II.

Pedro is much sharper than he was in Game 3, and has much the better of it. Roger gets knocked around for three runs in the third, and then gives up a leadoff homer to Kevin Millar in the fourth. A walk and a single follow, and Mr. T has seen enough, calling for Mussina, who has never thrown a pitch of relief in his career. He strikes out Jason Varitek on three pitches, and then gets Johnny Damon to hit into a 6-6-3 double play. Mussina has already lost two games in the series and given up five home runs; these are the most important outs he's gotten as a Yankee, and he doesn't stop there. He strikes out David Ortiz with two men on an inning later, and as I lie on the training table and get rubbed down by Geno, I am full of admiration for what he's doing.

He's getting every single out he has to have, I think.

In all, Mussina throws three scoreless innings, and now our bats finally wake up. Giambi belts Pedro's first pitch of the fifth inning, a changeup away, over the center-field fence, making it 4–1. It is only our third hit of the night. Two innings later, Matsui grounds out sharply to second and Jorge hits a sinking liner that Damon catches in right center, but I can see we're starting to get on Pedro's pitches more. Giambi comes up again and this time gets a fastball away, and he is all over it, ripping it over the wall in straightaway center, just over the leaping Damon's glove. Now it's 4–2, and when Enrique Wilson (who is in the lineup because he hits Pedro really well) gets an infield single and Garcia ropes a line single to right, there's more positive energy in the Stadium than there has been all night.

Then Pedro strikes out Sori for the fourth time, and the energy drains right back out of the place. Pedro points his finger to the sky, his trademark sign-off, and gets a hug from Nomar Garcia-parra in the dugout, and we all figure he's done. Pedro assumes he's done, too, until his manager, Grady Little, puts a question to him:

Can you give me one more inning?

Pedro says okay. He feels as if he has no option, even though he clearly thought his night was over. Ortiz homers off of Wells, another emergency reliever, to make it 5–2, and we have six outs left.

Sure enough, there is Pedro back out for the eighth. With one out, Derek hits an 0–2 pitch to right that Trot Nixon doesn't get a good read on, the ball bouncing just over his glove for a double. Bernie drives a single to center to score Derek, and then Matsui drills a ground-rule double to right. Still, Little leaves his ace in, and though Pedro gets Jorge to hit a flare to center, it falls and the game is tied. The Stadium erupts. Pedro exits. On the bullpen mound, the frenzy and noise are overwhelming, and so are my emotions.

I put down my glove, leave the bullpen mound, and run up a small flight of stairs, where there is a bench and a bathroom. I go into the bathroom, close the door, and start to cry. The moment is just too much to take in. We are down three to Pedro Martinez with five outs to go and now the game is tied. I don't know what else to do, so I thank the Lord for answering my prayers.

I let the tears come for a minute or two, wipe them away, and then finish my warm-up.

The Sox bullpen does the job and I come in for the top of the ninth, and end it by getting Todd Walker on a little looper to second with a man on second. When it leaves his bat, I crouch down, afraid for a second it might be another soft hit with terrible consequences. But Sori jumps to make the catch, and I jump on the mound with him. Mike Timlin sets us down in order in the ninth, and with two outs in the tenth, Ortiz takes me the other way with a double off the wall. I bite my hand on the mound afterward, upset that I didn't come in on him with the cutter instead of going away, but I get out of it by popping up Kevin Millar.

After Tim Wakefield and his knuckleball put us away in order in the bottom of the tenth, I have my own 1-2-3 inning, with two strikeouts. It's my first three-inning outing in seven years. When I get to the dugout, Mel comes up to me.

Great job, Mo, he says.

I can give you another, I say.

Mel doesn't want me going out there again, I'm sure. But there is no way I am coming out of the game. If I need to pitch a fourth inning, I am going to do it. A fifth inning? I will throw that, too. The season is just about over. I have a long time to rest. I don't just *want* to stay in the game. I have to. I feel that it is my duty. I am going to push Mr. T and Mel as hard as I have to. I am not going to let anybody else take the ball.

Aaron Boone leads off the bottom of the eleventh. He is hitting .125 for the series. Wakefield's first pitch is a knuckler that comes in about waist-high, on the inner half. Boone turns on it, and the minute he does, we know. Everybody in the Stadium knows — you can tell by the roar. The ball lands a dozen or more rows deep. We are going back to the World Series. The whole team pours out of the dugout to greet Aaron at home, but I have a different destination.

I am running to the pitcher's mound. I need to be on the

pitcher's mound. I get there just as Aaron rounds second and heads to third. I am on my hands and knees, kissing the rubber, saying a prayer to the Lord, crying in the dirt.

Thank You, Lord, for giving me the strength and courage to pull through. Thank You for the joy of this moment, I say. *Thank You for all of Your grace and mercy.*

Lee Mazzilli, our first-base coach, follows me to the mound and puts his arms around me as I weep. All around me guys are hugging and jumping around. I just keep praying and weeping. I am not sure what the depth of these emotions is about. Is it because I had left the field in such hurt after the last Game 7, two years before? I don't know. It doesn't matter. When I get to my feet, I share a hug with Aaron and then a long embrace with Mr. T.

I am named MVP of the American League Championship Series, but there is no real MVP. The trophy should be divided twenty-five ways. That is not a throwaway line. It's the truth. We never stop battling. We are a band of brothers. We stick together and believe together. I could've stayed in that dirt all night.

14

Losses

IN THE FIRST INNING of Game 3 of the World Series against the Florida Marlins, Josh Beckett, a twenty-three-year-old kid with a wicked fastball and a curveball to match, strikes out Derek Jeter on three pitches. Jeter spends the next three hours and eight innings doing more than anybody else on the team to make sure we win the game. As I watch him do this, I realize it has been ten years since we were teammates in Greensboro, the year he made fifty-six errors and I knew—*I knew*—he was going to be a great, great ballplayer.

What I saw then, in 1993, is the same thing I see now: a man with an insatiable desire to be the best, and to win.

You think about Derek's résumé of big moments, and it's staggering. The double that started the rally against Pedro in Game 3. The flip play. The home run in the tenth inning of Game 4 to beat the Diamondbacks in 2001. The leadoff homer in Game 4 against the Mets in 2000. The hit that started the big rally in Game 4 against the Braves, the one that culminated with Jim Leyritz's home run.

And now it is on display in Game 3 against Beckett and the Marlins, in a Series that is supposed to be about as competitive as a Globetrotters–Washington Generals game—a mismatch in star power, payroll, tradition, and pretty much everything else. We split the first two games in New York and know beating Beckett tonight can alter the course of the whole Series. So after that initial strike-out, here is what happens:

Jeter doubles to left and scores in the fourth inning. He singles to center to lead off the sixth inning. He doubles to right and scores the go-ahead run in the eighth inning.

Beckett pitches seven and a third and strikes out ten and gives up just three hits and two runs. All three hits, and both runs, come from Derek Jeter, a man who never stops competing and embodies the ethos of the Joe Torre Yankees: He gives his personal all but always wants it to be about the team.

I am warming up in the visitors' bullpen, getting ready to come on for Mussina, who is superb all night. Minutes after Derek's third hit and second run knocks Beckett out of the game, I am on the mound, throwing six pitches to retire Pudge Rodriguez, Miguel Cabrera, and Derrek Lee. We explode for four more runs on an Aaron Boone solo homer and Bernie's three-run homer, and then close it out in the bottom of the ninth.

We've beaten the Marlins' best pitcher and have Roger Clemens going in Game 4, and David Wells in Game 5. Nobody is taking anything for granted, but I like how we're situated, and when pinch hitter Ruben Sierra laces a two-out, two-run triple down the right-field line in the ninth inning to tie Game 4 at 3–3, it just seems familiar, like another Yankee workday in October.

It's a hit straight out of 1996 or 1998 or 2000, I think.

And from that point on, very little else goes right for the Yankees in the 2003 World Series. We are the ones who become the Washington Generals. As much as it stings to think about, the truth is undeniable: We are not the same team we used to be. It's not even close. The Marlins are fast and aggressive and play with spunk, but, I am sorry, those teams of ours that won four World Series in five years would've hammered them. They would've found a way, and willed their way through *as a team.* Because those were guys who cared more about winning than anything else. And it's just not like that anymore.

We leave the bases loaded in the top of the eleventh, and then watch as Alex Gonzalez, the Marlins shortstop, hits a game-winning homer off of Jeff Weaver to lead off the bottom of the twelfth. It's a highlight straight out of the Aaron Boone playbook, only now we are on the receiving end.

So the Series is tied at two games apiece, and then Game 5 unspools faster than a runaway fishing line. During infield practice, Giambi tells Mr. T he's not sure he can play first base because of a bad knee, and then Wells has to leave after an inning with a bad back. We get one hit in eight at-bats with runners in scoring position. It adds up to a 6–4 defeat. We go back to Yankee Stadium, where Andy pitches really well and Josh Beckett is even better, spinning a five-hit shutout and striking out nine, doing it on three days' rest. We whimper off to clear out our lockers, to another off-season that doesn't include a parade.

Anything short of a championship tends to result in big changes for George Steinbrenner's Yankees, and 2004 brings about the biggest change you can have: the acquisition of Alex Rodriguez, the American League MVP, a man widely considered the best player in baseball. Alfonso Soriano goes to the Texas Rangers in the deal, and Alex, deferring to Derek, goes to third base from his natural position of shortstop. It's Alex's third team in four seasons, and I'm thrilled we have him, but as I look ahead to my own 2004 season, the final year of my contract with the Yankees, I have an overwhelming desire to not go anywhere. I do not want to chase the biggest contract I can, and I do not want to wear another uniform. Maybe this makes me an agent's worst nightmare, because I have no interest in playing the free-agent game, posturing about all my options and leaking stories about how I might be on my way someplace else.

Maybe it costs me money, too. I extend my contract for two years in 2004, a year before it's up, and a few years later, the Phillies offer me a contract for four years and $64 million, almost $20 million more than what the Yankees offer. Do you know how long I consider that? For about half the time it takes you to read this page. The reason is very simple:

I have never played the game for money. I like money as much as the next person, and am fortunate to be able to provide well for my family, but it has never been my motivation for playing. I always felt that if I played the game the right way, if I worked hard and tried to be a good teammate and honor the game, the money aspect of it would take care of itself, and that is exactly what has happened. There hasn't been one time in my career when I looked at what somebody else was earning and felt shortchanged. Why would I do that? Why concern myself with other people's business?

It would do me not one iota of good. It would make me restless and unhappy, tying my contentment to the size of my bank account. The Lord has given me much more richness through His wisdom, as it is written in Hebrews 13:5:

Keep your life free from love of money, and be content with what you have, for He has said, "I will never leave you nor forsake you."

Contentedness for me comes from the Lord, and is available to me wherever I am, at any time, whether I am surrounded by fancy walls or no walls. I don't need anything but the love of the people who matter to me. It's how I choose to look at life.

Not that I need it, but as we head into another postseason in 2004 I get a powerful reminder of how little money really matters. It's minutes after we beat the Twins in the Metrodome to take the American League Division Series in four games; I have just put the Twins away in a ten-pitch bottom of the eleventh.

We file into the clubhouse to begin with the Champagne-spraying.

It never gets old; it feels new to me every time. Mr. T puts a hand on my shoulder and asks me to come into his office. Derek and Mel and a few of the other coaches are there.

Mo, something happened, Mr. T says. His eyes begin to well up. He is struggling to find words.

I'm very sorry, Mo. I think Clara should be the one to tell you.

I have no idea what is going on.

They bring Clara down to the clubhouse. She is crying, too. I find out later she doesn't want anyone to tell me anything until after the game. She suffers with grief the whole night, getting comforted by other Yankee wives.

There has been an accident at our house in Puerto Caimito, Clara says. Victor and Leo were at the pool and they were electrocuted. Neither of them survived.

I can't believe what I am hearing. Victor is Clara's cousin and someone very close to us. I've known him my whole life. Leo is his fourteen-year-old son. As I try to take this in, all I can do is embrace my wife and weep with her in Mr. T's office. Soon I learn all the horrible specifics. Clara and I built the house several years earlier, a place for us to stay when we go back. Victor takes care of the yard and the pool. He and Leo are working there and it's a very hot day, and Leo decides he's going to cool off, so he jumps in the pool. There is an electric fence nearby that we use so our dogs don't get away. One of the cables for the fence accidentally got into the pool, electrifying the water. Leo gets shocked into unconsciousness, and dies from drowning. When Victor sees his boy in the water, he jumps in to rescue him, and the same thing happens to him.

Clara and I fly back to New York with the team and catch a flight the next day for Panama. I go to the funeral home to see the bodies of Victor and Leo. I want to see them. It may sound gruesome, but I need to see them, to say goodbye to them and express the depth of my sadness, and pray for them. It is a small room in the basement of a building in Panama City. They bring out the bodies, which are being prepared for burial. It is one of the saddest moments of my whole life, to see the lifeless bodies of a cousin who is like a brother, and his young son.

I begin to pray over the bodies.

Dear Lord, I know that Victor and Leo are in Your eternal kingdom now, and know that they are in perfect peace. Please bless them and keep them and help their family through the terrible grief they are experiencing. Please give all of us the strength we need in this hour, and help us to find comfort knowing that through Jesus Christ there is eternal life. Amen.

The funeral is held at Church of God of Prophecy in Puerto Caimito on Tuesday morning, October 12, a two-hour service attended by hundreds of people. Rev. Alexis Reyes talks about how fame and money do not matter in this world. It is our love of Jesus Christ that matters. We go to the cemetery nearby and release balloons into the sky. I leave Panama City at about 2:30 p.m. on a private plane provided by the Yankees, and I land in Teterboro Airport in New Jersey a little after 7:00 p.m. The Yankees arrange for my documentation to be handled quickly so I can get on my way. They have a blue Cadillac waiting for me and we drive through north Jersey, across the George Washington Bridge and down the Major Deegan to the Stadium. It's the second inning when I arrive. I've spent a good part of the day crying and am emotionally exhausted, but it's good to be back at work and to immerse myself in game preparation, mental and physical. I want to compete. I want to get in this ball game and help my team win.

That would be the best healing agent of all.

I head right for the clubhouse. Geno is there, waiting for me. We share a long hug. It feels so good to see Geno's kind face. We talk as I get rubbed down and go through my routine. In the bottom of the fifth inning I arrive in the bullpen, with the Yankees leading, 6–0. Every guy out there comes up and hugs me. The fans in the bleachers spot me and a "Mariano" chant begins. It is exactly where I need to be. The guys give me a quick update on the game—Matsui has four RBIs, including a three-run double that helped chase Curt Schilling after three innings—and soon the lead goes to 8–0. I sit down and watch the artistry of Mussina, who has a perfect game into the seventh, before the Red Sox suddenly throw up five runs, making this a game that I will almost certainly pitch in. When Tom Gordon gives up a two-run triple to Ortiz with two outs in the eighth, the lead is down to one and the phone rings, and it's time.

The hitter is Kevin Millar. I fall behind, 2–1, and then bring a cutter that Millar rips at but pops to short. Bernie's two-run double in the bottom of the inning gives us a three-run cushion, and with two guys on, I get Bill Mueller to bounce into a 1-6-3 double play, a rousing finish to a wrenching day.

Nobody needs to remind us that this Red Sox team has a bunch of guys with pit-bull makeup, guys who are gamers, even after they go down two games to none one night later, when we win, 3–1, behind Jon Lieber, who outpitches Pedro. I get another four-out save, striking out Damon, Ortiz, and Millar, and off we go to Boston, but Red Sox hopes that the sight of the Green Monster and the Pesky Pole will change their fortunes get buried beneath an avalanche of Yankee home runs, over the Monster and other walls, too. Matsui hits two of them and goes five for six with five RBIs. Alex Rodriguez has another, drives in three and scores five. Gary Sheffield also homers and has four hits, and Bernie has four hits, too. It is a nightlong BP session and a 19–8 triumph for us, and with Duque matched against Derek Lowe in Game 4, it doesn't even look as if it will be a fair fight.

We hold to a 4–3 lead through seven innings of Game 4. The bullpen phone rings.

Mo, you got the eighth, Rich Monteleone says. As I stand up and start getting loose, a drunken fan begins to holler at me. I ignore him, but he continues. It is impossible not to hear him. He is right in my ear.

Is he really doing this? I think. *Is this where we are now?*

The drunken fan decides it would be fun to taunt me about my cousin and his son. He is going on about it, one sick and twisted insult after another. I can't even write what he says, it is so ugly. I wouldn't even want it in my book. I put all my attention on Mike Borzello's target. I am not going to let a drunken fool take me away from my task at hand. More than angry, I am sad. Sad that a human being could stoop so low, sad that this man is so full of poison, and so miserable in his own life, that he would bring up the deaths of two people I love, one of them a child.

It is a new low.

I enter the game with us leading, 4–3, in the bottom of the eighth. Manny singles, but I strike out Ortiz and get through the heart of the Sox order with no drama. In the ninth, the leadoff batter is Millar. He has had success against me, so I am extra careful, especially after he smokes a foul line drive early in the at-bat. My 3–1 pitch is high and Millar walks, and is immediately replaced by Dave Roberts, who is in the game to steal a base. I know it. Jorge knows it. The whole park knows it. Roberts stole thirty-eight bases in forty-one tries this year, and his lead is big. I throw over to first, fairly easily. Then I throw over again, and then a third time. He just beats the tag of our first baseman, Tony Clark.

I am thinking we might pitch out, but the call never comes. On my first pitch to the next hitter, Bill Mueller, Roberts is off. He gets a good jump. The pitch is up and away and Jorge makes a strong throw to Derek, who slaps the tag on just an instant late. Roberts is in scoring position with nobody out. Mueller fakes bunt and takes a strike. I throw a cutter over the plate, not where I want it, and he spanks it up the middle. I try to spear it as if I were a hockey goalie, even kick out my leg, but the ball goes into center and Dave Roberts goes home.

Mueller had hit a game-winning homer off me in July, a big emotional boost to the Red Sox in a game that featured a fight between Alex and Jason Varitek after Alex got hit with a pitch. Now he has gotten me again, and the fans in Fenway are loving it.

I get out of the inning, but the damage is done, and it becomes much worse, when Ortiz, the hottest hitter on earth all through the playoffs, blasts a two-run homer in the bottom of the twelfth.

The game lasts five hours and two minutes, and it not only gives the Red Sox a game, it gives them hope. In Game 5, we're up, 4–2, in the eighth and lose in fourteen innings. We come back to the Bronx in Game 6, Schilling outpitches Lieber, and we lose, 4–2, and with each passing inning, we look tighter than spandex on a fat person.

It's as tangible as the interlocking N and Y in our logo. We are waiting for something bad to happen, mired in negative thinking. It's another round of evidence of how the makeup of our team has changed. The guys from the championship years wouldn't have succumbed to it. They would've found a way. This team does not. The Red Sox complete the greatest comeback in postseason baseball history with a 10–3 drubbing. A year after Aaron Boone, the Red Sox have four games' worth of epic moments of their own, and nobody feels worse about it than I do.

I am the one who left the door ajar, after all, blowing the save in the ninth inning of Game 4. That inning changes everything. But even as I leave Fenway Park and head back to our hotel that night, I have a very clear thought:

We have a 3–1 lead. If we can't win one more game, we don't deserve to go to the World Series.

And we didn't.

15

Cheers and Jeers

It's opening day in Boston, April 11, 2005, and I am more popular than Paul Revere. The Boston Red Sox—the world champion Boston Red Sox—are getting their World Series rings and hoisting their championship flag, and wouldn't you know it, the New York Yankees are in town for the occasion. One by one, we are introduced. Everybody gets booed, some more than others, Alex Rodriguez most of all. After Randy Johnson, No. 41, gets his booing, it is my turn to be on the Back Bay griddle.

The public address announcer says:

Number 42, Mariano Rivera...

And the Fenway Park crowd goes nuts, people standing and cheering as I run onto the field, taking my spot next to Chien-Ming Wang and Randy. When I reach the baseline, I take off my cap and wave and bow. I laugh, and laugh some more, and the cheer keeps going, as if I were one of their own. Of course I know that I don't rank with Ortiz or Damon in their hearts. Of course I know the cheer is derisive—that I am being saluted for my contributions to the Red Sox's first world championship title in eighty-six years.

And that is okay. I am willing to play along. My reaction is not phony in the least, and I'm not brimming with private rage. The fans are happy, and it is as great a day of celebration as Boston has had in a long time, and I can appreciate that. Their team won after making a historic comeback against their fiercest rivals.

Why wouldn't they want to celebrate? What would be the point of taking this as a personal affront? Let them rejoice. I will be doing all I can to get them out the next time, and perhaps to make me a bit less popular around town. In a way I actually enjoy watching the depth of the Sox fans' Fenway celebration, its intensity fueled by passion and decades upon decades of perseverance. So it is easy to tip my cap and smile to thirty-three thousand people who are cheering at my expense, because this is not about me.

There is Scripture, after all, that is setting me on the right path. In James 1:12, it says:

Blessed is the man who remains steadfast under trial, for when he has stood the test he will receive the crown of life, which God has promised to those who love Him.

I have bigger matters to be concerned about than ovations in enemy ballparks as the 2005 season begins. The main one is getting booed in my own ballpark. I blow back-to-back saves against, yes, the Red Sox, during our opening home stand, and in the second of them, I am so ineffective (three walks, three singles, and five runs, one earned) that Mr. T comes and gets me, earning me a resounding Bronx cheer on my trip to the dugout. Some of my teammates are appalled that I got booed, but I don't expect to get bouquets tossed my way when I don't do my job. Why would I? Nor do I expect a lifetime pass because I've had a lot of saves. If people want to boo, they should go right ahead. It really doesn't bother me at all.

Much more than fan reaction, I turn my attention to improving the performance that triggers it. In other words, stop messing up. My whole issue is not having my usual command—a result, I'm sure, of the elbow tenderness that cost me time during the spring. I count on hitting spots, especially against the Red Sox, a patient team that sees me so much that it's hard to surprise them with any-thing. In the outing that gets me booed, I throw thirty-eight pitches and only eighteen are strikes. If that's not the worst ball-strike ratio of my career, I'd be surprised. The fans may be alarmed, but I am not. I know it's a question of fine-tuning things. I throw more, tighten up my delivery, and I know the results will be there.

I convert my next thirty-one save opportunities—a stretch of more than four months. One of the appearances comes in Detroit in early July, in a game that does my heart good. Bernie Williams is thirty-six now and is gradually being phased out as the regular cen-ter fielder. In a recent series against the Mets, we lose two of three at the Stadium, and Bernie drops a fly ball in right center in one game, lets a runner advance on another, and gets run on repeat-edly. Mr. T says he wants to give Bernie a couple of days off to clear his head. Bernie doesn't want time off but gets it anyway.

You can't call Bernie an unsung hero, not when he is a guy who to this day has more postseason RBIs (80) than anybody; when he has won a batting title and driven in a hundred runs five times; when he's hit .435 in an ALCS, as he did against the Mariners in 2000. Lost in all the spilled ink about our ALCS collapse against the Red Sox in 2004 is that Bernie had ten runs batted in, two homers, and a .306 batting average in the seven games, all pretty much without a peep. This is one of the things I admire about him: He's much more eager to play his guitar than sing his own praises.

Bernie has never changed from the time I met him in 1990. There's this innocence, almost an artist's fragility, about him, not something you often see in star athletes. Ten minutes before first pitch, he'd be strumming chords on his guitar, as if it were going to be his main activity for the night.

Like Derek, Jorge, Andy, and me, he comes through the farm sys-tem and does his work, and becomes one of the rarest commodities you can find—a switch-hitting All-Star center fielder who can hit for power and average, run, and field. I know he's not the most gifted natural base runner, but I still love to see him in full stride, knees coming up high, almost prancing, a beautiful athlete flying gracefully around the bags.

But the season has not been an easy time for Bernie. The Yankees are about to bring up Melky Cabrera to play center field, and more and more, Bernie is either a DH or nothing. Age happens to every athlete, but that doesn't make it any easier to watch when a player has been such a champion and brought so much honor and grace to the team.

We're only a .500 team (39–39) when we head into Comerica Park that afternoon, Mussina going against Sean Douglass, a six-foot-six right-hander.

Bernie's in and he singles in the fourth, the 2,154th hit of his career, moving him past Don Mattingly on the Yankee hits list, trailing only Lou Gehrig, Babe Ruth, Mickey Mantle, and Joe DiMaggio. Then he belts a line-drive single to bring home two runs in the sixth. He hits another line-drive single off of Kyle Farnsworth in the eighth, and in the ninth, he breaks open a one-run game with a three-run home run off of Troy Percival.

Bernie is the star of the game. And when the press comes in the clubhouse to talk to him, he is already gone. He has been a special teammate, and a big-time player for the Yankees for a long time. I am happy to see him have such a huge day.

With the way the season started, getting hailed as a hero in Boston and botching those first two save chances against the Red Sox, I can't imagine a better way to finish it off than being back in Fenway Park—to clinch another AL East title. I decide it's time for another dugout appearance, a little impromptu motivation from a bullpen interloper. Let's finish the job right now, I say. This is our division. Let's leave it all out there today.

The guys always seem amused when I go into cheerleader mode. I have no problem amusing them if it produces the desired result.

On the final Saturday of the regular season, Alex, Gary Sheffield, and Matsui all launch homers off of Tim Wakefield, and Randy Johnson pitches into the eighth. For Alex, it's home run No. 48 in another monstrous season, an MVP season. When Johnny Damon swings and hits a ball back to me with two out in the ninth, we are AL East champions for the ninth straight season (the Red Sox finish with the same 95–67 record as we do, but we win the division because we won the season series against them).

We draw the Angels in the division series and fly to Anaheim for the first two games. We take the first, knocking Bartolo Colon around early, mostly thanks to a three-run double by our rookie second baseman, Robinson Cano, in the top of the first. We kick away a prime chance to take a two-game lead by making three errors in Game 2. Still, we're even as we head back to New York, and we have Randy Johnson matched up against Paul Byrd, and you have to like your chances with a future Hall of Famer on the mound.

Byrd isn't good at all that night, but Randy is much worse. He gives up nine hits and five runs in three innings. We climb out of a five-run hole and take a 6–5 lead, but the bullpen gets strafed and we lose, 11–7, and now we're down, 2–1. We fight back to win Game 4, 3–2. I get the final six outs with two strikeouts and four groundouts, but the best part may have been the outpouring for Bernie, who gets four standing ovations and has his name chanted over and over again, the same way Paulie did four years earlier. It's not clear if Bernie will be back next year, and if this is goodbye, Yankee fans want to do it properly.

As we prepare for the decisive game, it's impossible for me not to conjure up my enduring image of Bernie: falling to one knee after catching Mike Piazza's fly ball in Game 5 of the Subway Series to give us our fourth World Series in five years. It was a perfect ending—a humble act and a respectful celebration. It was the essence of Bernie.

We fall behind, 5–2, in Game 5 against the Angels, but Derek leads off the seventh with a home run to cut the lead to two. We still have nine outs to go. We've come back when things have looked bleak before. I pray that we will summon such strength and resolve again. Think about Game 7 against Pedro, just two years ago, down three in the eighth. Why can't we do it again?

Alex grounds out, and after Giambi doubles, Sheffield flies out and Matsui pops out. We don't do anything in the eighth, either.

In the ninth Derek leads off with a single, but Alex hits into an around-the-horn double play. Giambi and Sheffield single, and then Matsui hits a shot wide of first that Darin Erstad makes a great play on, throwing to Francisco Rodriguez covering for the final out.

It's my least favorite kind of game...the kind we lose and the kind I do not get in. It's a helpless, hollow feeling, getting ready to compete and wanting to compete, and then never getting the chance. We shower and change in a somber clubhouse and head for the airport. Red Bible in hand, I pray my way through another cross-country flight in Row 29, taking comfort in knowing that I am in the Lord's hands, and that the frustration and disappointment I am going through will ultimately make me a stronger man and a better person. I listen to the comforting Christian songs of Jesus Adrian Romero. I feel the presence of the Holy Spirit. Sleep beckons.

16

Count Me Out

NUMBERS MEAN VERY LITTLE to me. Much as I'd like to blame it on Mrs. Tejada, my old math teacher, I can't. It is just the way I am. I play a sport that is infatuated with records and milestones, that churns out enough numerical nuggets to fill a barge. Me, I don't keep track of such things, and never have. I would be a terrible guy to have as your fantasy advisor. You know when I know about a milestone? When somebody tells me about it.

In early June 2006, I have a five-pitch, three-out save in Fenway (no, they didn't cheer), which was No. 391 for my career, moving me past Dennis Eckersley into fourth place on the all-time list.

About six weeks later, I throw two scoreless innings at Yankee Stadium against the White Sox for save No. 400. On September 15, 2008, also against the White Sox at home, I retire A. J. Pierzynski on a tapper in front of the plate, saving a game for Phil Coke — and, with save No. 479, passing Lee Smith for second on the all-time list.

If Jason Zillo, the Yankees' director of media relations, doesn't clue me in, or a reporter doesn't ask me about it, it slips right by. It's different when I pass Trevor Hoffman's 601 saves, because it's a big topic all over the media, but otherwise, just open the bullpen door, cue up "Sandman," and tell me where I stand in the history department later.

What these milestones mean to me could not be simpler: I am doing my job—and we are winning a lot of ball games.

I hear stories over the years about closers—some big-name closers—who refuse to go into the game if it is not a save situation.

Sorry, Skip, I can't get loose, they might say.

Or:

I don't think I can give you anything today.

In other words, *If it's not helping my bottom line, I am not taking the ball.*

Their rationale, I guess, is that they get paid based on saves, so why would they want to take on duties that are not going to get them paid?

If I were a pitching coach or manager and I had someone with that attitude, I'd try to get rid of the guy faster than Brett Gardner can get to first. Why have somebody on the team who doesn't care about the team? If you are that concerned with yourself and your money, maybe you should go play tennis or golf.

Early in September 2007, we are in a pennant and wild-card race and we have an eight-run lead against the Mariners—not a save opportunity—and Mr. T brings me in to get the final three outs. In the final moments of our collapse and the Game 7 defeat to the Red Sox in the 2004 ALCS, Mr. T calls for me to get the final out of a 10–3 game that is one of the sorriest nights in all of Yankee history.

You know what I am thinking?

My manager wants me to pitch, I pitch. That's it.

I can't imagine not taking the ball, ever.

So, my numbers? Unless you are talking about my team's numbers or Numbers, the book in the Old Testament (*The Lord bless you and keep you; the Lord make His face shine upon you and be gracious to you; the Lord turn His face toward you and give you peace*), I will leave them to others, and let them be.

*   *   *

From start to finish in 2006, we put up numbers as a team to make your calculator smoke. We score 930 runs for the season, 60 more than the next closest team. We hit .285 as a team and clobber 210 home runs, and with a lineup that includes names such as Rodriguez, Jeter, Sheffield, Damon, Abreu, Cano, Williams, Giambi, Matsui, and Posada, it's a wonder we don't score ten runs a game.

We finish with 97 victories and end the regular season at home before the usual 50,000 fans (we set an American League record by drawing 4.25 million fans), and with a new manager, Bernie Williams. Bernie is playing what turns out to be his final regular-season game with the Yankees, and with the division safely clinched, Mr. T continues his tradition of letting a player manage the final game if nothing is at stake. This year, he decides it is Bernie's turn.

For a reticent musician, Bernie is a managerial maestro. Derek is battling the Twins' Joe Mauer for the batting title, and when Derek singles in the first, he is only half a point behind. But Mauer winds up getting two hits, and when it's clear Derek can't catch him, Bernie sends a minor league call-up, Andy Cannizaro, No. 63, out to replace Derek in the top of the ninth. Derek points to his chest, as if to say, *Me?* and leaves to a huge ovation. Later, in the ninth, Bernie pinch-hits himself for DH Miguel Cairo and doubles to right center. The first-base coach, Tony Pena, makes sure to retrieve the ball—it turns out to be Bernie's 2,336th and final hit—and tosses it into the dugout, where Jorge grabs it, looks at Bernie on second, and pretends to heave the ball into the stands.

Bernie blows the game by bringing in Kyle Farnsworth, who gives up a two-run homer in the ninth to Adam Lind of the Blue Jays, and then, in his postgame press conference, conducted in Mr. T's chair, Bernie announces that George Steinbrenner has fired him.

It's all good fun, and we are upbeat going into the division series against the Tigers, who lose 31 of their last 50 games but still find a way to climb from 71 victories to 95 in one year. We seem to have stabilized after a crazy year of turnover, even by Yankee standards. We endure so many injuries, every day seems to bring three new guys through the clubhouse door. In the pitching ranks alone, we use twenty-five different guys. It's hard to keep track of their names. I want to be a good teammate to everybody, but often guys are not around long enough for me to do much more than shake hands with them.

(*Excuse me, are you Colter Bean or T. J. Beam?*)

Pitching has always been the core of our championship teams, so I am not completely sold on the idea that we can just bludgeon teams out of our way with the bats. But plenty of people do think that, including Al Kaline, the Tigers' Hall of Fame outfielder, a man who played against Mickey Mantle and the great Yankee teams of the 1950s and early '60s and goes on record as saying that this Yankee lineup is deeper and better. The big-bat formula works fine to begin the series, as Derek hits a homer over the center-field fence and goes 5 for 5. Giambi homers, Bobby Abreu has four RBIs, and we bang out fourteen hits. I save an 8–4 decision for Chien-Ming Wang, and when Damon clocks a three-run blast off of Justin Verlander early in Game 2, Mussina has a 3–1 lead and I am thinking we are in a very good place.

But the Tigers have the best pitching staff in the majors, and if the old cliché that good pitching stops good hitting seemed like a joke in Game 1, nobody is laughing now. We go 1 for 8 with men in scoring position, wasting all kinds of chances; Alex strikes out three times, once with the bases loaded. Alex is already upset that he's batting sixth instead of cleanup, and I can't say I understand Mr. T's thinking there. Alex hit 35 homers and drove in 121 runs batting cleanup, and even though that's a down year for him and he hasn't hit at all in the postseason the last two years, do you just bump him from his spot? He was in a great groove going into the playoffs. It's not my decision, obviously. I don't know whether Mr. T is looking to take the pressure off Alex or using the demotion to motivate him. Alex is a staggering talent, but sometimes he gets in his own way and makes things much harder for himself than they need to be.

Don't worry about it, I tell him. You can't change the lineup. Just go out and hit the way you can and everything will take care of itself. You don't have to prove anything to anybody. Just play your game.

Alex is a very proud man, though. Appearances are important to him. Being a cleanup hitter is important to him. He hasn't hit this low in a lineup since his first full year with the Mariners ten years earlier. It weighs on him, I'm certain, and I want to be sure his head is where it needs to be. I talk to Alex a lot—especially when stuff is going on around him (which is often).

Relax, Alex. Not trying to do too much is the best gift you can give yourself, I tell him.

Alex is back in the cleanup spot in Game 3 in Detroit, but it doesn't change anything. Kenny Rogers, a member of our '96 championship team, hasn't beaten a Yankee team in a dozen years, but he might as well be Sandy Koufax on this night. He gives up only five hits and strikes out eight and pitches into the eighth, Randy Johnson gets smacked around, and we lose, 6–0.

What is it with these division series? Why do we seem to be in a fight for our playoff lives every year? I haven't pitched since the first game of the series, and that is not part of our game plan. But I am forever optimistic. All we have to do is win a game. That's it. We win Saturday, and then we have a deciding Game 5 at home, with our best starter, Wang, on the hill. We put up one good at-bat, then another. We throw one good pitch, then another. We keep battling. That is the championship recipe. You fully embrace each moment, and winning all the little battles allows you to win the greater one.

The Tigers do these things superbly, and the Yankees? Not so much. With our season on the line and with Alex now hitting in the eight hole, we are as flat as a boat deck. Alex looks so lost it's hard to blame Mr. T for batting him there at all, or even for considering sitting him down. Our team is on the brink, and we have to put players out there who can help us win. As great as he is, Alex doesn't look as if he can help us win right now. Jeremy Bonderman, the Tigers' hard-throwing starter, pitches a perfect game through five. Our starter, Jaret Wright, gets reached for two homers to fall behind, 3–0, in the second, then gives up an unearned run in the fourth after Alex makes an error. The lead grows to 8–0, and we only get to 8–3 because Jorge, who hits .500 for the series, hits a two-run homer with two outs in the ninth off of reliever Jamie Walker.

The Yankee highlights are otherwise nonexistent. Alex goes 0 for 3 and finishes the series with an average of .071 (1 for 14) and no RBIs, and he is far from alone. Sheffield hits .083, and, as a team, we get two hits in our last twenty-one at-bats with runners in scoring position. For years we win with top-notch pitching and a lockdown bullpen, and one clutch hit after another. We don't have stars all over the field; we just have guys who grind, and win.

Even I can keep track of the numbers in this series. I throw twelve pitches and complete one inning.

The idleness is crushing.

Spring may bring renewal, but as I report to Tampa in 2007 it also brings sadness. Bernie Williams is not in camp, and he won't be in camp. He wants to return to the Yankees to fulfill a part-time role similar to what he did very well in 2006, for very little money. The Yankees are not interested. They tell Bernie he can come to camp, but only as a minor league invitee, not with a major league deal. It's contractual semantics, but to Bernie, a four-time world champion who has been a Yankee since 1991, it is a major affront.

They want him to see if he can play his way onto the team, after hitting 22 postseason home runs and those 80 playoff RBIs—and after everything else he has contributed? Bernie says no thanks, and that's it. There's no goodbye, no Bernie Williams Day, just a beloved Yankee sent on his way. It's not my job to tell the Yankees how to run their business. Brian Cashman and those around him make decisions that they believe are in the best interests of the team. I just don't think that this is the right way to treat Bernie, and I don't think it's the right baseball decision for the team. I am going to miss the guitar. I am going to miss No. 51 even more.

It's what makes the return of No. 46, Andy Pettitte, so impeccably timed.

Andy left as a free agent after the 2003 loss to the Marlins in the World Series, signing with his hometown Houston Astros. Now, four years later, he's back, and just the sight of him walking in the door brings joy to my heart. Andy isn't just a man who leaves it all out there every time he pitches; he's as good a teammate as you could ever find, a devout Christian who is totally forthright and fully accountable, and he shows it at a difficult time, after his name comes up in the Mitchell Report on the use of performance-enhancing drugs in baseball. Most guys in similar circumstances either go silent, swear on the Bible that they are clean, or release some generic apology through their agent. Andy faces it straight on and admits that he took human growth hormone. It takes a ton of courage to do that, and it makes me respect him even more.

Andy brings the same courage with him out to the mound. He is a man who proves over and over again that you can't scout heart. The 594th pick in the 1990 June free-agent draft, taken in the 22nd round, Andy is a chubby kid out of Deer Park High School in

Texas who is projected to do basically nothing. He doesn't blow people away with his arm or his athleticism. But he winds up winning 256 games in the big leagues and nineteen more in the post-season, pitching some of the biggest games in recent Yankee playoff history.

He is a guy you want on your team, for sure.

It's no fault of Andy's, because he pitches superbly, but when he falls to the Blue Jays in late May, we are in an unimaginable spot: last place. Our record is 21–29. We've already had ten different starting pitchers, and all sorts of guys are not playing to their level. We are so far behind the Red Sox—fourteen and a half games— that we're in danger of getting lapped.

We head into Toronto, where things get even messier, and Alex Rodriguez is at the center of it. He is photographed with a woman who is not his wife, and it's plastered on the cover of a tabloid newspaper. I know none of the particulars. I just know media hysteria ensues. In the same weekend we have a 7–5 lead on the Blue Jays in the ninth inning when Jorge hits a pop fly to third. The Jays' Howie Clark camps under it. Alex is running with two out, and as he passes Clark he shouts, Ha! A startled Clark backs off the ball, thinking the shortstop had called for it, and it drops. We score three more runs and win, 10–5. Later, Blue Jays manager John Gibbons rips Alex for what he considers a bush-league play. Other Blue Jays chime in, too.

There is no doubt that Alex has a knack for finding himself in the middle of things, and for sometimes making his life a whole lot harder than it needs to be.

As a friend, I just want to help him see that. Help him think through the consequences of things. Help him understand that, probably more than any other player in baseball, he needs to exercise discretion or it's going to blow up on him.

But I also think that people come after him much harder

because he is Alex Rodriguez. If Jorge or Derek had yelled at a fielder the way Alex did, I don't think it would have become nearly as big a deal. You know how many times hitters and base runners have pulled similar stunts to try to distract me? You know what I hear when I go to field a bunt?

Third! one guy yells.

Second! another guy yells.

People are screaming at me from everywhere, trying to confuse me and get me flustered so that I will throw to the wrong base. It doesn't work, because I keep my focus on what I have to do. If you are listening to what other people are yelling, then you aren't as professional as you need to be. How is that different from what Alex does in this case?

And what about when infielders pretend to be fielding a throw from an outfielder to trick a runner? Is that okay, even though it's outright deceit and could even result in a base runner getting injured pulling up at a base to slide?

I thought the whole brouhaha between the A's pitcher Dallas Braden and Alex was also ridiculous. Braden had a fit a few years back when Alex ran across the mound to return to first base from third after a foul ball. Braden cursed him out and made Alex out to be the most evil person this side of Whitey Bulger.

Running across a mound? Are you serious? You are really going to worry about that, as if it were some kind of holy land? You think I'm going to get upset if you run across the mound after I get an out? You can do whatever you want. You can roll on the mound. You can dance on it. I don't care. Because I'm going to get right back on it and go back to work, trying to get you.

I get the save in the "Ha!" game and just hope this is the start of a turnaround. It is my first save in almost a month, and only my fourth in a season that has had many more lowlights than highlights. Four weeks into the season, I have an ERA of 10-something, and there is the annual chorus of doubters starting up, suggesting that I have lost it and that my days as a dominant closer are done. The doubters do not include me, so I honestly am not worried. I know how I feel and what my cutter is doing. I know things will come around and I will get sharper. The day I go out there feeling overmatched, or ill-equipped to get guys out, I will be out of there, and I won't need anybody else to tell me.

The worst moment for me is probably a game at home against the Mariners when we start a rookie pitcher, Matt DeSalvo, who arrives from the minors and pitches a wonderful game in his big league debut, giving up three hits and one run to the Mariners, without striking out even one guy, a seven-inning effort straight out of soft-toss heaven. In the eighth, an ump blows a call when Willie Bloomquist tries to steal second, calling him safe even though Willie is out by the length of a fishing pole, and the Mariners wind up tying the game. In the ninth, I blow the game when Adrian Beltre mashes a misplaced cutter—supposed to be up and in, but it is out over the plate—for a home run, and we lose. The sting is always bad when you lose that way, but for me to shortchange young Matt DeSalvo, who spoke afterward about the "majesty" of the moment when he was about to throw his first big league pitch to Ichiro, really eats at me. The poor kid has nothing to show for his phenomenal debut.

In the clubhouse afterward, I seek him out.

You pitched a great game. I am sorry about the ending, I say.

That's okay, Mo. It happens. I know you did your best, Matt says.

We head to Fenway for three games, and one of the tougher weekends Alex has probably ever had. He doesn't know what the fallout will be from the photograph and how he is going to handle it with Cynthia, his wife and the mother of their young daughter, who is going to meet us in Boston.

It is not for me to judge Alex or lecture him on what to do. I am my own man with my own shortcomings. I know that he and Cynthia have a lot of talking to do, and the last thing I would ever do is inject myself into that process. I just always think that the best thing is to be honest and direct. Look inside yourself. Ask the Lord to purify your heart and share His strength with you. Humble yourself and try to set yourself on a better path, a righteous path, and know that the Lord's forgiveness is boundless.

At the ballpark, to nobody's surprise, the Fenway fans find great humor in the whole thing, wearing masks with the face of a blond woman and riding Alex unmercifully. With the score tied with two out in the ninth on Sunday night, Alex rips an 0–2 pitch from Jonathan Papelbon into the Red Sox bullpen. He has never had a happier trip around the bases, I guarantee you that. It's the biggest hit of our season. I get the save. We take two out of three in Fenway. It is something to build on.

A few weeks later, we have a scheduled trip to Colorado. Our oldest son, Mariano Jr., is graduating from middle school. It is our first graduation as a family. I walk into Mr. T's office.

You got a minute?

Sure, Mo. What's up?

I know this is a lot to ask, but would you be okay if I didn't make the Colorado trip so I can attend my son's graduation? It means so much to me, and to our family.

I can't recall ever asking Mr. T for a favor before. I've definitely never asked out of a road trip. He looks surprised. He pauses for a long while before he answers.

Mo, I would love to accommodate you. I really would. I understand how important it is to you and Clara, and to your son, but it would be really hard for me to do that. It sends the wrong message.

It wouldn't be fair to let you do this and then not extend the same courtesy to others.

I hear him out, and I know that even asking this is putting him in an awkward spot. But for once, I am not my compliant, team-first self. I don't think Mr. T understands the significance of this to me. I dropped out of school when I was just a little older than my son. My father dropped out even earlier. This day is something that needs to be celebrated properly, in my mind.

I am sorry, but I am going to go whether I have permission or not. It's very important that I be there, I say.

I can't stop you from going, Mr. T says, but if it comes to the eighth or ninth inning and we have a lead and we need you and you're not there, what do I say to people? You tell me what I'm supposed to say. That you are gone without permission? I don't know what you want me to say, but I can't tell people I gave you permission when there are twenty-four other guys counting on you. I can't do that.

Okay, I reply. I need to think about it. I leave his office and talk it over with Clara. I explain the conversation to her, and the more I reflect on it, the more I realize I cannot defy my manager and go to the graduation. It's just not how I operate. When it comes down to it, I'd feel that I really let everybody down.

Next time I see Mr. T, I let him know I've reconsidered.

I will be on the trip to Colorado, I say. It wouldn't be right not to be with the team.

I explain to my son: I want to be at your graduation more than anything, but the Yankees won't give me permission to miss the trip. I love you and I'm proud of you, and I wish I could share this moment with you, but it's not possible for me to be there.

Mariano Jr. is very understanding. The sad truth is that he, Jafet, and Jaziel are very accustomed to my being away and missing occasions and events. Baseball has given our family an awful lot, but the schedule is not very forgiving.

We get swept in Colorado and I don't even pitch. It's pretty much how the season is going. Every time I think it's going to turn around, we backslide again. We manage to get to .500 (43–43) for the All-Star break, so, psychologically speaking, it's a new season. We forget the mess we made in the first half and start resembling the New York Yankees. In back-to-back games against the Rays, we outscore them, 38–9, pound out 45 hits, and wind up scoring the most runs in the majors again. We go 24–8 out of the break and suddenly are within four games of the Red Sox. A big part of the surge is our new secret weapon out of the bullpen, a hulking kid from Nebraska named Joba Chamberlain, who is twenty-one years old and overpowering the world. Joba throws 99-mile-per-hour fastballs, and his slider is an even better pitch. In his first twelve games, he doesn't give up an earned run and strikes out way more than a man per inning, pumping his fist after every punch-out. By the end of the regular season, he has 34 strikeouts and 6 walks in 24 innings, and an ERA of 0.38. Of the 19 games in which he has pitched, we've won 17 of them. It's fun to see a kid who has so much belief in himself, attacking from the first pitch to the last. I'm not one to get carried away and anoint someone as a future star after such a short sample of games, because to me that status is only achieved over time, but he's been the next best thing to unhittable, and it is something to behold.

We're in the playoffs for the thirteenth straight year, but for the first time in ten years, we are not the AL East champions. As the wild-card team, we open on the road against the Cleveland Indians. Johnny Damon drives a CC Sabathia pitch over the fence to start the game, and then Chien-Ming Wang takes the mound, a steady sinkerballer who won nineteen games for us in each of the last two years. There is no reason not to have a ton of faith in Wang.

He has won six of his last seven starts and handled the playoff pressure well the previous two seasons.

Then the game starts, and Wang is all over the place. In the first inning alone, he walks two, hits one, and gives up three singles and three runs. His sinkerball not only isn't sinking; it is flying all over the park. By the time he leaves in the fifth, his line says nine hits and eight runs, and even though Sabathia is wild and we're hitting him, it doesn't matter. We lose, 12–3, and that makes Game 2 a must-have, and we've got just the guy we need on the mound: Andy Pettitte. He needs to go deep in the game, and hand the ball to Joba, who will hand the ball to me. It's worked almost flawlessly from the day Joba arrived.

Andy proves yet again that his competitive makeup ranks with anybody's. He has base runners on in every inning and gets out every time. In the sixth, Grady Sizemore hits a leadoff triple, and never budges; Andy gets Asdrubal Cabrera on a bouncer back to the mound, then strikes out Travis Hafner and Victor Martinez.

The game moves to the seventh, the only run coming on Melky Cabrera's homer off of Indians starter Roberto Hernandez in the third. With one out in the bottom of the seventh, Jhonny Peralta doubles and Kenny Lofton walks, and Mr. T calls for Joba, who makes his postseason debut by striking out Franklin Gutierrez and getting Casey Blake on a fly to right.

The kid is amazing and without fear.

It's still 1–0 as Joba comes out for the eighth and I warm up in the bullpen for the ninth. As Joba prepares to face Sizemore, he begins swatting and waving his arms around on the mound. It is not a stray mosquito or two. It is a swarm of little bugs called midges, and in the heat of an unseasonably warm fall night (it's 81 degrees when the game starts), they are descending on Joba and his sweat-soaked neck and face by the hundreds, if not thousands. They are covering his neck. They are in his ears. Flying around his mouth and nose and eyes. He keeps flailing and it does no good, and neither does the insect spray Gene Monahan brings out.

The bullpen is completely midge-free. I am not bothered once. Seeing Joba's reaction, I can't believe the umpires aren't stopping the game. They stop it for a torrential rainstorm. Why not stop it for a torrential bug storm? Maybe because the midges aren't nearly as bad by the dugout, Mr. T doesn't fully grasp what Joba is going through and doesn't push the umps to halt play. So it continues, and for the first time since he got to the majors two months before, Joba Chamberlain, strike machine, turns from a smoking-hot sports car into a wild and sputtering jalopy. He walks Sizemore on four pitches — a first in his big league career. He wild-pitches him to second, and two batters later, he wild-pitches him home to tie the game. The poor kid is doing all he can to keep his composure, but with the midges continuing the attack, he hits one guy and walks another, before finally getting Peralta on a slider away to end the inning.

Joba leaves the game. And the midges leave the field as mysteriously as they came.

We have a man on second in the top of the ninth, but Alex strikes out. I get the Indians in order and it goes to extra innings. After I get through a bumpy tenth — I strike out Peralta with the bases loaded — we do nothing in the top of the eleventh, our all-world offense so weak it has produced just two singles since the fourth inning.

When Hafner lines a single with the bases loaded off Luis Vizcaino, the Indians have a 2–1 victory, and we have another serious divisional hole to escape from.

Back in the midge-free Bronx, Mr. T starts forty-four-year-old Roger Clemens, who was lured out of retirement to help stabilize our rotation; but he has battled injuries and inconsistency, and tonight is no different.

Phil Hughes is stellar in relief, Damon and Cano sock big hits, and I save an 8–4 victory. So we need one more to take the series back to Cleveland for a fifth game. It's Wang's turn again, and, pitching on three days' rest, his fortunes do not change, the Indians smacking him around for five hits and four runs in one-plus innings. We fall behind, 6–1, and though Alex homers and Abreu homers, it's another game where we don't pitch, or hit, well enough to win.

Our season ends with a 6–4 loss.

When I go into the off-season, I am like a fisherman going out to sea. I'm going to be gone awhile, and I don't look back. I don't think about baseball, and I don't watch baseball. As much as I love the game, if I am not playing in the World Series, I don't want to watch the World Series. It is no different this year, when the Red Sox are playing the Rockies, but it doesn't take me long to find out that my friend Alex Rodriguez is back in the news. In the top of the eighth inning of the fourth and final game of the Series, FOX reporter Ken Rosenthal apparently reports that Alex is going to opt out of his contract with the Yankees.

Why now? What are you doing, Alex? Couldn't you have waited until tomorrow?

Those are my thoughts when I find out about this.

Alex has the right to be a free agent by the terms of his contract. That is completely his right, and he should go for the opt-out if that's what he thinks is best. But what is the point of doing it during the World Series? Why hijack attention from the game you love? I am no psychologist, and I am not going to pretend that I am. You know by now that I am not one to judge harshly; I try not to judge at all. I don't know what Alex's motivation is. Maybe his agent convinces him that this is a great way to kick off a bidding war by showing the world what a big deal Alex Rodriguez is . . . so big that they interrupt the World Series to talk about his contract situation. Or maybe it's important for him to feel, well, this important. I don't know. Controversies may not swarm Alex the way the midges swarmed Joba that night in Cleveland, but sometimes it's close. I have spoken to him time and again about the beauty and benefit of keeping things simple.

I am hoping and praying that one day he will listen.

It's November 29, my thirty-eighth birthday, the Series put to bed and another month closer to spring, but I am not in the mood to celebrate. I am in Panama for the funeral and burial of my friend and mentor Chico Heron, who has passed away after a long illness. I've known Chico for most of my life, and I loved him. If he hadn't scouted me and believed in me, I would've had no shot at making the big leagues. If he hadn't taught me the things he taught me, I don't know where I would be.

Chico was a funny little guy, a man completely about Panamanian baseball. You could be playing on a rock-ribbed sandlot that was miles from everywhere, and you'd look up and Chico would be there. Then you'd be at the biggest stadium in Panama City, and he'd be there, too. Chico loved baseball and loved scouting, and he loved helping guys he believed in. Chico didn't worry that I was skin and bones and only throwing in the mid-eighties when he scouted me as a pitcher. He saw potential. He saw what I might become — a kid who, with more weight and a lot of work, just might be a legitimate prospect. He recommended me to his boss, Herb Raybourn, and soon enough I was on my way to Tampa.

Even more than his eye for talent, though, Chico had goodness in his soul. He knew the right way to do things. Over and over, he would talk to me about giving everything I had at all times, about being respectful and keeping my focus and persevering through the tough times that are definitely a part of the game and of life.

Trust yourself and believe in yourself, and trust in the Lord, Chico would tell me. When you have that trust, and you are willing to work and work, there's no telling what you can accomplish.

I listened, and it changed my life.

17

Closing Time

You can't have a stranger way to begin a baseball season than this. The last time I saw Roger Clemens, in the fall of 2007, he was in the Bronx, wearing a pin-striped uniform, trying to keep our season alive against the Cleveland Indians. Now I see him on the television screen, wearing a pin-striped suit in Washington, DC, trying to keep his legend alive against the accusations of his former trainer, Brian McNamee. It's another low moment for baseball, with the issue of performance-enhancing drugs getting hotly debated in a hearing room on Capitol Hill. I know it's important, and nobody wants baseball to be a clean sport more than I do. I still wish it would go away, and that almost everyone who ever cheated would go away, too.

It's a time of big transition in my baseball life as well. Mr. T is gone, and Mr. G — Joe Girardi — is here. He's the third manager of my career, and the first, of course, who had been not just a team-mate of mine but a catcher of mine. The first time we were actually a battery in a real game was the first week of the 1996 season — in Texas, against the Rangers. I struck out Rusty Greer and sailed through two quick innings with Joe. He was upbeat and high-energy, a small guy with a big, positive presence who was really good at blocking pitches and calling games. He was all about the team, too. Batting eighth, right ahead of Derek, he had the most sacrifice bunts on the team that year, stole thirteen bases, and had one of the biggest hits in the Series—the run-scoring triple off of Greg Maddux that got us going in the decisive Game 6 at Yankee Stadium.

Having a new manager may be a big change, but just as Joe was easy to play with, he is easy to play for. His moving into the manager's office isn't a problem in the least. I will work and prepare the same way as always, and I am going to do whatever he asks me to do.

He tells me he wants to limit me to one inning whenever possible, and be judicious when it's my turn to pitch.

Whenever you call, I will be ready, I say.

Whether it's the new manager or my new catcher, Jose Molina (Jorge misses much of the season with an injury, so the Yankees go out and get a Molina brother), I begin the year as if I'm about to turn twenty-nine, not thirty-nine. Two months into the season, I have twenty-six strikeouts, two walks, an ERA of 0.38, and fifteen saves. We go on a seven-game winning streak after that, and I get my nineteenth save by striking out the side against the Padres. It would feel a whole lot better if we weren't just five games over .500 (50–45) when the All-Star Game arrives at the old Yankee Stadium for the final time.

It's my ninth All-Star Game, and the most special to me of all— baseball's best gathering to say farewell to a shrine. The most powerful part of the experience for me is seeing George Steinbrenner back at the Stadium. He hasn't been around all year. We keep hearing about his failing health and his diminished faculties, so it is great to see him in person.

And you can't mistake how much it means to him to be here. In the pregame ceremony, riding in from the outfield in a golf cart, Mr. George is weeping as he rolls along toward the pitcher's mound. He hands baseballs to four Yankee Hall of Famers—Whitey Ford,

Yogi Berra, Goose Gossage, and Reggie Jackson. They embrace him—and then throw the balls to their designated catchers: Whitey to Derek; Yogi to Joe Girardi; Reggie to Alex; Goose to me.

I'm not even sure when I first officially met Mr. George, but I am positive I was already in the big leagues. If he was around spring training when I was younger, I watched him from afar, but mostly I just went about my work and tried not to get noticed.

Mr. George is surrounded by his family at the All-Star Game, and he looks overcome through almost all of the festivities. It's sad to see a man who has always been such a commanding (and demanding) presence, such a forceful leader, with his vitality gone. I want to thank him for giving me a chance, and giving me the honor of wearing the uniform of the New York Yankees, but I am not sure what to say or do—whether to approach him and risk an awkward moment if he doesn't know who I am. I decide it's best to let him enjoy his family and the farewell to the Stadium, a place he has helped make one of the legendary venues in all of sports.

It is one of the last times I ever see Mr. George Steinbrenner.

We come flying out of the box to start the second half, winning eight in a row. Joba, now a starter, pitches a 1–0 masterpiece in Fenway on a Friday night in late July, and after I finish it by striking out Mike Lowell and J. D. Drew, we are just three games out of first—the closest we've been since the first week of May.

And then we slide right back to mediocrity again. We lose four of five games and give up forty-four runs in the process, not the sort of pitching that is going to take you places. We lose Wang in June to a freakish ankle injury when he's running for home in a blowout victory over the Astros in Houston (sadly, he has never been the same pitcher since), and we have only one starter—Mussina—with an ERA under 4.00. Plus, we're no better than an average offensive team this year, and that's not a good combination.

The Red Sox come to town in late August, and it's a series we really need to win, if not sweep. We do neither. Andy gets roughed up in the opener, a 7–3 defeat, and in the next game we send out Sidney Ponson, and soon a Red Sox rout is on, and so is the Dustin Pedroia Show.

He gets three hits, scores four runs, and drives in four on a grand slam off of David Robertson. He runs and dives all over the place, is covered with dirt from beginning to end, and plays with such passion you'd think it was the last ball game he'd ever get to play.

Until he comes back the next day, and the day after, and plays the same way.

There are a lot of players I admire, and Dustin Pedroia is right at the top of the list. Nobody plays harder, gives more, wants to win more. He comes at you hard for twenty-seven outs, every time. It's a special thing to see, a little guy like that who is willing to do whatever it takes. I've seen many top-notch second basemen in my years in the big leagues. Roberto Alomar was a staggering talent who made the game look easy, who could beat you with his glove, his legs, or his bat. Robinson Cano has a beautiful stroke and is as good in the field as almost anybody. Before he started having his throwing problems, Chuck Knoblauch was another guy who could take over a game with his speed and grit. But if you are looking for a guy who's going to go full-out and do whatever it takes to win, Dustin Pedroia has to be right there with anybody.

Just over three weeks later, our season is effectively over, and so is our postseason streak of thirteen years. The Rays are the AL East champions, the Red Sox are the wild-card winner, and the Yankees are out of luck, six games behind at 89–73. Like Derek and Jorge, I've been to the playoffs every year of my career, but the simple truth is that we don't deserve to go this year. I finish with one of the best statistical years of my career (39 saves in 40 chances, 1.40 ERA, 77 strikeouts, and 6 walks), but all of that and 45 cents will get me on the bus to Chorrera.

Our final piece of business in the 2008 season is to say goodbye to Yankee Stadium. After 85 years and 26 world championships, the final game is played on Sunday, September 21. The Orioles are in town. The gates open seven hours early so fans can walk around and have a proper farewell. From the time I leave home for the Bronx that day, emotions flood me like water over the bow.

I think about the first time I stood on the mound in the postseason — top of the twelfth inning in the 1995 ALDS against the Mariners, striking out Jay Buhner to begin three and a third innings of relief, before Jim Leyritz belted his homer in the bottom of the fifteenth.

I remember celebrating the Series sweep of the Braves four years later with Jorge and Tino and everybody, and I remember kneeling in prayer in the dirt as Aaron Boone rounded the bases four years after that.

These moments, of course, are merely a small, personal sample, a few special memories of a Panamanian boy who was going to be a mechanic. What about all the other historic moments, and all the iconic players, from Ruth to Gehrig to DiMaggio to Berra to Mantle and now to Jeter? What about their feats and memories, and their glories?

Derek says the aura and the tradition are just going to move across the street, but are they? Can the spirit and soul of this Stadium ever really be recaptured? I don't know — still don't.

Yankee Stadium is not just a home office for triumph. It is a place where I grow up as a pitcher, and as a man, a place with special, spiritual retreats deep within it. There is the trainer's room, where I spend all those middle innings for all those years with

Geno, an athlete and a healer, a young man and an older man bonding over balm and shared values and a mutual belief in the importance of thoroughness and hard work.

There is the tunnel beneath the left-field stands, where I make the walk to the bullpen, turning left out of the clubhouse and following the corridor around, behind home plate, and continuing down toward the left-field foul pole, where I turn right and wind through Monument Park toward the pen.

There is the bullpen bench, which is where I watch the game, taking in the verdant splendor of the field before me, sharing the time with my bullpen soul mates. I love that bench, and how I mark the nightly rhythms of my job there, playful and silly at first, then turning more introspective almost by the batter—until I am transformed into someone else entirely, into a man whose whole world is centered on getting people out and securing a victory.

I love that bench. I love it so much that the Yankees were kind enough to let me take it home when the old Stadium closed for good.

And then there is the bullpen mound, where I go to work after I get the call, going through my precise warm-up routine and waiting for the doors to open, and making my solitary run toward the mound.

I cherish this place and I want to honor this place. I want to be the last man to stand on that mound. I want to throw the last pitch, and get the last out.

The power and poignancy of the day never let up. It seems as though half of Cooperstown is on the field before the game, and Yankee greats are everywhere. Bobby Murcer, one of the most beloved of all Yankees, passed earlier in the summer, but his wife, Kay, and their children are there, all wearing Bobby's No. 1 jersey, basking in a huge cheer. Bernie is there, of course, and he probably gets the biggest roar of all. Julia Ruth Stevens, the daughter of the

Babe, throws out the first pitch to Jorge. Yogi is in his old heavy flannels, talking about how the place will always be in his heart.

Julia's father homered in the first game ever played in the Stadium, and the homers continue. In the bottom of the third, Johnny Damon rips a three-run blast that gives the Yankees an early lead. Andy does his best to protect the lead, but the Orioles tie it up in the top of the fourth, before Jose Molina, who has had two homers all season, hits his third into the netting in left center, giving us a 5–3 lead.

In the trainer's room, Geno finishes up his rubdown.

Thanks, Geno, I say.

Just doing my job, he says. And I know you'll do yours.

Thank you, and God bless you, I say.

Andy gives way to Jose Veras in the sixth. I make my way down the left-field corridor beneath the stands. I don't want to leave this place. I don't want this to be the last time.

Nostalgia doesn't hit me very often.

It is hitting me now like a freight train.

Now, for the last time, I am in the pen that has been my baseball home for fourteen years.

Joba (back in the bullpen now) pitches a strong inning and two-thirds and we tack on two more runs. The phone rings in the pen in the eighth. Mike Harkey answers.

Mo, you got the ninth, Harkey says.

Derek grounds out to third to end the bottom of the eighth, and it's time. The blue doors open, and "Enter Sandman" starts up and I make my last run across the outfield in the old Yankee Stadium. The crowd is standing and cheering. It is surreal.

I get to the mound and pick up the ball. I need for this to be business as usual; I need to focus on these three outs, even if it is not business as usual at all.

The first Orioles batter is Jay Payton. He hit a three-run homer off of me in the ninth inning of Game 2 of the Subway Series eight years before, down the right-field line. You do not forget things like that.

I get Payton on a weak grounder to short, which is ably handled by Derek. I get ahead on the next batter, 0–2, come with a hard cutter inside, and he bounces it to second. Two outs. One to go. But before I even get on the rubber to throw another pitch, I see Wilson Betemit running from the first-base dugout toward shortstop. Joe wants Derek to leave the old place in a fitting way, with one last massive ovation.

And that is exactly what happens.

Derek Jeter, the last Yankee icon in a fabled Stadium, runs to the dugout and is summoned again to do a curtain call.

The next Orioles hitter is Brian Roberts. He has always been a tough out for me. On a 2–1 pitch, he hits a grounder to Cody Ransom at first. I break off the mound, but Cody takes it himself for the final out. He tucks the ball in my glove and shakes my hand. The Yankees didn't win enough games this year, but we won this one, the last game ever played at 161st Street and River Avenue.

And for that I am very grateful.

I know exactly what I am going to do with this ball. I am going to give it to George Steinbrenner. He is the one who deserves to have it.

18

New Digs and Old Feelings

You don't want to make hasty judgments, but the early returns on the new Yankee Stadium are pretty unmistakable. Home runs are flying out of the place, and from a design standpoint, the new park—for all of its grandeur and luxury and state-of-the-art amenities—is a much more open place: It doesn't hold noise, or home-team fervor, anywhere near the way the old place did. It's not that we worry about such things as players, but when you are used to having a full-throated full house connected with every pitch, it's a little hard when people either aren't in their seats or have no idea what a hit-and-run is.

The old Stadium was our tenth man—a loud and frenzied cauldron of pinstripe passion, with a lot of lifers in the stands. Maybe I'm wrong, but it's hard to see that the new place can ever quite duplicate that.

Some things are completely unaffected by new construction, though, and one of them is Derek Jeter's swing. He's had that hands-inside-the-ball magic going for fifteen years, and here it is on display across the street for the first time, in the eighth inning of our second game, with the score tied at five against the Indians. On a 3–1 pitch, Derek swats it to right, flings his bat away as if it were spring-loaded, and is off and running until the ball clears the fence.

Now it's on me. After a long fly to center, I give up two singles, and Grady Sizemore steps in. He fouls off a couple of cutters in, and on 1–2, Jose Molina sets up outside for the backdoor cutter. Sizemore swings through it. Mark DeRosa comes up. The count goes full and the runners are on the move. I throw the cutter away, hoping to nick the outside corner upstairs. As I wind and deliver, it's right where I want it. Jose barely has to move. DeRosa thinks it is breaking outside and takes it, but it is right there. Umpire Phil Cuzzi rings him up, DeRosa has a fit, and I have my first save in Yankee Stadium III.

The Yankees have dug deep to have a shiny new team for the new ballpark, spending tens of millions to bring in CC Sabathia, A. J. Burnett, and Mark Teixeira, but it doesn't stop us from getting off to another sluggish start, including a forgettable weekend in Fenway in late April. We get swept, and the most painful loss comes Friday night. I strike out Ortiz and Pedroia and am one out from saving a 4–2 victory for Joba when I leave a 1–0 cutter over the heart of the plate to Jason Bay, who hits it to straightaway center, halfway to Boston Harbor. It's another muffed save against a team that has gotten to me more than any other by far. I think about it and we talk about it and we look at film, and still I cannot pinpoint one thing the Red Sox are doing against me that others don't. It's not as if they are standing in a different place in the box, or altering their swings. I think it comes down to familiarity. They see me more times than any other team, so they have a much keener sense of how and when my ball moves.

I wish I had some epiphany about what the Red Sox are doing so I can attack them differently, but I don't. I just have to pitch better against them—or maybe change my pattern so it's not at all predictable.

We wind up losing in eleven on a Kevin Youkilis walkoff, and lose Saturday when Burnett can't hold a six-run lead. In the Sox triumph on Sunday, Jacoby Ellsbury has a straight steal of home off Andy, who actually picks two guys off of first in the game but gets caught by Ellsbury as he pitches from the windup.

A couple of weeks later, I give up back-to-back homers to Carl Crawford and Evan Longoria of the Rays, the first time I've ever done that in my career. I've already given up more homers than I did all of the previous year. I am not where I want to be velocity-wise; that much I know. I am coming off minor shoulder surgery in October and know that my arm is going to get stronger and that it's just a question of building it back up. I have less margin for error than I did when I was throwing 96 or 97 miles per hour all the time, so I also know that regaining my command is critical.

My struggles, of course, bring a fresh round of panic that I am finished. It is almost comical. I love playing in New York, but it's also the home office of overreaction. People are always searching for trends where none exist.

With the exception of our results against the Red Sox—we lose eight straight to them to start the season—I see something in this club that I haven't seen in a long time. We are fighting to the end, game in and game out. Teams always say they do that, but not that many really do.

Example? Early in June at the Stadium, I have a brutal outing against the Rays, giving up three hits and three earned runs in two-thirds of an inning in a really bad loss.

The next day? We score three times in the bottom of the eighth and I pitch a clean ninth, and we win to move into first place. It's the twentieth come-from-behind victory for us and the season is barely two months old. And then we keep the comeback theme going to start a Subway Series with the Mets, thanks to the all-out hustle of Mark Teixeira.

We are trailing, 8–7, down to our last out, after I give up an RBI double to David Wright in the eighth. Derek, who singled, is on second, and Teixeira, who was intentionally walked, is on first. Alex is at the plate. Frankie Rodriguez, the Mets closer, fires and gets Alex to pop up a fastball to second base. Alex slams the bat down, because he had a fastball to hit and missed it. The pop floats into short right behind second baseman Luis Castillo. It is way up there. Castillo settles under it and the Mets are about to take the opener, and then somehow the ball glances off Castillo's glove. Derek is running hard, of course, and right behind him, Teixeira is running all out, busting it from the time Alex swings the bat. He makes it all the way home and we win that game, not just on an error you might see once every five years but on the hustle of a star player who doesn't assume anything...who goes hard until the game is over.

That's what winners do.

Three games out of first, with a 51–37 record at the All-Star break, we take off on our best roll of the season. We win eighteen of our first twenty-three games after the break, sweep the Red Sox four games at the Stadium, and blow right past them into first place.

The last of those games is a microcosm of our season. Down 2–1 going into the bottom of the eighth, Damon and Teixeira blast back-to-back homers, and Jorge follows with a two-run single. I close it out by getting Ellsbury to ground out to Teixeira. I go seven weeks and 21 appearances without giving up a run, and by the time we pull off another four-game sweep, this time of the Rays, in early September, we are 41 games over .500 (91–50) with a nine-game lead. I am pretty darn sure this is not going to be another year when we have a division series meltdown.

I have 39 saves, and my ERA is 1.72. By mid-September, I have converted 36 consecutive save opportunities.

The panic has subsided.

Then, on a Friday night in Seattle, I come on in the ninth with a 1–0 lead to save a game for A. J. Burnett, who outpitched the great Felix Hernandez. I strike out the first two batters looking and then Mike Sweeney hits a long double. The next hitter is Ichiro. He is so good at going the other way that I want to come in hard to him, jam him. I deliver a cutter, but he is not jammed.

The ball stays over the inner part of the plate. He is one of the best hitters in the world and knows just what to do.

He hits it over the right-field fence, a stunning turnaround in the space of two pitches. Against a hitter that good, you have to be better. I miss my spot. Save blown. Game over.

My bad.

I'm sorry, I tell A.J. You deserved to win that game.

Don't worry about it, Mo. You've saved plenty for me, A.J. says. I walk out of the clubhouse with a chocolate ice-cream cone. It does nothing to take away the sting of letting down the team.

We draw the Twins in the division series and win Game 1 at the Stadium behind CC, but the best news is that Alex looks better than he has in years in October. We get homers from Derek and Matsui, and two big hits and two RBIs from Alex, and win, 7–2.

You see what happens when you don't try to do too much and just let your ability take over? I tell him.

Game 2 is much more tense. The Twins rally to take a 3–1 lead into the bottom of the ninth, with Joe Nathan, one of the best closers in the league, on for the save. Nathan has saved 47 games during the regular year, but before he even gets an out, Teixeira lines a single to right and Alex hits one into the bullpen in right center and the game is tied. It's the first magical October moment in the new ballpark, and it's followed by another two innings later in the eleventh, when Teixeira hooks a ball around the left-field foul pole off of Jose Mijares and we're up two games to none.

We head to Minneapolis and take a 2–1 lead thanks in part to another Rodriguez home run, and then get saved by a tremendous defensive play by Derek and Jorge. Nick Punto leads off the bottom of the eighth with a double off of Phil Hughes, before Denard Span bounces a ball up the middle. Derek does well to snare it before it bounds in the outfield and knows he can't throw out Span. He sees Punto has rounded third aggressively, as if he might try to score. Derek stops, turns, and fires to Jorge, who rifles a throw to Alex, whose swipe tag has Punto nailed. It's a colossal baserunning blunder, but only perfect execution gets us the out.

I am warming up in the bullpen and you can almost feel the air come out of the Metrodome.

One batter later, I come in to face Joe Mauer, with the tying run on base. Mauer is a .365 hitter that year, the AL MVP, but you can't worry about that. You trust your stuff and know that if you throw your best pitch and truly believe in it and put it where you want, you can get your man, even if it's Joe Mauer. When you have that belief, you are in attack mode, ready to bring your very best— and that's when you finish it well, with all that you have.

Against a hitter like this, if you back off just a little bit, it could mean the difference between a hit and an out.

I bust Mauer's bat and he grounds out to first.

Jorge and Cano get RBI singles in the ninth off Nathan, I save the victory for Andy, and now it's on to meet the Angels in our first ALCS since 2004. We take Game 1 behind CC, 4–1, and then Alex saves us in Game 2, drilling a Brian Fuentes fastball over the right-field wall in the eleventh inning, answering an Angels run. It's Alex's third game-tying homer of the postseason, and we win two innings later when Jerry Hairston singles, gets bunted to second, and scores on a wild throw.

After the Angels win in extra innings back in Anaheim, CC pitches another great game in a Game 4 blowout, we head home, and suddenly I am having a new experience. I have never been the subject of a little Internet tempest before. It happens courtesy of a video that supposedly shows me loading up the ball with spit as I stand behind the mound with my back to the plate.

The video looks convincing, I admit, but I do not throw a spitball, and have never thrown a spitball. That is the truth. Major League Baseball looks into it and clears me of any wrongdoing, and even though I answer whatever questions the reporters have, even though I have always done everything legally, there are still some reporters who seem to be positive that they've unlocked my secret fifteen years into my career.

It doesn't bother me, and it changes nothing. If somebody wants to try to get in my head or throw me off my game, they are going to have to come up with something way better than that.

We wind up closing the Angels out in six games, Andy winning, me saving my third game of the series, giving up a run in two spitless innings. Next up: the Philadelphia Phillies, baseball's defending World Series champions.

Being in the World Series doesn't seem as if it comes with the uniform anymore — not with six years passing since our previous appearance. I have a new appreciation for how hard it is to get here. I am a month away from turning forty. I pray that I will glorify the Lord and savor the experience.

I don't know if I am going to pass this way again.

My first big test comes against Chase Utley, with two on and one out in the top of the eighth in Game 2. Cliff Lee was dominant in Game 1 in a complete-game 6–1 victory, Utley belting two homers in support of him. Now here Utley is again, after Burnett delivers a superb effort in getting the better of Pedro Martinez. The Phillies acquired Pedro for games like this. He pitches well, but Teixeira and Matsui get him with solo homers, and then Jorge has a huge pinch single. So I am protecting a 3–1 lead as Utley works the count full. I go at him with nothing but cutters, mostly working on the outside, for good reason. He is trying to pull everything, and Jorge and I both see it. I don't know if this is another instance of a lefty hitter getting seduced by the short porch, but Utley sure seems to be thinking that way. On a 3–2 pitch, I come at him with another cutter away, and he does just what we are hoping for— tries to pull it. He makes solid contact but hits a bouncer that goes from Cano to Jeter to Teixeira for an inning-ending double play.

An inning later, I get Matt Stairs swinging to finish things up, and we square the Series at one.

With Alex, Matsui, and Nick Swisher homering in Game 3, and Andy pitching around two Jayson Werth homers, we take an 8–5 decision in Citizens Bank, and then score three in the ninth to break a 4–4 tie in Game 4, the big hits coming from Alex and Jorge. I nail down a 7–4 victory with a 1-2-3 ninth and we are one game away.

After the Phillies push the Series to a sixth game by winning their last game of the year in Citizens Bank, we return home for Game 6, Andy vs. Pedro. Matsui hits a two-run homer in the bottom of the second to get us going, then hits a two-run single in the third and a two-run double in the fifth. He has six RBIs in three at-bats.

If only he would start hitting in the clutch.

A two-run Ryan Howard homer makes the score 7–3, but Joba and Damaso Marte shut them down from there, and I get the final two outs in the eighth and then two more in the ninth, sandwiched around a Carlos Ruiz walk. Shane Victorino steps in. The Stadium crowd is on its feet. Victorino battles. He always battles. He's another one of those guys, like Pedroia, who can play on my team anytime. He falls behind, 1–2, then keeps working it, fouling off four straight pitches on 2–2. Finally, he works the count full.

Utley, Howard, and Werth are the next three hitters, and this is no time to complicate things or make things exciting. I need to get Victorino right now. I throw one more cut fastball, down, and Victorino pounds it down into the ground, a harmless bouncer to

Robby Cano. I start to run toward first, thinking I might need to cover, but Cano tosses to Teixeira and I start pumping my fist before the ball is even in his glove. I turn around toward the infield and keep running, and now it feels as if the whole team is chasing me.

I am laughing like a little kid playing keep-away. This is the fourth time I've gotten the final out in the World Series, and the best one of all. Maybe because it has been so long. Maybe because the last time I was this close to winning I had that debacle in the desert in 2001—eight years earlier, to the day. I don't know. I am not stopping to analyze it. It's beautiful not just that we won but how we won. Hideki Matsui, a total pro, hits .615 and knocks in eight runs in six games. Damaso Marte retires the last twelve hitters he faces, among them Utley and Howard, both of whom he strikes out in the final game. Andy pitches his second clincher and does it on three days' rest. Derek hits .407 and Damon hits .364. Alex, a new man this October, has six RBIs; Jorge, five.

What is also beautiful is that for the first time Clara and the boys are at every game, and so are my parents and in-laws. We share the whole ride together. What could be better than being surrounded by the people you love the most?

Later that night, after a half-hour ride home and congratulations and good nights from my family, I get on my knees beside our bed. My Bible is on the nightstand. I begin to pray, purely and completely overcome with gratitude to the Lord for my life and my health and my family. None of it would've been possible without Him.

19

Passages

IF AMERICA EVER WANTED to have a queen, Rachel Robinson would be the perfect choice. She is regal and gracious, intelligent and tireless — a champion of freedom and equality for her whole life. I am not in awe of too many people, but I am in awe of Rachel Robinson. More than forty years after she lost her husband — the most courageous and important baseball player in the history of the sport — Rachel continues to honor Jackie Robinson, No. 42, through the foundation that bears his name, and through her efforts to make the world a more just place.

Before I report for my twenty-first season of professional baseball, I begin 2010 by getting to meet Rachel for the first time. It happens at a fund-raising event in Lower Manhattan for the Jackie Robinson Foundation. I am there with Henry Aaron, in an informal question-and-answer session, speaking about the privilege and the pressure of being the last player to wear Jackie's 42, after all of the other guys who'd been grandfathered in had retired.

The privilege part couldn't be more obvious; who would not want to share a uniform number with the great Jackie Robinson? The pressure is living up to the measure of a man who changed the world, and conducted himself with dignity every step of the way.

I don't know if any person can match that standard. I am no pioneer, I can tell you that. Roberto Clemente was the first Latin star, and there were many others, including Vic Power and Orlando Cepeda, who followed. Humberto Robinson, a relief pitcher, was the first big league player from Panama. I am a simple man who measures his impact in a smaller way: by being a humble servant of the Lord, and trying to do my best to treat people—and play the game—in the right way.

The home opener carries on with the big moments—it has always been a festive occasion, especially when there is a ring ceremony attached. But this year it is not so festive at all. Sure, we get our rings and standing ovations, the biggest of them all reserved for Hideki Matsui, World Series hero, who is now a member of the Angels—our opening day opponent. The fans salute him for his quiet excellence and years of service and send my heart soaring, the exact opposite direction my heart is going when Gene Monahan is introduced.

Through all these years and all those rubdowns, Geno remains a man who radiates kindness in all he does. So it's a body blow when I find out a month before spring training starts that he has been diagnosed with throat cancer. He has spent four decades caring for his Yankee ballplayers. Now he has to take care of himself.

It turns out that Geno felt a lump in his neck when he was shaving one day during the postseason. He does exactly what he tells us not to do; he puts off getting it checked out. He finally goes and sees a doctor in December and gets his diagnosis in January. He has to get his tonsils and an affected lymph node taken out, and then begins a course of thirty radiation treatments. Geno knows, because he counted. He is a man who is more precise than a Swiss watch. His training room is almost as spotless as his car, which he washes and vacuums the way most people brush their teeth. Everything is in its place, right down to the antique brass scale that Babe Ruth used to get weighed on. The room is so...cared for. And that's exactly how I feel when I am in it.

Geno takes a leave from the team while undergoing treatment. He has radiation the morning of opening day and then heads to the Stadium. He is introduced right after Joe Girardi. Jorge asks Michael Kay, the master of ceremonies, to wait before he introduces anyone else. The crowd rises and cheers for Geno, and the Yankee players who owe him so much move to the dugout railing and cheer for him, too. Geno is choking up, tapping his heart. I am choking up, too. I miss him terribly, miss all the talks about his daughters and my sons, about everything. Geno wants to rejoin us by early June. I pray that the Lord will give him the strength he needs to get through this and help get him back to the job that he loves.

We celebrate our rings and Geno with a victory that day, even if another former teammate, Bobby Abreu, gives us a scare when he hits a grand slam off of David Robertson in the top of the ninth to make the score 7–5. Joe calls for me to get the last two outs. I strike out Torii Hunter and up steps . . . Hideki Matsui. A few hours earlier, I am clapping for him, and now I want to put him away so people will clap for us. It's weird stuff sometimes, this free-agency racket, but when I look in at Jorge's glove, Godzilla himself could be in the batter's box and I wouldn't be ruffled.

Hideki pops up my first pitch to second, and the game is over.

Geno actually makes it back ahead of schedule, and maybe it's the inspiration of a sixty-five-year-old trainer that makes me feel, well, almost young. We have the best record in the majors (44–27) as we take the field on a Tuesday night in Phoenix against the Diamondbacks, and we rally to tie in the ninth and go ahead in the tenth when Curtis Granderson, our new center fielder, smokes a line-drive homer into the right-field stands. After a clean ninth, I come out for the tenth looking to nail down a victory. I have retired twenty-four straight hitters, a streak that ends when Stephen Drew singles to right and Justin Upton cracks a double. Joe orders me to walk the cleanup man, Miguel Montero, to set up the force at home.

So the bases are loaded with Diamondbacks, and Joe and every-body else is wondering if I am having flashbacks to the 2001 World Series.

I give them the answer later:

No.

That was November 4, 2001. This is June 23, 2010. I had hair then. I have no hair now. I had Scott Brosius and Tino Martinez on the corners then. I have Alex Rodriguez and Mark Teixeira on the corners now.

I was thirty-one then. I am forty now.

I don't carry things that do me no good to carry. I let them go, so I can be light and free.

The batter is Chris Young, the center fielder. I bust him inside and he pops up to Francisco Cervelli, my catcher. Next up is Adam LaRoche. He has all five RBIs in the game for the Diamondbacks. I run a cutter in on his hands and he pops to Alex.

Now the hitter is Mark Reynolds. He leads the team in homers, leads the majors in strikeouts. Not a guy you want to miss your spot with.

I get strike one on a cutter away that Reynolds looks at. I miss away, then hit the outside corner with another cutter away. On the 2–2 pitch, I want to go up the ladder—change his eye level. I wind and fire—another cutter, but up now. Reynolds swings through it.

It is not nine years ago. You can tell by the outcome.

Two days later, we are in Los Angeles to face the Dodgers, our first game ever against Mr. T. I give him a big hug before the game. It is great to see his face and look into his eyes. He is not just the man who led us to four world championships; he's a man who saw something in me, who was willing to give me a chance to become the Yankees closer. You never forget that.

Take it easy on us tonight, okay, Mo? he says. These guys have never seen a cutter like yours before.

I laugh and am on my way. CC Sabathia pitches four-hit, one-run ball through eight, and I take the ball for the ninth, three outs away from saving a 2–1 victory.

Due up are Manny Ramirez, Matt Kemp, and James Loney. I strike out all three. I make sure not to look into the Dodger dugout for a reaction.

While we're in town, my old bullpen buddy Mike Borzello, who came to the Dodgers with Mr. T, asks if I would be willing to talk to Jonathan Broxton, the Dodgers' closer. He's a kid the size of a boxcar, a young man with a great arm who has a strong start to the year but is suffering from some confidence issues. I walk up to him in the outfield during Dodgers batting practice.

Nice to meet you, he says.

I've heard a lot about you. How are things going?

Okay, I guess, he says. I'm just not doing the job the way I did last year.

Broxton talks some about how confident and in control he felt when he was blowing away the league in 2009. I can see how hard he's trying to get back there, all but putting himself into a vise, and tightening it up. I talk to young pitchers often, and it's never about grips or pitch selection or on-the-fly tutorials about throwing a cut fastball. It is always about the mental approach to closing. That is what separates the guys who are good for a year or two and the guys who get the job done year after year after year.

This is going to sound boring and obvious, I say, but you know what I think about when I come into a save situation? I think about getting three outs and getting them as fast as I can and getting out of there.

That's it. The job is hard enough without overcomplicating it. You don't want a lot of noise playing in your head. You don't want doubts. You just have to think about making every single pitch the best pitch it can be, so you can get that first out. And then the second out. And then the third out.

I also tell him: Don't worry about getting beat. It is going to happen. It happens to me. It happens to everybody. These are major league hitters and they are going to get you sometimes, but the best thing you can do for yourself is have a short memory. You can't take what happened yesterday out to the mound today. Because if you do that, you've got no shot at succeeding.

Every time I have gotten beat, it has made me better. Every time. I am not happy it happened, but I am happy it made me better. You only pay attention to the positive, not the negative.

In the series finale, Clayton Kershaw holds us to two runs and four hits. Broxton comes in to close it. I wish him well, but not right now. He can find his way and change his mental approach after we leave town.

Broxton strikes out Teixeira looking for one out. I'm thinking I may have been better off talking to him after the series. Then Alex singles. Cano doubles. Jorge singles. Granderson walks. Chad Huffman singles, and we score four times to tie the game at six, smacking Jonathan Broxton with as rough a blown save as he will have all year. We win it an inning later when Robby Cano hits a two-run homer off of George Sherrill in the tenth.

Thanks for talking to Brox, Mr. T says the next time I see him. Whatever you said, he got a whole lot worse.

We go into the All-Star break in first place, with a record of 56–32, and even though I am selected to the team for the eleventh time, I sit it out so I can rest a cranky knee and a tender oblique muscle. The game is played in Anaheim. The date is July 13, and it brings with it prayers and one more tearful goodbye: Mr. George Steinbrenner dies of a heart attack in a Tampa hospital, nine days after his eightieth birthday. It is two days after the passing of Bob Sheppard, the Yankees' legendary public-address announcer. Death and illness are part of life, of course. Still, I am reeling. First Chico Heron passes, now Mr. George and the great Bob Sheppard, who graced us with his dignity and a voice that seemed to come straight from the Lord Himself.

It's hard to know why anything happens in life, or why we seem capable of terrorizing the Minnesota Twins on command. We sweep them again in the postseason this year, making it nine straight October victories against them, and twelve out of the last fourteen. We have eliminated them in division series play four times in eight years and always seem to do it by coming from behind, as we do in two of our three victories this year, including Game 1.

I have more success against the Twins than against any other team. I feel it at the time, of course, but, looking back, and seeing that my career ERA in the Metrodome and Target Field is 1.09 and that, overall against the Twins, it is 1.24? I can't explain it. I blew a save against them earlier this year at Yankee Stadium, allowing a grand slam to Jason Kubel, but otherwise have gone through them like a machete in a cornfield, especially in the playoffs; I have pitched sixteen and two-thirds innings against the Twins in the postseason and have given up no runs and only eight hits. The funny thing is that most of their big guns have hit me pretty well. Joe Mauer hits .286 against me. Justin Morneau and Michael Cuddyer hit .250 off of me. It's not as if we have some master game plan against this club. I just always make the pitches I need to make and get the outs I need to get. You do that over a number of years, and you naturally develop confidence and positive associations when you are facing that team, fortifying you for the battle.

And the battle, for me, is what makes me so passionate about the game, even after all these years. If it weren't a battle, then it wouldn't mean nearly so much to prevail. It is the prospect of the battle that makes you put in all the work, all the preparation, readying yourself to deliver your best, and that is all I am thinking of as I stare in at Jorge Posada's glove, with Michael Young at the plate in Game 1 of the ALCS against the Texas Rangers in Arlington.

There is one out in the bottom of the ninth, the tying run on second. We have climbed out of a massive hole, taking a 6–5 lead on a Robby Cano homer in the seventh and a five-run outburst in the eighth. These two innings have left Rangers president Nolan Ryan with his arms crossed and his face pained, looking as if he'd eaten a bad piece of steer. I come in for the ninth, and after a single and a bunt, here comes Young.

He is a consummate pro and a tough out, a guy who never gives away an at-bat, and a career .320 hitter off of me. I don't fear any hitter, but I have come to respect some more than others, and Michael Young has totally earned my respect. Jorge and I know it's going to take work to get him — that I need to move the ball around and make sure I keep him guessing. So I start him out with a cutter up and a cutter in, and he fouls both of them off. I barely miss with two more cutters, one in, one away. I am positive the 1–2 pitch is a strike — it's knee-high on the outside corner — but I don't get the call. I take the ball back from Jorge. I'm not going to start staring down umpires or showing them up now.

I have a pitch to make.

I come in with a two-seamer that is in and higher than I want, probably the best pitch to hit of the at-bat; Young fouls it off. Now I come set again. Jorge sets up outside, and wants it up, and I throw a nasty cutter right to his glove.

Young swings through it. Jorge points his glove at me. Getting him has everything to do with working both sides of the plate, and then hitting that last spot. Some outs are more gratifying than others; this is a very good out.

One pitch later, I get Josh Hamilton in on the fists and he hits a slow bouncer to third for the final out, and a stirring comeback victory. But being three victories away from returning to the Series doesn't mean anything, because we don't come close to getting them. Almost every battle for the rest of the ALCS is won by the Rangers, who outpitch us, outhit us, and outplay us. They also outscore us, 38–19, winning in six games. Hamilton so terrorizes us with his four homers and seven RBIs in six games that we give him the Barry Bonds treatment and intentionally walk him three times in one game. He is named the ALCS Most Valuable Player, and deservedly so.

Some things change. In the World Series, Hamilton's bat goes cold and the Rangers lose in five games to the Giants.

But some things don't.

I don't watch.

I turn forty-one a month after our season ends and am already well into my off-season routine, which includes lots of fitness work and little throwing, just enough playing catch to keep my arm loose. I make very few concessions to age. I eat properly and prepare properly and take care of my body, so I don't think it's a miracle that I am still doing what I am doing. I just try to listen to my body and give it what it needs.

If there is one thing I have changed, though, it is trying to be more economical about everything. Who knows how many rocks I have left to throw? If I can get a batter out with one or two pitches, why throw three or four? I throw 928 pitches in 2010, over 60 innings. They are both the lowest totals of any full season of my career, and for a reason: There is no reason to stress yourself unnecessarily.

In 2010, I threw seven innings in spring training and was ready to go. This year, I might not even throw that many. In my first game action since I pitched the ninth inning of Game 6 against the Rangers, I face three Twins in the middle of March and strike them all out. One of them is Jason Kubel, who hit that grand slam the last time he faced me. This time he is caught looking at a 92-mile-per-hour two-seam fastball. It doesn't take me long to get loose for a game, and it doesn't take me long to get ready for the season. I don't aim to be low-maintenance; I aim to be no-maintenance. My mechanics are simple, and, as with any machine, the fewer moving parts the better. I think again about my message to Jonathan Broxton and to Alex. Why complicate things?

On opening day of the 2011 season, at home, I keep up the economy and throw twelve pitches to three Detroit Tigers to save a victory for Joba. It's an exhilarating way to start, but it still comes with mixed feelings, because my catcher is not Jorge Posada.

Nothing against Russell Martin, our new catcher, but when you grow up with a guy, and go to Applebee's in Columbus with a guy, you have a different sort of connection. Jorge has caught more of my pitches than any man alive. That he's not doing it anymore is sad for him, I know, and it's sad for me, too. Apart from being a tremendous player and teammate, this man is like a brother to me, the two of us connected by one ball, two gloves, and a shared mission: Get outs, win games, and go home.

I go about my job with stoicism and calculated calm; he goes about his with fire and passion that spew like lava from a volcano. We complement each other perfectly and communicate so effortlessly after all these years that we barely need to use words. I can tell a lot just from being with him.

Jorge is thirty-nine, and in what will be the final season of a superb seventeen-year career. He is a full-time designated hitter now, and he's having a difficult time adjusting to being a hitter and nothing else, to the point that he's not hitting nearly the way he usually does. His frustration reaches a breaking point during a weekend in Boston. Joe makes out his lineup and puts Jorge in the nine hole. An hour before the game, Jorge, in a fit of anger, pulls himself out of the lineup. Things only get worse when Brian Cashman goes on national television and details the reason for the late scratch.

Jorge and I have a long talk that night. His emotions run hot, sure, but Jorge is a man who can take an honest look at himself and make amends if he needs to.

I tell him, I know you feel disrespected, but this is not you—a guy who refuses to play. Sure, it hurts, but you need to make this right and do right by the team, because we need you and we need your bat.

You are right, he says. It was just the last straw, but you are right.

Jorge apologizes to Joe and Cashman and gets back to playing ball, and he shows what he is about on the most memorable day of the season, standing at home plate in the third inning of a game at Yankee Stadium against the Rays. It is July 9, a Saturday, and Derek Jeter has just belted a home run off of David Price for his 3,000th big league hit, another staggering achievement in a career that has been full of them. Jorge is the first to greet Derek, and he wraps him up in a massive bear hug, and I am next. Derek is on his way to a 5-for-5 day as we win, 5–4, and even for someone who supposedly doesn't care about milestones, I am filled with joy at this whole experience, seeing a guy Jorge and I have played with for almost twenty years get to a place that even players such as Babe Ruth, Joe DiMaggio, and Mickey Mantle never got to.

Jorge is there again just over two months later, this time to give the hug to me, on the day that I pass Trevor Hoffman and become baseball's all-time saves leader with my 602nd career save. Martin is behind the plate for the occasion, and the Twins are the opponent, and when I catch Chris Parmelee looking at a cutter on the outside corner, umpire John Hirschbeck comes up with his right arm and Jorge comes out of the dugout, already celebrating before "New York, New York" starts up, letting me know how happy he is for me, and what it means to him to be my friend. He and Derek push me out to the mound to soak up all the adulation from the crowd. He doesn't want me going anywhere until I am properly feted, and not long after, Derek and I have a chance to celebrate Jorge, when he knocks in the go-ahead run in the victory that clinches another AL East title.

We do not defend our World Series title or even come close. We outhit and outpitch the Tigers in five games in the division series but fall in the fifth game at Yankee Stadium, 3–2. We get ten hits, but very few of them when we need it—the story of the series.

But the other story of our series is our leading hitter, who hits .429 and has an on-base percentage of .579, reaching base on ten of his eighteen trips. His name is Jorge Posada, and I am proud that he is my catcher, teammate, and friend.

20

Wounded Knee

THE OUTFIELD HAS ALWAYS been my favorite playpen. It's a place where you can roam free, chasing fly balls, trying to outrun them before they hit the ground, defeating gravity. It's where I learned to love the game. If you ask me, there isn't a better feeling in baseball than catching a fly ball on the dead run.

Even when the Yankees signed me as a pitcher, I still was a closet center fielder, harboring private fantasies of being an every-day player. In my heart, I knew I was going to make it as a pitcher or not at all, but I kept my little dream alive.

The next best thing to being an outfielder is playing there in batting practice. Or shagging, as it is known in baseball slang. A lot of pitchers shag, though for many of them it's more of a social event than an athletic one. They hang out and talk, and if a fly ball happens to be in the neighborhood, they grab it. That's not how it is for me. I am out there to catch every fly ball I can. I am out there to run hard. Loops around the warning track, running sprints from foul line to foul line, doesn't do it for me. I want to run and sweat and get dirty. If batting practice is canceled because of rain or because it's a day game after a night game, I am the most bummed-out guy in the ballpark.

A month into the 2012 season, we leave New York for Kansas City to start a four-game series with the Royals. The date is May 3, our twenty-fifth game of the season. It is a Thursday. We get in late, so I sleep in and spend the day around the hotel, watching a little bit of the Animal Planet channel before going out to P. F. Chang's for lunch. I eat by myself. I get to the park about four o'clock. I haven't pitched since Monday, when I saved a game for Hiroki Kuroda against the Orioles. I don't like to go so long without pitching; I'm hoping I get in the game tonight.

Before I head out to shag, I go over and greet my newest teammate, Jayson Nix, a utility guy who has just been called up from Scranton/Wilkes-Barre to replace Eric Chavez, who suffered a concussion. Joe puts Nix right in the lineup, batting ninth and playing left field.

I change quickly and head out to the field. It is a beautiful spring night. I haven't made any official announcement, but I am almost certain this is going to be my last season, and that makes me want to savor everything, every day, every pregame fly ball, even more.

I am standing in center field of Kauffman Stadium, wearing a navy blue Yankee Windbreaker and gray running shoes — my shagging uniform. It's almost always windy in Kansas City, and today is no exception. Not far away are our bullpen coach, Mike Harkey, and David Robertson, my bullpen buddy.

Hark is a strapping man with a strapping son, Cory, who is a tight end for the St. Louis Rams. Hark is a good soul, a guy who helped launch my career, a fact I remind him of often. On the day I won my first major league game in Oakland, the losing pitcher was Big Mike Harkey, a former No. 1 draft choice of the Chicago Cubs who was taken fourth overall in 1987, just three picks after Ken Griffey Jr. My catcher that day was Jim Leyritz and my first baseman was Don Mattingly, and my shortstop, of course, was Robert Eenhoorn, a Dutchman. We raked Hark for seven hits and four runs, and I was the beneficiary.

Thanks for throwing all those cookies, Hark, I tell him.

No problem. Happy to help, he replies.

Hark is the perfect man to have in charge of a bullpen. He believes in keeping things loose and keeping guys relaxed, because he knows that when the time comes at the end of the game it's often not relaxed at all. He once said that what he was going to miss most about me was the element of calm I brought to the pen. I do bring calm, but I also bring mischief. After I spend the first five-plus innings of games in the clubhouse, I typically arrive in the pen in the middle or end of the sixth. I fist-bump everybody and then start in, usually with my gum. It's amazing how a bunch of grown men turn into a pack of adolescents when you throw them into a bullpen. I am at the head of the pack. The command I have with my cutter is nothing compared with what I can do with gum. An earlobe from ten feet away? I nail it almost every time. Either ear. When they are onto my gum heater, I change things up and stick the gum on somebody—Hark, ideally. On the seat of his pants, his back—there are plenty of good spots on Hark's big body. My favorite is his jacket pocket, so when he jams his hand in there it gets good and gooey.

You got me again, he tells me.

You're easy, I reply.

Batting practice is more than halfway finished when Jayson Nix, the new guy, gets into the cage. He swings and hits a long line drive toward the wall in left center and I am off, turning to the right, running hard, no mischief in mind now, only the ball, and getting it in my glove. Nix has tagged this ball, and it's knuckling in the wind, but I am pretty sure I can catch up to it. I keep running on a diagonal line toward left center, eyes fixed on the ball the whole time. As I near the warning track, I notice the ball is drifting a bit back toward center. The KC wind is playing tricks again. The ball is on its descent now. I am almost there, about to make maybe my best catch of the BP session. I feel the crunch of the track beneath my foot as I turn back slightly toward my left.

And before I take another step, a shot of pain blasts through my right knee.

It feels as if it's ripped out of whatever is holding it in place, wobbling in and out. It's the most pain I have ever felt. The ball bounces onto the track. My momentum takes me on a hop-step into the wall before I crumple in a heap in the dirt.

I try to scream, but no sound comes out. My teeth are clenched. Hark and David see my teeth and think I am laughing—just goofing around and pretending to be hurt. I am not pretending. My face is in the dirt and my knee is throbbing. I don't know what happened, but I do know it's not good. I can feel my knee moving around. You know me. I pray all the time. At home, behind the wheel of the car, behind the mound. I am not praying now. The pain is too fierce. I keep rubbing my knee, hoping that somehow takes the edge off of it.

In a second or two Hark and David and Rafael Soriano, who is also right there, realize that this is for real. Hark whistles to Joe Girardi and waves for him to come out.

Joe runs out to me and so does our assistant trainer, Mark Littlefield. Batting practice stops. I keep writhing.

Did you hear a pop? somebody asks.

No.

No sound at all?

No.

That's a good sign.

I appreciate the encouraging diagnosis, but it's not an easy sell right now. After a few minutes I am able to sit up. Hark and Joe and Rafael carefully lift me up and put me on the back of a green John Deere cart. It has groundskeeping stuff in it. Now it is hauling baseball's all-time saves leader. My leg is propped up on the bed of the cart.

I hope it's okay, Mo, says a fan from just over the center-field fence.

I wave to the guy as the cart starts to pull away, following the track by the third-base dugout, all the way around. A few other fans yell encouraging things, shout my name. I wave again. The whole thing is completely surreal.

What on earth am I doing on the back of a John Deere cart right now? How could something I've done thousands of times, with no problem, result in this?

As the cart continues into a tunnel, I start to think that maybe it's not all that serious. Couldn't it be that it felt terrible when it happened but it's just a sprain or something I can come back from in a week or two? I actually can walk on it, and it doesn't feel so bad anymore. It's not even swollen.

Maybe this is just a freak thing and I'm going to be fine. That's what I tell myself.

I get into a waiting car with Mark Littlefield. It's a little before six o'clock now and I am off to Kansas University MedWest Hospital for a magnetic resonance imaging test. It's about a half-hour ride, which gives me time to run various scenarios through my head. I stay positive, because that is my default position, but I also am realistic. I am forty-two years old, and if the news is not good, well, what comes next?

Could my career actually end face-first on the Kauffman Stadium warning track? One of the writers asks Joe what it would mean if it turns out I need knee surgery.

If that's the report, if that's what it is, that's as bad as it gets, Joe says.

We pull up to a boxy brick building and I get through the half hour of jackhammering. The tug of war in my head between optimism and realism keeps raging. When the MRI is finished, I ask the doctor how it looks.

He seems uncomfortable.

I haven't seen the results yet. We're going to get them as soon as we can, he says.

Something tells me he just doesn't want to deliver bad news to me. I walk out to the car unaided, putting a good amount of weight on my knee.

It's hard to believe it can really be that bad if I can stand and walk like this, I think.

Another doctor I'd seen inside approaches the car.

I'm sorry to hear about your injury, he says. I know you are a Christian. Would you be okay if I prayed with you?

Thank you. Sure, I'd like to pray with you.

We both clasp our hands.

Lord, You are in control of everything, the doctor begins. *Sometimes You do different things, and life doesn't go as we want or plan. Lord, please help Mariano heal and give him the strength and perseverance to recover from this injury and get back on the mound. Amen.*

It's short and heartfelt and I thank him, and soon we are heading back to the ballpark. It's the fifth inning before I am back in the clubhouse. I am not going to be heading out to the pen. Somebody else will have to play gum tricks on Mike Harkey.

I meet with Dr. Vincent Key, the Royals' team physician. He is a young African American guy with a goatee and a shaved head not unlike mine. We are in the trainer's room of the visiting clubhouse.

How does it look, Doc? I ask.

Well, I am sorry to be the one to tell you this, Mariano, but the MRI shows that you have a torn ACL and a torn MCL in your knee, Dr. Key says. It is going to require surgery. This can have excellent results, but you will almost certainly be out for the rest of the year.

I let his words sink in for a moment:

Torn ACL.

Torn MCL.

Surgery.

Out for the year.

The year.

They are hard to take in. Three hours earlier, I am romping around the outfield, doing what I love most, maybe in the last season I'd ever play, taking in every moment. Now I have the first serious lower-body injury of my entire professional career. I am looking at major reconstructive knee surgery and a long and grinding rehab.

Now who really knows what my future is going to be?

I thank Dr. Key and wait in the clubhouse for the game to end. We lose, 4–3. I stand in front of the whole team. I am fighting tears and not winning the fight. I share my diagnosis with them, and my orthopedic horror story:

Shredded knee. Major surgery. Goodbye, 2012.

I don't know what to say about it, really, so I just start.

I'm sorry. I feel like I've let you down, let the Yankees down, I say. I feel really bad about that. You count on me and now it looks like I will not be able to pitch for the rest of the year. I know this happened for a reason, though, even if I don't understand what the reason is right now. And I will tell you this...I am glad this happened to me, near the end of my career, and not to one of you younger guys, with all your baseball in front of you. I'm not glad it happened, but I know that with the strength of the Lord I can handle this.

Derek comes over and gives me a hug. So does Andy. Lots of other guys do, too. This is why I love being on a team. You share your triumphs and your troubles. You share everything. You are all in it together. You will do anything for the guys on your team.

When I meet with the writers, one of the first questions they ask is whether I will definitely come back. I've been dropping hints about retirement since spring training—so they logically want to know:

Is this how it ends?

Almost instantly, I can feel all sorts of emotions welling up in me. I don't know what to say, or think, and that's pretty much what I tell them. I take a breath and remind myself I am not alone and that the Lord will give me whatever I need to get through this. I never ask, Why me?

I know that will not take me anywhere good.

I go back to the hotel and have a long talk with Clara. I cry on the phone with her for a long time. We pray together and she offers me the comforting words she often uses during difficult times. It is Clara's balm, words that are almost as soothing as her hand on my back:

Tomorrow will be a better day.

The pain and swirling emotions make for a fitful night of sleep. I do not believe in agonizing over things. I cannot undo my knee injury, any more than I can undo the ninth inning of the 2001 World Series. When I wake up, my knee is as stiff as a piece of cement. Forget about walking unaided. I call Mark Littlefield and ask for crutches. It feels like a defeat, having to ask for them. But I am in a much better place, and have a completely refreshed outlook.

I am sitting at my locker in the visitors' clubhouse, reporters all around me, my crutches propped nearby. It's not even twenty-four hours since I lay writhing in the warning-track dirt, but a lot has happened in those hours. A lot has happened inside of me. I won't be shagging, or saving games, any time soon, but I am not going anywhere.

I'm coming back. Write it down in big letters. I can't go out this way, I tell the reporters. Miracles happen, I'm a positive man.

*   *   *

My surgery is delayed for a month because doctors find a blood clot in my leg that they need to break up. On June 12, Dr. David Altchek of the Hospital for Special Surgery in New York operates, and it goes well. He says the tear wasn't as bad as it looked in the pictures. I spend the rest of the summer going through the pounding process of rehab, treating it as seriously as a World Series appearance. Four or five times a week, for three hours a day, I go through the array of torturous exercises I need to increase range of motion and strength, pushing, pulling, punishing myself. The pain on many days is as bad as, or worse than, the original injury, but I am dogged in my perseverance.

This is what I need to do if I want to make it all the way back.

If there's one unforeseen positive in the whole ordeal, it is that I discover the joys of summer with my family. I haven't been off for an extended time during a summer since I was twenty years old.

We have a family barbecue on the Fourth of July while the Yankees are winning in Tampa.

I could get used to this, I think.

I can go to my boys' ball games, and have more relaxed time with Clara. I am much more in sync with the daily rhythms of our family. Of course I'm not ready for retirement; I have a comeback season, 2013, ahead of me, Lord willing. But these feelings let me know that when the time comes to retire, I am going to be fine with it.

Just as I am getting set for surgery and beginning the rehab work, the Yankees take off in the East, winning twenty of twenty-seven games in June, a charge led mostly by Robinson Cano. Every time I tune in to a game it seems Robby is crushing another baseball. He has 11 homers for the month, hits .340, and maintains a 23-game hitting streak, all while playing world-class defense.

Without a doubt, Robby is one of the greatest players I've ever played with. He is also one of the most confounding players I've ever played with. Go back a few years to a game in Anaheim. The Angels have won two straight lopsided games, and we are in dire need of a victory if we want to stay in the pennant race.

Joe calls for me with one out and men on first and second, the score tied in the ninth. I either get two outs or we lose. The hitter is the leadoff man, Chone Figgins. On my first pitch, I get him to hit a six- or eight-hopper to second. Robby is shading a step or two toward second, but the ball is hit slowly enough that I know he has time to get there. Robby takes a couple of steps toward the ball. And then he stops.

No dive, no attempt to block it.

Nothing. He just stops.

The ball trickles into the outfield. The runner, Howie Kendrick, comes around from second to complete the sweep. Nobody can understand why Robby doesn't dive or smother the ball somehow to save the game.

I definitely don't understand. Even if you think the first baseman is going to catch the ball, how do you not get ready in case he doesn't? How do you stand there like a department-store mannequin and watch the ball roll into the outfield?

How can you not give all you have in that moment to prevent our team from losing?

I do not talk to Robby after the game. Reporters are all around. Emotions are running high. That's the worst time to have this conversation.

We fly to Minnesota that night, and the next day, I seek out Robby in the clubhouse in the Metrodome. Robby and I have had these discussions before. We are standing near his locker.

What happened on that ball Figgins hit yesterday? I say.

I don't know. I thought Wilson [the first baseman] was taking it. I just didn't read it right, Robby says.

When he didn't make the play, why didn't you go after it? I ask.

I didn't think I could get there, he says.

Robby's head is down, and it's obvious he feels bad about what happened. He knows he doesn't have a bigger fan than me on the club. I am not trying to drop a safe on him. I am trying to help him, the way an older brother helps a younger brother.

Robby, you are way better than what you showed yesterday, I say. In that situation you have to do whatever it takes to keep the ball in the infield.

Robby nods.

I know it wasn't good. Next time it won't happen.

Robinson Cano and I were teammates for nine years by the time I retired. This guy has so much talent I don't know where to start. Sometimes I question if he knows how much talent he has — knows that he can be much better even than what he is, better than what anybody is. He is that gifted. I used to tell him, I don't want to see you give up at-bats. Ever. I want to see you fight at every at-bat.

It would drive me crazy when I'd see Robby swing at balls at his eyes and basically get himself out. And how many times did I see him swing at the first pitch with the bases loaded? That's what a guy without confidence does. Not what one of the best hitters in the game does.

Over and over, I tell him just that: Robby, you are too good to do that. On the first pitch, the pitcher often is going to throw something bad to see if he can get you to go fishing and hit a weak grounder or pop-up somewhere. Don't help him. When you do that, it's not just your at-bat that gets wasted. It's a letdown for the whole team when the best hitter we've got gets himself out.

Why would you want to help the pitcher?

You're right. I won't do it.

His baserunning is another one of our topics. When he gets going, he's a very good base runner. He gets a good secondary lead, reads the ball well. His instincts are solid. He just doesn't always run hard out of the box, and then there are those times — way too many — when he doesn't put pressure on the defense by running all-out on routine grounders. You never assume everything is going to be an out, because it isn't always going to be.

You can ask Luis Castillo, the former Met, about that.

A month later in New York, Robby trots after a ball Cliff Floyd hits in a game at the Stadium against Tampa Bay. It allows Floyd to get to second base. At the end of the inning, Joe pulls Robby from the game.

You don't want to hustle? Take a seat, Joe says.

I stay on top of Robby more than any other teammate, precisely because of the gifts the Lord has given him. If somebody else gets himself out or doesn't hustle, it bothers me, but not in the same way. I hold him to a higher standard — and want him to have the same expectation of himself.

To his credit, Robby never makes excuses or tells me to back off when I approach him. Not one time. I think he trusts that I come to him in the spirit of helping. He is always very respectful — and he always says thank you.

Trust me, there are plenty of guys who can't take that kind of honesty.

Robby has gotten better and better as he's gotten older. He plays harder now, and I hope he keeps it going in his new home in Seattle. There's no doubt he is a Hall of Fame–caliber talent. It's just a question of whether he finds the drive that you need to get there. I don't think Robby burns to be the best. I think he's content to enjoy the game and help his team and go home. You don't see the red-hot passion in him that you see in most elite players. He is a laid-back guy. Maybe because he came up surrounded by so many star players who were older, he just slipped into that role, but now that he is the leading man for the Mariners, it is his time.

How often do you see a player with this beautiful a swing, who can play this kind of defense, and hit for this kind of power? It's amazing. He steps in the box and has those quiet hands and then uncoils and the hands come forward, so strong, so quick. You see him rip a ball into the gap, and you think: *With a swing like this, you should hit .350 in your down years.* That's the kind of ability he has. It is all there for Robby Cano. I hope he goes and gets it.

After two months of painstaking rehab on my knee, I am feeling so good that I am convinced that I can come back and pitch this season. I meet with Dr. Altchek to give him the glowing report.

Doc, my knee feels great, I say. I really think that I can—

He cuts me off. He knows athletes, knows where this is going— that I am about to make a case for why I should get back to the mound this season. He tells me it would be foolish and risky to try to rush back. I am a runner barreling toward home, and he is a Molina-sized catcher blocking the plate.

I am not going to get close to scoring.

Your arm may feel fine, but isn't being a major league pitcher more than that? he says. Can you field bunts? Can you sprint off the mound, plant, turn, and throw a guy out? Can you defend your position, and beat a runner to first on a 3–1 play?

I wish I had a counterargument, but I don't. He is right.

I know how much you want to get back to the club for the playoffs, but you're not ready to be on a big league mound yet, Dr. Altchek says. You want to give your knee all the time it needs. You should be in great shape for spring training.

Spring is next up for us, since we have another disappointing October, beating the Orioles in the division series before getting swept in the ALCS by the Tigers. A bunch of cold bats do us in. After a regular season in which he hit .312 with 33 homers and 94 RBIs, Robinson Cano goes 3 for 40 in the postseason. It turns out to be his final October in a New York Yankee uniform.

21

Exit Sandman

I AM ON A back field at our spring training complex in Tampa, having just spent an hour working on bunt defense and pickoff moves. Mike Harkey, our bullpen coach, is nearby. The year is 2008. Or 2010. Or 2012.

It could've been the odd years, too.

This is it, Hark, I'm done. I'm not going through another year of this.

You are full of it, Hark says.

No, this time I mean it, I say.

You're like the little boy who cried wolf, Hark says. You will be back here next year and probably the year after and we'll be having the same conversation. You will never retire.

Hark and I have this exchange six times, or is it ten? We have it often, because spring training is my least favorite time of the year. You hear people wax poetic about spring training being a metaphor for life, a symbolic rebirth that comes packed with hope. I never really get the rapture. I am a homebody at heart. Leaving Clara and the boys has never been easy for me. Home is where we pray and laugh. It's where we nurture one another. I see my sons having fun in the family room right before it is time to leave one year, and I begin to cry.

The feelings are like a tsunami from nowhere.

I feel like I've failed these boys, because I leave them so often, I tell Clara.

Leaving home wasn't easy when I was twenty-three and it is harder still when I am forty-three. I am a creature who finds comfort in routine, and it's unsettling when the routine gets upended.

It's not that I don't want to prepare and do the work. I understand that there is rust to scrape off, fundamentals to lay down, but how many times can you cover first or work on cutoffs? To me, spring training is more boring than waiting for fish to bite. Give me a handful of innings, a couple of weeks, and I'm ready to go. There are so many monotonous drills and so little rush of competition.

In my twenty-fourth and final spring training, though, my attitude is completely different. It's not because I know this will be the last one. It's because I am able-bodied. Nine months removed from the pain and tears of Kansas City, my knee feels strong. My whole body feels strong. To be running in the outfield and taking ground balls and practicing with the guys—I am so grateful to the Lord for the opportunity to play again.

When I throw twenty pitches in live batting practice, my old catcher and friend Jorge Posada teases me.

Twenty pitches is a lot for you, he says.

Let him tease. Let anybody say whatever he wants. I am back in uniform, throwing baseballs. It is a blessing that I am not taking for granted.

I throw a couple of bullpen sessions in the following days, and it's all good, and then I make my spring debut on the afternoon of March 9, a few hours after I officially announce my retirement at a press conference. Our opponent is the Atlanta Braves. I get Dan Uggla to pop up to second for the first out, then strike out Juan Francisco and Chris Johnson looking, to wrap up a quick inning. As first outings go, it couldn't have been better. I am overflowing with optimism.

I wish I had the same feeling about Derek Jeter.

Derek also makes his spring debut against the Braves. It's the first time he has played for the Yankees since the twelfth inning of Game 1 of the American League Championship Series, when he snapped his ankle as he moved to his left fielding a ground ball. In a strange way it reminded me of what happened to me in Kansas City, because it's a play I've seen him make ten thousand times. It's so completely normal, and then in a flash it isn't. Derek has surgery a week later and says over and over that his goal is to be back by opening day.

Playing as a DH for his first game, Derek rips the first live pitch he's seen in five months into left field for a single. It is vintage Derek Jeter. The fans go berserk. He plays shortstop for the first time a day or two later and insists that all systems are go for starting opening day.

The only trouble is that I don't believe it. I have been around Derek so long that I know his movements, the anatomy of his game, as well as I know my own. And he does not look right to me. He's not moving freely. Doesn't have the same burst, or quickness. I know it's extremely early in the spring, but I'm concerned about what I'm seeing and his insistence that everything is on course.

I watch him closely as camp continues. Derek had a devastating injury to his left ankle. No matter how well the surgery went, sometimes you just need more time to heal. I think he wants to be in the lineup so bad that it might be clouding his judgment.

I know how much you want to start the season, but you need to be careful and not rush back, I tell him one day in the trainer's room. It's not worth it. You should wait until you are one hundred percent healed, because if you push it too much too soon, it could backfire.

I'm fine, Mo. I feel good. I understand your point, but I am not going to do anything reckless, don't worry, he says.

He says the doctors are telling him it's getting better every day. A little stiffness and swelling are to be expected. He insists it's all good.

Of course medical professionals know what is going on inside that ankle much better than I do. I just know what I see. In late March, Derek has some extra stiffness and inflammation and has to get some cortisone shots. He insists it's a minor setback. Then word comes out that he is going to start the season on the disabled list, and basically the bad news never stops coming. He doesn't play his first game until July 11. Soon he gets hurt again, his body breaking down all over the place.

Derek is one of the most driven people I have ever known. It's what makes him great. But I also think in this case his drive just blinded him, and maybe everybody else, too. To me it was obvious he wasn't ready, and yet somehow he kept pushing and pushing and nobody stopped him—or protected him from himself—the way that Dr. Altchek protected me from myself. I believe it was an organizational mistake—a big one—not proceeding more deliberately.

Nobody had anything but his best interests at heart, no doubt, but sometimes you have to forget what the diagnostic tests say and trust your eyes. Derek plays in a total of seventeen games in 2013. If he doesn't rush it and plays even fifty or seventy-five games, the whole season plays out differently. We have our captain, our Hall of Fame–bound shortstop. With a healthy Derek Jeter, I can't see our season ending in September.

Six weeks into the season, with thirteen saves in thirteen chances, I am standing on the mound of Kauffman Stadium in Kansas City. I am not a patient this time around. I am a closer. I like this much better.

It is a day of deep emotion for me, in all kinds of ways. Five hours before the game, I meet with eighteen people from the Kansas City community. All season long, at every stop, I make it a point to do this, meeting people whom I might not ordinarily get to connect with. They might be fans, or ushers at the stadium, or cafeteria workers, or ticket takers, folks who work behind the scenes to make ball games happen, folks who in many ways are the lifeblood of the game. In Cleveland, I even get an audience with the legendary drummer John Adams, who has been banging on his drums at the top of the bleachers, trying to start Indians rallies, almost since the time I was born. Jason Zillo, the Yankees PR director, does a phenomenal job taking care of the logistics, and these intimate meetings are truly as memorable as anything in my last year. I'm not trying to be noble or heroic; I'm simply taking an opportunity to thank people for their contributions and their steadfastness, to join them in their world, not mine. Or, in the case of visiting with people who are facing adversity or tragedy, it's just a way to offer whatever I can that might make a difficult time just a little better.

I connect with wonderful people all over the country, and the memories of all of them will stay with me forever, though none are more poignant than my visits with the Bresette family and with a young pitcher named Jonas Borchert before our May 11 game in Kansas City. The Bresettes, of Overland Park, Kansas, had just suffered an unimaginable loss while traveling home from Florida. Their ten-year-old son, Luke, was killed when a huge display board in the Birmingham, Alabama, airport landed on him. Heather Bresette, his mother, was seriously injured as well, and so were sons Sam and Tyler. When I hug Ryan Bresette, the boys' father, I don't know what to say or do, other than to express my sorrow and tell him I will be praying for his family.

You are giving us a special gift in a time of a lot of tears, Ryan says.

You are giving me a gift, too, by sharing your family and your time with me, I say through tears of my own.

We all have a laugh when another young Bresette, thirteen-year-old Joe, lets it be known that Luke loved baseball but hated the Yankees.

The power, and the inspiration, go on and on as I meet so many special people that day. I am uplifted by the Bresettes' strength in the face of such a devastating loss, just as I am uplifted by fifteen-year-old Jonas Borchert, a dominant closer from Lee's Summit, Missouri, who has a form of cancer but is fighting it with all he has, and by Ricky Hernandez, a young man in a wheelchair who built a place in his backyard for children with disabilities to play.

Everybody wants to make a big deal out of how nice it is for me to take an hour or so out of my day, but I try to tell them that they are the ones who should be thanked, for what they've given me. Even in a room that is overstuffed with pain and adversity, the Lord's blessings, and people's goodness, are everywhere, and I am so much richer for having been there.

Returning to the scene of the accident isn't traumatic at all. It is a joy. I shag before the game (though I admit I am not going at it as hard as I did before the knee surgery), and I laugh when I see the big "No 'Mo' Zone" sign my teammates have hung on the outfield wall, right at the spot where I collapsed. I can't wait to get out there and pitch. In the bullpen, the phone rings in the eighth inning. Hark picks up.

Mo, you got the ninth, he says.

I come on to try to save a victory for Andy, who has a fine duel with James Shields of the Royals. I get two outs on grounders to short. Salvador Perez, the Royals' catcher, hits a double to right and now the hitter is Mike Moustakas, a left-handed-hitting third base-man. He battles hard, fouls off four pitches. With the count full, I throw a cutter up and away and he hits it to left center, fairly deep. The ball is going right toward the spot where I got hurt. I turn and watch left fielder Vernon Wells run into the gap and haul it in. It's our fourth straight victory, and we make it five a day later when I save a victory for Kuroda, getting Moustakas again, this time on a short fly to right.

I save twenty-nine games in my first thirty chances and am feeling as good as I ever have. We're up and down as a team, and the barrage of injuries — suffered not just by Derek but by Mark Teixeira, Curtis Granderson, Francisco Cervelli, and Alex Rodriguez (still recovering from hip surgery) — is like nothing I've ever seen.

We keep trying to find our way and head out west, and at our stop in Oakland I get to visit an old friend and language teacher, Tim Cooper. It's been twenty years since we were teammates, but Coop is somebody I won't ever forget. He was there when I needed him, teaching me English and helping me escape my loneliness. I leave him tickets and have him and his family in the dugout before the game. It is great to see him.

You look good, I tell him.

I'd cut your hair, but you don't have any, he tells me.

We're six games back as I head for my final All-Star Game, another game I'm thankful I can drive to, since it's just across the bridge in Queens. Jim Leyland, the American League manager, calls for me in the bottom of the eighth. When I walk through the bullpen door and begin to run across the Citi Field outfield, "Enter Sandman" starts to play and the fans are standing and cheering. Everything feels the same, normal, and it's not until I am almost at the mound that I realize something.

I am all alone on the field.

Completely alone.

My American League teammates stay back in the dugout to salute me. They are all at the railing, clapping. The National League players are doing the same thing on the first-base side of the field. I am so humbled, so blown away, by the outpouring that I am barely conscious of what I am doing. I bow my head and blow a kiss. I wave my hat and touch my heart, and all I can think is:

How blessed can one man be?

I wish I could go all around Citi Field and thank every single person there.

Before the game, I had stood in the middle of a room full of All-Stars and told them how proud they should be of their accomplishments, and what an honor and privilege it was to be among them. Torii Hunter got up and implored the AL stars to win it for me, getting a rousing cheer as he did a rap-star impersonation.

And now here I am, three hours later, trying to help win it for them, for us. I throw my warm-up pitches to Salvador Perez and have a three-run lead to protect. I retire Jean Segura, Allen Craig, and Carlos Gomez in order. After Gomez grounds to short, I walk slowly toward the third-base dugout. The fans are standing again. This whole season is full of lasts...a last visit to this park, and that park, to all these places. It is winding down now. This is my last All-Star team. It's the best imaginable way to go out.

After the break, we are in Chicago for a three-game series with the reeling White Sox—and not in a good place. We are stuck in fourth in the American League East, 6–9 in our first fifteen games after the All-Star Game, and now we have The Greatest Sideshow on Earth changing into his uniform just across the clubhouse. The story of the night isn't our sluggish and inconsistent play or the White Sox's ten-game losing streak. It is the return of our third baseman, Alex Rodriguez, who is finally making his season debut following hip surgery. The hip is the least of Alex's problems, though. He has just been suspended for 211 games for his alleged role in the Biogenesis scandal, getting performance drugs and then trying to block baseball's investigation of the case, according to Major League Baseball. It's the heaviest drug suspension ever handed out. A bunch of other players accepted 50-game bans for their involvement with Biogenesis, which used to bill itself as an anti-aging clinic but turns out to have been more of an anti-playing clinic, for the way its customers got hammered.

Alex appeals the suspension on the same day he gets hit with it, making him eligible to play—and turning the clubhouse in Chicago into a full-blown nuthouse. I've seen World Series games where there wasn't so much commotion, or so many reporters. I don't care. I am happy to have him back. This is not a regular guy. This is a superstar guy. In his prime, he is one of the greatest ballplayers I've ever seen. He is not that anymore, but he is still a good player who can help get us out of our funk.

There is plenty about Alex that I can't say I understand, but he has every right to appeal his suspension, and every right to pursue every legal avenue he wants to. He is my friend and my teammate, and, as I've said, to me that makes him like family. And you don't cast aside a family member because he has made a mistake, or even many mistakes.

When I see Alex at his locker, I go right over and give him a hug.

Welcome back. What took you so long? I say.

Thanks, Mo. It's great to be back. I'm ready to play some baseball, he says.

Let's get this thing moving forward, I say.

Alex Rodriguez may love baseball more than anybody I've ever known. Baseball is everything to him. I love to play and compete, but after a game, I want to go home or go back to my hotel and not even think about baseball until the next day. He'll watch another game, and then another game, and search for replays of the games he's already watched. He's as smart a ballplayer as I've ever played with. It's why it's so hard to understand some of the decisions he has made, not just with performance-enhancing drugs but in his spotlight-seeking ways. It's not enough to be an all-time great player, it seems. He wants to be at the top of everything. He wants to be the best, look the best, get the most attention, and all it does is make him baseball's No. 1 whipping boy.

And this is exactly what I tell him, starting in 2009, when *Sports Illustrated* came out with its story that he had tested positive.

I think it's wrong what you did, I say. I don't like what you did. But I still am going to be there for you, pushing you forward, not dragging you down.

Alex's return to the lineup doesn't make much of a difference. We get pounded in the opener of the White Sox series when Andy has one of the worst starts of his career, and we lose the second game, too. We're now just two games over .500 and have dropped two straight to a club that was out of the pennant race before Memorial Day, which makes the final game of the series that much more important. We need to get righted, and fast, because we're ten and a half games out of first.

CC Sabathia delivers a big effort and we go up, 4–0, early, before the White Sox narrow it to 4–3. I get the ball for the ninth. The fans at U.S. Cellular Field give me a standing ovation on my final visit. I appreciate the sentiment and tip my hat, but I am pretty good by now at getting right down to business. I say my prayer behind the mound. The White Sox's two most dangerous hitters, Alex Rios and Paul Konerko, are the first two guys I have to face. I get Rios on a foul pop-up to first. Konerko steps in, and on an 0–1 pitch he lifts a short fly to center. Two outs on five pitches, all of them strikes. I like it.

One more and we're out of here, I think.

Gordon Beckham, the second baseman, is at the plate. He has never gotten a hit off of me. I fall behind, 2–1, and leave the next pitch a little too far out over the plate. Beckham gets good wood on it and drives a double to right center. Now the tying run is at second.

I have thirty-five saves for the year and have blown only two. Adam Dunn is the pinch hitter. I have faced him four times and he has never hit a fair ball off me, striking out four times. I throw two cutters, down and away, and he takes them both for strikes. Doesn't even budge. From the start of my big league career, John Wetteland, the Yankee closer before me, always stressed one thing above all else: Never let yourself get beat with your second-best pitch. When you absolutely need an out, you bring your best. Nothing else.

I need an out. Dunn, a big left-handed power hitter, is going to get another cutter. Dunn's reaction to the first two pitches tells me he is looking inside, so I figure I will stay outside. Austin Romine, the catcher, sets up outside. The pitch isn't quite on the corner, gets too much of the plate. Long known as a dead-pull hitter, Dunn has spent the last couple months of the season staying back and hitting to all fields. He swings and hits the ball sharply on the ground toward third. I wheel around, just in time to see the ball elude a diving Alex. Beckham comes around to score and tie the game.

I am incensed at myself for staying outside with the cutter again. He was so obviously waiting for an inside pitch he'd probably have jumped at it. I should've come inside, off the plate, and seen if I could get him to chase. But I never tried that. I stayed outside, missed my spot, and the game is now tied.

I strike out Carlos Wells to end the inning, but the save has already been blown. I have one more out to get in a game we really need, and I don't get it. After the Wells strikeout, I make the walk that every closer hates: back to the dugout after you've lost the lead, if not the game. It's the longest walk there is.

I can't dwell on the failure, though. I have another inning to pitch, and I set them down in order, and when Robby crushes a homer in the top of the eleventh, I feel much better. When the

White Sox score two in the bottom of the eleventh, I feel much worse.

We head home to face the Tigers, and it's another supercharged night in The Rodriguez Chronicles—Alex's first game back in the Bronx since his return and since all the uproar about his suspension and appeal. Thousands of people boo him. Thousands cheer him, too. I wonder how the whole thing is going to play out, and if he can stay focused throughout the saga. We take a 3–1 lead into the ninth, and it's my time again.

After I get the first out, Austin Jackson hits a double to left center. I get Torii Hunter on a comebacker. Now Miguel Cabrera, hulking Venezuelan ball crusher, the best hitter in baseball, walks to the plate. It's down to the two of us. Cabrera is hitting .358 with thirty-three home runs (it's early August, mind you), and as usual, he's hitting the ball to every part of every ballpark. I approach him the same way I approach every hitter; it doesn't change because of who he is. Sometimes I might pitch to a particular weakness a guy might have, but in the case of Cabrera, there really is no weakness, so I just go after him.

The Stadium crowd is on its feet. My first pitch is a cutter up in the zone, out over the plate, and his swing is not his best. He lofts a fly ball toward the first-base dugout. Lyle Overbay, our first baseman, goes over to the railing of the camera well but overruns the ball a bit and has to lean back. He stretches for the ball, but it falls probably an inch from his glove. Cabrera gets a big break and he knows it. I get another foul ball to go up, 0–2.

One strike away again.

One strike.

Finish the job. Close this thing, I tell myself.

I throw a ball high out of the zone, but he won't chase. The next pitch is in and Cabrera fights it off, grazes a foul ball off his knee and hobbles around, gets attended to by the trainer and Jim Leyland.

After a few minutes he limps back in the box, and I fire again on the inner half, and this time he fouls it off his shin. Now he is limping even more.

All I want is to get this game over with. I try to get him to go after a pitch that breaks off the outside corner. He doesn't bite. The seventh pitch of the at-bat is coming. The way he is swinging at my cutter tells me he could be vulnerable to a two-seam fastball; it's a hard sinker and if I hit the right spot down and in I think it will get him. It is my best shot, I believe, because it's a given that he is expecting another cutter. I make my deep forward-bend and come set, then fire a two-seam fastball, violating Wetteland's gospel, because I believe I can fool Cabrera by throwing what he's not expecting. I might've, too, except that the ball goes over the heart of the plate, and just sits there. Now he rips away and the minute he makes contact I drop my head on the mound. I know where it's going to land.

In the black.

Over the center-field fence.

No need to watch Brett Gardner give chase.

Wow, I say, as Cabrera hobbles around the bases. The wow is as much about what just happened as it is about the gift of hitting Miguel Cabrera has been blessed with. He handled two pitches that usually would've ended the game. He extended his at-bat.

And then he beat me.

For the second time in two games, one strike away from locking down a victory, I make the long walk to the dugout, mission not accomplished, feeling almost dazed, as if I'd taken a punch to the jaw. I have let the guys down.

We win in ten innings on a clutch single by Gardner, so that helps soften the blow, but the hurt just can't get airbrushed out of the picture by a happy ending.

Somebody is going to pay, I tell myself again, same as I did sixteen years earlier in Cleveland, when Sandy Alomar Jr. hit that homer off me in the division series. Somebody is going to pay. How or when they are specifically going to pay, I can't tell you. It's the voice I give to my determination.

What happened tonight is going to make me smarter, stronger, better. It's not going to shake my faith in myself. If anything, it's going to deepen it. It's going to make me redouble my resolve to get the next one.

When I get home that night, Clara rubs my back and says what I know is true:

Tomorrow will be a better day.

They are just about my favorite words on earth.

We get drilled on Saturday, so if we want to start turning things around we better get after Justin Verlander on Sunday. Alex hits his first homer of the season into the seats in left in the second inning, and we have a two-run lead as I take over in the ninth.

The first batter I face is somebody I know. Miguel Cabrera. I bring a sharp cutter that he swings through for 0–1, and after a ball, I put another cutter right on the inside corner. It's 1–2. I go away with a cutter and he takes it for a ball, and on 2–2, I am not going the two-seam route, the way I did Friday night.

I am going with Wetteland, and my best. The pitch is up a bit, and it is over the plate. It is not where I wanted it—not at all. I know it before Cabrera even swings. He knocks it over the fence in right and now it is 4–3, and I am on the mound, talking to myself.

How could this happen again? I know he's a great hitter, but I felt in charge of that whole at-bat.

And then, boom—he takes me over the wall again.

I get Prince Fielder on a line drive to third base, and now Victor Martinez steps in. At 0–1, I come in with a cutter, but again, I miss my spot, and Martinez takes a rip, and there goes another ball into outer space, into the seats in right, tying the game and clinching a history I want no part of: For the first time in my big league career, I've blown three consecutive saves.

I stand on the mound and try to take this in. It is not easy. For the third time in five days, I have failed to do my job. Gardner is the hero again, hitting a game-winning home run off Jose Veras with two outs in the bottom of the ninth. We take two out of three, no thanks to me. I have seven weeks left in my career. I am not having a crisis in confidence. I believe as much as ever that I can do all things through Him. Somebody did not pay today, though, and that really bothers me.

It means everything to me to be dependable, trustworthy.

And I have not been either this week at all.

A week later, we are in Fenway against the Red Sox, and Sox starter Ryan Dempster decides he's going to drill Alex. After a couple of awkward misses, he finally gets him. I can't believe Dempster is so blatant about it, nor can I believe the way the fans cheer in delight. The venom coming from the stands — what people are screaming at Alex, and the looks on their faces — is ugly. Benches empty. Alex gets his revenge when he homers against Dempster in the sixth, and I wind up with my thirty-sixth save. I am hoping that this is just the spirited victory that will get us going.

Five games out of the wild-card spot with five weeks to play, we struggle through an up-and-down September, and it becomes clear that my final days are not going to include a pennant race. But what a memorable month. On September 22, the Yankees host Mariano Rivera Day. Clara and my kids and parents are there, and former teammates are there, and so is Rachel Robinson and her daughter, Sharon. And my dear friend Geno, too. They retire my number — Jackie Robinson's number — and mount it on the Monument Park wall, and Metallica even plays "Enter Sandman" live.

It is beyond what I could've imagined, and leaves me filled with so much gratitude and warmth, I don't know what to do with it all. I pitch a scoreless inning and two-thirds in the game that day, and the perfect ending would've been a victory, but we fall, 2–1.

And now, four days later, we are there…the 1,115th and final appearance of my New York Yankees career. It comes against the Tampa Bay Rays. The gate opens and I make my last run in from the pen, the crowd standing and cheering. I enter with two on and one out in the top of the eighth, doing my best not to think about the weight of the moment, or saying goodbye. It is not easy. I quickly retire two batters, and then I walk back to the dugout and head into the trainer's room in the clubhouse. My forearm is tight. I ask Mark Littlefield, the trainer, to put some hot stuff on it. He is working on my arm when Andy Pettitte walks in.

What are you doing here? I ask.

Jeet and I want to come and get you before you finish the ninth. What do you think?

Don't do that, I say. Please don't do it. You guys know me. I want to finish the game. That's my job.

Okay, Andy says, and off he goes. With my forearm loosened, I get back to the dugout and sit on the bench. I don't move right away even after our at-bat is over. I just sit for a moment and look at the mound and the field, before I go out there for the last time.

I have no idea how I am going to get through this. I've been good at holding off the torrent of emotions so far, but I pray to the Lord for strength, since I can feel the dam starting to weaken.

Finally, I get off the bench and go out to the mound. I throw my warm-ups. The crowd is once more standing and cheering. The first hitter, catcher Jose Lobaton, hits a cutter away right back to me on a high hop. I jump to grab it and make the play.

One out.

The next hitter is Yunel Escobar, the shortstop. He takes a cutter away for 1–0. I come back again with a cutter that is up a bit, over the plate, not the best spot by any means, but Escobar swings and lifts a pop-up to Robby Cano.

Two outs.

The next hitter is Ben Zobrist, one of my All-Star teammates at Citi Field. I take a deep breath, hoping I can finish this up without losing it, hoping I can do my job one last time. I am about to get back on the rubber when I look to my left and see Andy and Derek walking out of the Yankee dugout toward the mound.

I thought I told you not to do this, I think.

Andy and Derek are both smiling at me. I am smiling, too.

Andy's face says, *I know you told us not to do it, but we're doing it anyway, because this is the way you need to go out.*

Andy motions to the home plate umpire, Laz Diaz, that he wants the right-hander, and he and Derek keep walking, and now they are on the mound.

Andy holds out his left hand and I put the ball in it. I won't be needing it anymore.

Andy wraps his arms around me and I put mine around him and now the dam finally bursts, the emotions flooding me, overwhelming me, the finality of it all descending on me like an anchor. I weep like a child in his arms. Andy holds the back of my head and the sobs keep coming, deep heaves of joy and sadness and everything, all at once.

It's okay, Derek says. It's okay.

The embrace lasts a long time, and then I hug Derek, and I don't want any of this to end, with the Stadium drenching me in applause, the two teams doing the same.

I walk off the mound and wave my hat to the crowd, to my teammates, to the Rays. When the game ends I sit in the dugout by myself, just trying to be still, to drink up the glory of the Lord and the power of the moment. The crowd files out. Everybody gives me space. A few minutes pass.

I don't want to leave. But I am ready. I decide I need to go back to the mound, my office for the last nineteen years, one more time.

I toe the rubber a couple of times and then bend down and scoop up a handful of dirt and pack it into my right hand. It makes sense to me. I started playing in dirt so I might as well finish playing in dirt, the perfect keepsake for a simple man.

EPILOGUE

——

Refuge of Hope

FOR THE LAST NINETEEN seasons, the Lord has blessed me with the opportunity to play professional baseball for the New York Yankees. My job was to save games, and I loved every part of it. Now I have a new job—probably better described as a calling—and that is to glorify the Lord and praise His name, and show the wonders that await those who seek Him and want to experience His grace and peace and mercy.

From saving games to saving souls? I'm not sure I would put it that way, but I will say this:

With the Lord, all things are possible.

About four years ago, Clara and I started an evangelical Christian church called *Refugio de Esperanza,* or Refuge of Hope. We held services in a former home of ours in a town not far from where we live. The services were sparsely attended at first but quickly grew, attracting people of varying ages and ethnic and religious backgrounds. We had Spanish-speaking people and English-speaking people; wealthy people and poor people; devout believers and some skeptics, too, who were curious to find out what all this rejoicing and singing was all about. And before long we knew we needed a much bigger space. Now, after a two-year, $4-million restoration project, we are moving into that space...a magnificent House of the Lord in the city of New Rochelle. It used to be known as North Avenue Presbyterian Church.

Now it is known as *Refugio de Esperanza*.

North Avenue Church was built in 1907, a stately stone building with a slate roof and stunning windows. I first saw it two years ago after a friend told me about it.

It doesn't look like much on the outside. In fact, it's a wreck, my friend said. But it has all kinds of potential.

When I first walked in the place, it wasn't just abandoned. It was on the verge of being bulldozed. I mean, it was nasty. Just about everything was in disrepair. There were holes in the roof and windows, the sickening smell of dead animals, more debris and neglect than you can imagine. But the Lord was with me that day, and I truly believe He gave me a vision of what this church could be. In spite of the horrid condition, I saw only beauty. I saw the most majestic wood framing the sanctuary. I saw a soaring ceiling. I saw the glory of the Lord. Ankle-deep in garbage, surrounded by shards of windows and busted pews, I called Clara—the pastor of *Refugio de Esperanza.*

Clara, I have found our church. It's perfect. You have to come and see it right now, I said.

Clara arrived a short time later, and she, too, saw the possibilities. She, too, could envision it being full of people worshipping the Lord, a place rich with the Holy Spirit, a place that knows only goodness.

It's going to take a lot of time and work, and money, too, but it will be so worth it, she said.

Clara is the senior pastor of the church, and it is her profound faith and humility that are the spiritual bedrock of all that we do. The mother of our three sons and a woman who is the real superstar of the family, Clara grew up with the Gospel, but it wasn't until the age of twenty-five that she had a personal encounter with God that changed her life.

I believe in God and my desire is to always please Him, Clara says.

Our plan—the Lord's plan—is for the church to be not just a Refuge of Hope but a community hub that will include a food pantry, educational programs, tutoring, faith-based initiatives for kids and families, and more. It will be there for people of all walks of life, and seek to serve those among us who may not have had the easiest time of it.

It will be a place of giving, and love, following the lead of Jesus Christ.

There are so many troubles and tragedies in this world that sometimes it's hard to know where to start if you want to make a difference. It is equally hard to hold on to optimism. We know we can't solve every problem at *Refugio de Esperanza,* but what we can do is try to touch people's hearts, one at a time, to offer comfort and support in a way that might make people's burdens easier, and their road less difficult.

It is a daunting task, but the idea of spreading hope is a wonderful thing to contemplate. In our old home and our new home, our services at Refuge of Hope are without a doubt the greatest moments of my life. Eighteen hours before Mariano Rivera Day at the Stadium in September, we have one of the most beautiful services I can remember. I am so overcome by gratitude and lightness during the service that I just begin to weep. There is no containing the joy I feel in that moment. It is the presence of the Lord, the wonder of living in His light and sharing His goodness with others. Joy and goodness are what the Lord wants for us. That is the truth.

I loved saving baseball games for the New York Yankees, and I am grateful every day for my experiences in baseball. I have the dirt from the new Stadium and the bullpen bench from the old Stadium, and I have memories and friendships that will last a lifetime. I will never forget how it felt to put on that uniform every day. Through all of my years as a closer for the New York Yankees, I tried to honor the Lord; to live and play with a pure heart; and to give everything I had, every day, to the team and its fans.

And that is just what I seek to do with my new calling.

I know the possibilities are without limit, and the best is yet to come, for it is written in Philippians, chapter four, verse thirteen:

I can do all things through Him who strengthens me.

Acknowledgments

When you say goodbye to a sport you've played your whole life, as I did in 2013, there's a lot of reflection that goes along with it. When you write your life story in the same year, it makes the reflection, and the soul-searching, that much deeper.

Writing *The Closer,* in many ways, was not unlike getting a save. I may be the one with the statistic (or my name on the cover), but a whole team full of people made huge contributions to allow that to happen. I could fill another chapter with the names of all the people I am deeply grateful to, and I hope and pray that any omissions here are understood to be due to limitations of space and my flawed memory, and not to what I feel in my heart.

Fernando Cuza has been my baseball agent, friend, and right-hand man for many years, and he and Relativity Sports senior vice president Aaron Spiewak were the guiding forces and caretakers of the book from the outset. Aaron, in particular, found the book a home with Little, Brown, a top-notch publishing house with top-notch people who have been with me from the very early innings of this project, starting with publisher Reagan Arthur. Senior production editor Karen Landry and staff did a remarkable job turning a manuscript into a finished book, just as publicists Elizabeth Garriga and Nicole Dewey did in getting the word out, creatively and persistently, about *The Closer.* John Parsley, my editor, is not just skillful at his job; he was a tireless and indispensable ally from start to finish. Thanks, too, to John's able assistant, Malin von Euler-Hogan.

Jason Zillo, the Yankees director of media relations, has been there for me throughout the years, a constant source of support and counsel, never more than in my farewell tour in 2013.

My first catcher and friend of twenty-five years, Claudino Hernandez, along with our Panama Oeste teammate Emilio Gaes, saw the possibilities for me before I did; how do you thank somebody for *that?* Claudino also doubled as a driver / Puerto Caimito tour guide for Wayne Coffey, my coauthor, when he went to Panama to conduct research. Wayne and I began this book with a prayer, asking for the Lord's strength and guidance so that my story would honor Him even as it tells the story of a humble man who has as many shortcomings as any other man. I believe our prayer was answered. In our countless hours together shaping the manuscript, Wayne helped draw out memories and find an honest and authentic way for me to interweave all the elements of my journey. Along the way, I discovered that writing a book is hard work, but also deeply rewarding work.

I would also be remiss if I didn't thank Wayne's wife, Denise Willi, and their children, Alexandra, Sean, and Samantha, for their patience; they did not see or hear much from my coauthor as we neared the finish line. Frank Coffey and Sean Coffey were among the early readers whose insights were invaluable. Wayne's literary agent, Esther Newberg of ICM, along with her associate, Colin Graham, put together our collaboration with Relativity, which set Wayne and me on our way. The esteemed sports team with whom Wayne works at the *New York Daily News*—Teri Thompson, Bill Price, Eric Barrow, Mike Matvey, and Ian Powers—were likewise staunch supporters, and I thank them for that.

My parents and siblings and cousins—most of them still in and around Puerto Caimito—were the foundation of my life before anybody knew who I was, and in so many ways shaped the man I became. I can't say that fans and players and employees of the clubs around the big leagues had any part in shaping me, but they did so much to make this journey of mine special. To all the people I met and the clubs that honored me in 2013 — to the fans of Detroit, Cleveland, Tampa Bay, Colorado, Kansas City, Baltimore, the Mets, Seattle, Oakland, the Angels, Minnesota, Texas, the Dodgers, San Diego, the White Sox, Boston, and Houston — I just hope with all my heart that you know how much your kindness and tributes touched me. To the fans of the New York Yankees: Well, you were there in the beginning and you were there at the end, and I will never forget the love and support you've shown me all these years. I never wanted to be anybody's closer but yours. So I'll just say thank you all, and bless you all.

It's almost impossible for me to describe how important Mario and Naomi Gandia are to the Rivera family — both as loving extended family members and as sources of Christian inspiration and wisdom. As much as any people I know, Mario and Naomi live in the Lord's light, share the Lord's love, and make the world better because of it. They always want to be behind the scenes, but just this once, they must be out front.

There aren't enough words in my native tongue, Spanish, or in English to convey the love and admiration I have for my wife, Clara. She is the rock of our family life, a very present help in good times and otherwise. To our boys, Mariano Jr., Jafet, and Jaziel, you are the greatest gift a father can have, and I am as proud of the young people you are as I am grateful for your love. I have been away for many times in your life, and one of the best things about retirement is that I can stop saying goodbye so often.

And to the Lord, who has blessed me with His grace and mercy, whose wisdom and love are the beacons of my life, I don't want to just say thank you. I want to glorify You and honor You with all I do, and pray that *The Closer* is a good way to start.

Index

About the Authors

MARIANO RIVERA spent his entire career with the New York Yankees. He is Major League Baseball's all-time saves and ERA leader, a thirteen-time All-Star, and a five-time world champion. He and his wife, Clara, have three sons and live in New York.

WAYNE COFFEY is one of the country's most acclaimed sports journalists. A writer for the *New York Daily News,* he cowrote R. A. Dickey's bestselling *Wherever I Wind Up* and is the author of the *New York Times* bestseller *The Boys of Winter,* among other books. He lives in the Hudson Valley with his wife and children.